Writing
ON DEMAND

Writing
ON DEMAND

**Best Practices
and Strategies
for Success**

Anne Ruggles Gere · Leila Christenbury · Kelly Sassi

HEINEMANN Portsmouth, NH

Heinemann
A division of Reed Elsevier Inc.
361 Hanover Street
Portsmouth, NH 03801–3912
www.heinemann.com

Offices and agents throughout the world

The authors and publisher wish to thank those who have
generously given permission to reprint borrowed material:

Excerpts from *The House on Mango Street* by Sandra
Cisneros. Copyright © 1984 by Sandra Cisneros. Published
by Vintage Books, a division of Random House, Inc., and in
hardcover by Alfred A. Knopf in 1994. Reprinted by permission of Susan Bergholz Literary Services, New York. All
rights reserved.

Excerpts reprinted by permission from *Making the Journey:
Being and Becoming a Teacher of English Language Arts, 2/e*
by Leila Christenbury. Copyright © 1994, 2000 by Leila
Christenbury. Published by Heinemann, a division of Reed
Elsevier, Inc., Portsmouth, NH. All rights reserved.

Excerpts from *The Best Test Preparation for AP® English
Language and Composition* by Bannister, et al. Copyright

© 2003 by Research and Education Association, Inc. Reprinted by permission.

Rubric from the 1998 Alaska Direct Writing Assessment
based on the Oregon Department of Education model.
Reprinted with permission of the Alaska Department of
Education.

Example of a persuasive prompt and the score points in rubric found in *Florida Writes: Report on the 2002 Assessment
Grade 10*. Appears by permission of the Florida Department
of Education, Assessment and School Performance Office,
Tallahassee, Florida 32399–0400.

Excerpts from the "IRA/NCTE Standards for the English
Language Arts" from *Standards for the English Language
Arts*. Copyright © 1996 by the International Reading Association and the National Council of Teachers of English. Reprinted with permission.

Excerpts from *AP ® English Language and Composition
2003 Free-Response Questions*. Copyright © 2003 by the
College Board. Reprinted with permission. All rights reserved. *http://apcentral.collegeboard.com.*

Sample excerpts from the ACT Assessment used by permission of ACT.

Sample excerpts from the DSTP used by permission of the
Delaware Department of Education.

This book contains material that has been released to the
public by the Massachusetts Department of Education. The
Department of Education has not endorsed this book.

Library of Congress Cataloging-in-Publication Data
Gere, Anne Ruggles.
    Writing on demand : best practices and strategies for suc-
cess / Anne Ruggles Gere, Leila Christenbury, and Kelly Sassi.
        p. cm.
    Includes bibliographical references and index.
    ISBN 0-325-00728-4 (alk. paper)
    1. English language—Composition and exercises—Study
and teaching (Secondary)—United States. 2. English language—Study and teaching (Secondary)—Standards—United
States. 3. Essay—Authorship—Problems, exercises, etc.
4. Curriculum planning—United States. I. Christenbury,
Leila. II. Sassi, Kelly. III. Title.
    LB1631.G42 2005
    808'.042'071273—dc22   2004023991

Editor: Jim Strickland
Production editor: Sonja S. Chapman
Cover and interior designs: Catherine Hawkes, Cat &
Mouse
Author photograph: Steve Bernier
Compositor: Technologies 'N Typography
Manufacturing: Steve Bernier

Printed in the United States of America on acid-free paper
09 08 07 06 05 RRD 1 2 3 4 5

Anne dedicates this book to Budge, who has shared her life and cheered her on for nearly four decades.

Leila dedicates this book to Tucker, best friend and constant support.

Kelly dedicates this book to two future writers, her sons, Alessandro and Massimo, and her husband, Enrico, for his understanding that a woman's work in the home may include long hours at a laptop.

Contents

Writing on Demand's Companion Website

We feel strongly that a book like *Writing on Demand* should contain many things teachers can pick up and *use*. To that end, throughout the book you will see material marked with a printer icon, called Online 1.1, 1.2, and so forth. This material is available online on our companion website ready for you to download and print (for classroom use only). Please visit *www.heinemann.com/writingondemand* where you will find the following:

Online 1.1 Thinking Backward: Three Steps
Online 1.2 Sample Student Essay 1
Online 1.3 Sample Student Essay 2
Online 1.4 Sample Rubric
Online 1.5 Sample Student Essay 3
Online 1.6 Sample Student Essay 4
Online 1.7 Sample Student Essay 5
Online 1.8 Sample Student Essay 6
Online 1.9 Sample Student Essay 7

Online 2.1 Questions to Consider for Peer Response Writing Groups

Online 3.1 Rhetorical Analysis of Prompt
Online 3.2 Five Prompt Analysis Questions
Online 3.3 Prompt 1
Online 3.4 Prompt 2
Online 3.5 Prompt 3
Online 3.6 Prompt 4
Online 3.7 Two-Column Notes Using Prompt
Online 3.8 Five Questions About Images

Online 4.1 Common Assessment Terms
Online 4.2 Selected Response Question
Online 4.3 Advanced Placement Prompt
Online 4.4 Error Chart

Acknowledgements

Anne is grateful for her association with the Puget Sound Writing Project and the Oakland Writing Project, which nurtured her understanding of best practices in the teaching of writing. She expresses gratitude to the many teachers who have shared with her their concerns about the negative effects of tests on writing instruction, and she thanks Crystal Summers for tracking down so many state writing tests.

Leila would like to thank the students in Roseann Blum's spring 2004 tenth-grade English class, Clover Hill High School, Chesterfield County Public Schools, Chesterfield, Virginia.

Kelly would like to acknowledge the assistance of the students, teachers, parents, and administrators of the Fairbanks North Star Borough School District, with whom she discussed approaches to preparing students for the Alaska State High School Qualifying Exam. In addition, Kelly values the discussion with AP readers at Daytona each year, who are experts at blending best practices with solid test preparation.

Together, Anne, Leila, and Kelly say a special thanks to their editor, Jim Strickland, who believed in this book from the beginning and saw it through to the end.

Writing
ON DEMAND

Preface

Experienced teachers know that writing can be taught, that it has become increasingly important to teach it well.

—ERIKA LINDEMANN

Teachers need opportunities to learn more effective procedures for teaching writing. Tests of writing cannot teach that.

—GEORGE HILLOCKS JR.

This spring we cleaned out office bookshelves, discarding duplicates of books and old texts and rearranging what was useful and still current. We should most likely have thrown it away, but we decided to keep a copy of *How to Prepare Students for Writing Tests* (Tuttle 1986), a National Education Association monograph whose pages are now yellowed and that has not been read or consulted in many years. More out of curiosity than anything, we opened *How to Prepare Students* and found, in its beginning pages, an eerily prescient warning:

> Throughout the 1970s a clamor arose over the apparent decline in the quality of writing by American students. As a result of this outcry . . . research has encouraged instructional changes in the schools, focusing particularly on direct instruction and more assessment of student writing. The emphasis on evaluation has placed great pressures on students to perform well in writing tests . . . The call for writing tests has been dramatically exemplified by the increasing requirement of writing samples as part of basic skills tests in many states, [samples that are] used to judge individual competency. Students who fail to achieve minimum writing standards usually receive remediation and continue taking the writing tests until they pass. In some cases, those who do not achieve minimum competency on these tests may not be granted high school diplomas . . . In addition to the state

1

requirements, some students also face other kinds of writing assessments as they elect to take tests for advanced education. These "tests" range from formal, commercial tests such as the Scholastic Aptitude Test Writing Sample to writing tasks such as essays on college applications. (5–6)

Today, writing on demand is not an occasional, in-some-cases situation but an omnipresent one that faces all our students at all levels of skill and ability.

And today here we are. This report of the state of writing assessment, published nearly twenty years ago and reaching back thirty-five years, is an accurate description of what is now occurring in schools all across the country. Today, decades after the data for *How to Prepare Students* was collected, we are squarely positioned in a world of high-stakes tests. Today, writing on demand is not an occasional, in-some-cases situation but an omnipresent one that faces all our students at all levels of skill and ability.

The World We Live In

We live in a world of high-stakes testing and, in the area of writing, of testing on-demand writing. This is serious for secondary school students, who must learn to write effectively within a narrow window of time. Further, because these tests often carry consequences, there is also sometimes an emotional component for students, a component we know is not conducive to good writing. Nevertheless, high-stakes tests are here to stay for the near future. Highly focused writing in response to a specific prompt, completed within a limited amount of composing time, and scored using a weighted rubric, is the norm for most large-scale writing samples currently required by states and schools, by the current Scholastic Aptitude Test (SAT) and American College Test (ACT) writing exams, by some colleges, and by Advanced Placement (AP) English exams. In addition, many colleges and universities have established their own writing tests, and some require all entering undergraduates to take a proctored writing exam. Further, once students are accepted into college, they find that many courses in different disciplines require them to write essay exams. By the year 2000, forty-nine states had established academic standards for their schools, and according to a recent study, thirty-six of fifty states now mandate some form of writing assessment (National Writing Project and Nagin 2003, 75). Those assessments range from under a half hour to a few hours long and have attached, as their consequences, grades, rewards, and even high school graduation.

The professional literature of English teachers is filled with critiques of large-scale tests. And there is no shortage of criticism for writing on demand. These criticisms proceed from the view that both current teaching practices and research in composition are at odds with writing on demand. As noted researcher George Hillocks Jr. observes of writing tests, "Certainly testing assures that what is tested is taught, but tests cannot assure that things are taught well" (2002, 204). In addition, writing process pedagogies are frequently cited when objections to large-scale writing tests are made. Critics point to the differences between timed writing samples and the multiple drafts produced in regular classroom work. They cite the limitations of prompts designed for mass audiences and the inability of large-scale tests to address the needs of individual students. They criticize the disjuncture between the constraints of writing on demand and the research on writing processes. Frequently, these critics also take exception to the processes and standards employed in scoring the writing produced by students under test conditions. In sum, many critics contend that writing on demand almost always results in impoverished writing.

There is no shortage of criticism for writing on demand.

As part of the preparation to write this book, we talked with a number of classroom teachers and language arts supervisors in several states. We found first, regarding writing tests, that most of the tests require a prompt that elicits a variety of rhetorical modes: persuasion, exposition, argument, analysis, narrative. At the time of our research, we found that the length of the tests varied from a few hours (California) to twenty-five minutes (the state test in Tennessee and the SAT writing sample proposed by the College Board). In Virginia, students are currently given fifty minutes to write but can ask for more time. In practice, few do. At the time of our conversations with teachers in various states, we found that a very few states, like Michigan, allow students to revise their drafts in a separate testing session.

Our discussions revealed that most teachers prepare students for state and district writing samples a few weeks in advance. In general, we found that teachers give students sample essays that are considered exemplary; they have students write sample essays in timed conditions; and they instruct students directly regarding topic sentences, transitions, sentence structure, prewriting, organizational strategies, and sentence expansions. Some teachers require students to use a template form (the template most frequently cited was, not surprisingly, the five-paragraph theme). Teachers also reported that they present rubrics to students, have students make their own rubrics, and also take time to discuss teacher-made check sheets. Materials to prepare students for these tests are not uniform. The overwhelming majority of people with whom we talked use their own materials, while a small number of teachers use state- or district-provided materials.

Advanced Placement English teachers described themselves as preparing students the entire year, and some did not see a relationship between Advanced Placement English courses and good writing instruction. Some said they worry about teaching only to the test, and others mentioned that the Advanced Placement English exam itself fosters academic prose that is not needed or required in college writing classes. As one person put it, these "pressure comps" are unrepresentative of the writing taught in a "best practices" model and, as many teachers claimed, they focus on analysis. In addition, they do not take voice into account. Also, some AP teachers fret over the timed aspect of the AP exam. One wrote of her concern in an email:

> The drawback is the timed aspect . . . I have had several students who were outstanding writers when they could take an essay home and have time to craft it. However, they never did do well in timed essay questions. They all passed the AP exam (score of 3 or better), but the scores were not 5's—which would have reflected their outstanding writing better in some ways. (Bouta 2004)

Many Advanced Placement English teachers, however, feel the exam is positive, citing in particular that the one open question (of three questions on the Advanced Placement English exam) is helpful and that the exam's concentration on tone, audience, logic, and critical thinking has brought rigor to the high school. Some Advanced Placement teachers, in fact, consider the course to be equivalent—or even superior—to freshman college classes and feel that they have to teach writing comprehensively in order to prepare students for the exam. We interviewed one AP teacher, who wrote:

> I like the free response questions very much. They ask students to think, analyze and then give back their answers in [an] organized format. I think it tests accurately a number of skills college freshman composition classes ask for. (Bouta 2004)

In addition, some teachers do feel that because of the burgeoning numbers of students in Advanced Placement courses, many Advanced Placement English instructors are not prepared to teach the course—or, presumably, prepare students to take the exam—effectively. This may be partly because of high teacher turnover in schools and budget cuts: experienced teachers are retiring, and when they leave, inexperienced teachers find themselves with AP classes for which they have no training.

Most clearly, the stakes are high. Acceptable scores on these writing samples can ensure a wide variety of benefits: high school graduation, college entrance, and college credit for English classes taken before the freshman year. On the other hand, writing teachers are not satisfied with what they must do to prepare their students and how that preparation might contradict their classroom instruction on a daily basis.

What Writing Teachers Need

While the current high-stakes writing assessments vary in detail and scope, what remains constant is the need for a student to produce a successful finished product on an unfamiliar topic and within a limited space of time. In addition, the ever present essay exam requires students to produce relatively polished writing on a more familiar topic. Regardless, writing on demand is a crucial skill for high school and college students, and it is imperative that we, their teachers, help them learn that skill.

However, this is easier said than done. As mentioned earlier, most teachers rely on self-developed materials to prepare their students for writing on demand or they turn to test-specific materials. In either case, preparation for writing on demand is often largely disconnected from the curriculum and puts teachers in the position of teaching to the test while students develop an impoverished concept of writing.

We acknowledge the problems with writing on demand, but we believe that focusing energy on objecting to writing on demand has left little time to consider the ways it might contribute to positive developments in teaching. We believe it is possible to integrate writing on demand into a plan for teaching based on best practices.

> *We believe it is possible to integrate writing on demand into a plan for teaching based on best practices.*

The Assumptions Guiding This Book

From our perspective, *most writing is writing on demand*. To see high-stakes tests as something separate from our teaching is to give those high-stakes tests unwarranted power over our teaching and our curriculum. In the chapters that follow, we look to the continuities between teaching and testing, and we offer approaches that simultaneously help develop student writing abilities and prepare students to write successfully on demand. In addition to providing guidance for teaching processes of writing, we offer ways of thinking about the relationship between the classroom and externally imposed tests of writing.

We proceed from several classroom-tested assumptions, the first of which is crucial:

1. *Good writing and writing on demand are not contradictory.*
   The essential skills that student writers need to craft effective prose—getting ideas, drafting, revising, editing, and working with sentence-level issues—are all part of an effective final writing piece that will yield appropriate scores for on-demand writing tests. There can be *a real sense of fit* between good writing and on-demand writing.

2. *Assessment is an integral part of effective writing instruction.*
   Students should learn how to use assessment (including the forms represented by writing on demand) to improve their own writing. By becoming effective evaluators of their own and others' writing,

students will improve as writers and, at the same time, perform better in contexts that ask them to write on demand. Teachers need tools for assessing student progress toward meeting the demands of timed writing *before* their students take an externally imposed test (see Chapters 1, 4, and 8).

3. *Writing prompts can be approached rhetorically.*
   Whether one considers an assignment given in a composition class or a prompt on a state-mandated test, the language used to tell students what and how to write provides rhetorical cues. Students *can learn* how to read writing prompts more effectively if they have a basic understanding of the principles of rhetoric (see Chapters 3 and 6).

4. *Close reading fosters good writing.*
   Although reader response approaches have their place, classes that focus on writing instruction need also to employ critical approaches that help students focus on the details of prose. Attention to how phrases, sentences, and paragraphs are put together will give students a broader repertoire to draw upon in their own writing, especially when they compose under the pressure of a timed test (see Chapter 7).

5. *Criteria for evaluation belong in the classroom.*
   For too long the process of evaluating writing has been shielded from student view. As research on the recent emergence of evaluative rubrics in composition classes shows, students can improve their own writing when they develop a better understanding of *what readers expect.* Furthermore, when teachers and students look at evaluative criteria together, the distance between classroom and large-scale assessment is decreased (see Chapters 4 and 8).

Finally, writing is not learned quickly or once for all time. It is learned best over an extended time period, and that learning is frequently recursive. If a school district pays attention to this concept, curricula will be similarly recursive, and thoughtful curricula will provide a scaffolding of concepts and skills. This is particularly helpful in preparing students for writing on demand because it fosters confidence and familiarity with many forms of writing. Citing the *Report of the National Commission on Writing in America's Schools and Colleges* we believe that "standards, curriculum, and assessment must be aligned, in writing and elsewhere in the curriculum, in reality as well as in rhetoric" (College Board 2003, 4).

Accordingly, this book moves through issues and repeats topics in the chapters. We consider the way that best practice and curriculum need to relate, and within this book's nine chapters, we return to and explore the same concepts from different perspectives.

Who We Are

The three of us, in these pages, offer our insight and our expertise. All of us have taught writing in middle school and high school; all of us have worked with state and national assessments, helping design prompts and giving feedback on test administration and test scoring. One of us, Anne, is a specialist in composition and rhetoric and has written widely on the subject. Another of us, Kelly, though on leave from her high school classroom, has taught AP classes and has served as a reader for the AP exam. The third of us, Leila, also taught AP English and recently returned to high school to teach junior English, where she prepared her students for her state's writing test.

More importantly, to produce this book, the three of us have talked and written and shared with many teachers over a period of some years. We have spent time in classrooms and considered the apparatus of testing and the development of test items. Thus we bring to these pages our knowledge, our experience, and, to a certain extent, our dreams and aspirations. We hope that what we offer here will be thought provoking, worthwhile, and, ultimately, beneficial to students everywhere. Finally, we believe—and we trust this book will confirm—that teachers *can* prepare students for on-demand writing without sacrificing best practices and without compromising ideals. Preparing students for tests need not be separate from delivering good writing instruction. To the contrary, it can underscore best practice and exemplify best teaching.

> *Preparing students for tests need not be separate from delivering good writing instruction.*

Key Points for Reflection

While we join many teachers who question the current climate of writing on demand and writing-on-demand tests, there are positive points to remember. We believe:

- Good writing and the requirements of writing on demand do not need to be in conflict.

- When teachers and students consider together the craft of effective prose—getting ideas, drafting, revising, editing, and considering evaluative criteria—there will be a real sense of fit between the writing that takes place in English class and the writing that successfully meets the criteria for on-demand tests.

WORKS CITED

Bouta, Katherine. 2004. Personal email correspondence with the authors. 17 May.

College Board. 2003. *Report of the National Commission on Writing in America's Schools and Colleges: The Neglected "R" and the Need for a Writing Revolution.* College Entrance Examination Board.

Hillocks, George Jr. 2002. *The Testing Trap: How State Writing Assessments Control Learning.* New York: Teachers College Press.

National Writing Project and Carl Nagin. 2003. *Because Writing Matters: Improving Student Writing in Our Schools.* San Francisco: John Wiley and Sons.

Tuttle, Frederick B., Jr. 1986. *How to Prepare Students for Writing Tests.* Washington, DC: NEA.

Thinking Backward

Perhaps what we need is greater faith in our students' abilities to understand that a test is an artificial construct. It requires a degree of expediency, but it's not a surrender of the soul.

—ANTHONY J. SCIMONE

Until thoughtful educators are in complete charge of schools and allowed to make and enforce sensible decisions about assessment, teachers will continue to live in a world where externally mandated, large-scale, high-stakes tests are an inescapable part of the educational landscape. The current testing juggernaut looms with its inequities, its inconsistencies, and its inherent unfairness. These include, but are not limited to the following:

- long delays in score reports (Educational Testing Service 2002, 2004; Michigan 2003);

- inaccurate scores due to both flawed questions and erroneous answer keys (math test, Minnesota 2001); and

- misleading questions based on reworded and rewritten literature excerpts (New York Regents Exam 2002).

In our schools and wider communities we can continue to point out these issues, work for modification and change, and, as a last resort as in some communities in America, even encourage the boycott of the tests themselves. But at this writing it appears that high-stakes tests and large-scale assessments are not going away anytime soon.

The testing system is undeniably flawed, but until real change is initiated, our students must face those tests and must, if they wish to advance their academic careers, do well on those tests. With that reality in mind, we think it is irresponsible to leave our students to fend for themselves.

Teachers who choose to stay in the educational system—and certainly some teachers have left their school systems over the issue of testing—must not just curse the darkness but light candles. The current climate demands measurable, specific educational accountability, and while it clearly has flaws, the major manifestation of that accountability is through testing and test scores. At all levels—K–12, university, and teacher preparation—teachers live in an era of standardized, high-stakes testing, which is administered, assessed, and reported to the public. Often funding is tied to these reports.

Teachers who remain in the classroom *must* actively help students meet the demands of these high-stakes tests and give them strategies for success. It can be helpful to adopt Anthony Scimone's idea that our students may know more surely than we that this kind of writing test is part of a system that they must negotiate, a temporary hurdle, even an artificial and necessary evil, but not an invitation to lose their souls.

In addition, teachers must be aware of and sensitive to the psychological consequences of a test-drenched atmosphere. For many students there is an emotional component to tests and testing, and caring teachers can do much in instruction and in classroom affect to help students not only meet the demand but remain unthreatened by it. When students feel they have a mastery of skills, they are confident, and the perceived threat of tests, testing, and their consequences is far less overwhelming. While no teacher can make stress and tension disappear in the face of an on-demand writing test, he or she can do much to boost student confidence, depersonalize the test, and even neutralize testing's often negative atmosphere.

The Ideal of the Process Writing Model: Time, Ownership, and Response

One thing we need to consider is the relation between the requirements of on-demand testing and the ideal of how we feel writing should be taught in a best practice classroom. The composition theorists we've learned from all ascribe to a number of constants when they consider the ideal of the process writing model, principles considered essential for students and their writing. According to respected teachers and theorists (Janet Emig, Donald Murray, Donald Graves, Lucy Calkins, Nancie Atwell, and Erika Lindemann, among others), those principles are *time, ownership,* and *response.* Let's take a look at all three.

Regarding the first, insufficient time is the enemy of good writing, forcing students to draft without preparation and reflection and to edit without real revision. Regarding ownership, most theorists believe that students must have input into the shape and definition of the writing topic, that they should be able to form it in a way that makes the topic mean something to them. Finally, theorists agree that writers cannot produce in a vacuum: writers deserve response from other writers, that is, from peers and from teachers.

Countless writing teachers across the country have subscribed to this trinity of time, ownership, and response. Teachers who believe with Emig and Atwell and others that these are nonnegotiable ingredients ask how they can prepare students for writing on demand, writing that limits time, limits ownership, and, beyond a test score, limits response. The answer, sure and simple, is that students are capable of distinguishing the kinds of writing that occur in the classroom over weeks and months and in pursuit of a rich topic from the kinds of writing that they need to demonstrate on a test. Teachers can remind students that they will experience writing in a testing situation differently from the writing they regularly do in our classes. As Anthony Scimone already notes at the beginning of this chapter, students know the difference. Teachers need to make a distinction between the kind of writing environment that theorists and others so rightfully advocate and the kind of writing skills that an on-demand test requires. To do less is to abdicate their responsibility as teachers and as guides to success. At the same time, as we argue through most of this book, good writing instruction is not necessarily inimical to good test preparation: while the two diverge in some areas, they can also be made harmonious and consistent.

That said, how can teachers help our students meet the challenge of writing on demand in the context of instruction that meets student needs and satisfies standards for best practice? We believe, along with teacher Jeffrey Schwartz, that "a process-based curriculum with high standards is in itself valid preparation for the [AP] exam" (2004, 57), as long as that curriculum includes attention to the special skills required by writing tests. In other words, we don't think that drilling students in a disconnected practice is the best test preparation. Instead, we emphasize strategies that are both effective in the testing situation and intellectually defensible in light of what we know about how real writers write. In this chapter we begin at the end by showing how teachers can help students work inductively and think backward from rubrics and polished writing to the way such writing is produced.

We emphasize strategies that are both effective in the testing situation and intellectually defensible in light of what we know about how real writers write.

Thinking Backward: Three Steps

Teachers can begin to help students prepare for writing on demand by inviting them to think backward. Specifically, before they practice any kind of timed, prompt-driven writing that also uses a rubric for evaluation (and a

rubric toward which students would write), they should follow three prepara-
tory steps. Over a series of days, both with literature and student-written samples of writing, students should do these things:

- read and discuss in general terms a range of models;

- assess in specific terms the qualities of those models; and

- speculate on the impetus for each model and what it is trying to
  accomplish.

ONLINE
1.1

Thinking Backward: Three Steps

1. *Read and discuss in general terms* the models of writing, considering these questions:

   How do you *generally react* to this piece of writing?
   What do you think makes it *effective?* Less than effective?
   What is, for you, the model's *overall impression?*
   How do you *compare* this writing to other pieces you have read?

2. *Assess in more specific terms* and within certain parameters (i.e., using or even creating
   an evaluative rubric) the qualities of these models, considering these questions:

   What are the *dominant characteristics* of this model of writing?
   How would you describe its *language?*
   > Structure?
   > Sentence rhythm?
   > Transitional words or phrases?
   > Word use?
   > Organization?
   What, if any, is the personal *appeal?*
   What is its persuasiveness?

3. *Speculate on the impetus for this model* of writing and what you think it is trying to accomplish (i.e., what might be the prompt that would have generated this model?),
   considering the following questions:

   What do you think the writer is *trying to accomplish* in this piece?
   What do you think is the writer's *point of view?*
   Who do you think might be the *ideal audience* to read and appreciate this piece of
       writing?
   Who might be a *less than ideal audience?*

It's worth remembering that students may need instruction and discussion regarding terminology. While teachers might assume that students understand the terms *structure, sentence rhythms, organization,* and *transitional words,* such may not be the case at all. If students do not have a working vocabulary in these terms, it is important to provide discussion and examples. Otherwise, students will be relatively clueless regarding rubrics and evaluative terms.

When students are comfortable with this kind of consideration —working backward from writing to rubric to prompt—they are then ready to move forward.

When students are comfortable with this kind of consideration and can address texts and answer questions such as the ones in Online 1.1 with a sense of ease and confidence—working *backward* from writing to rubric to prompt—they are ready to move *forward*. Using an established rubric and a prompt, students can create a writing sample response within a time limit. With this kind of background they may well have a better appreciation of how a prompt and a rubric can govern and help create an effective piece of writing.

Thinking backward is part of literary study, and it is what teachers can most effectively do to help students consider and meet the requirements of writing on demand. Rather than have students immediately practice writing to a prompt in a timed situation and then scoring that writing using a rubric, thinking backward takes students from acknowledged models back to their rubric and then back to the prompt. Once students are confident that they can speculate about why a good piece of writing is good, how it fulfills the requirements of a rubric, and how it addresses a prompt successfully, they are then better able to move forward, looking at prompts with an eye to a rubric and to creating their own successful writing samples.

Thinking Backward with "My Name"

The model for this kind of thinking backward is not artificial or even, in the broad scope of the English language arts class, unfamiliar. As noted earlier, it has precedent in literature teaching, especially when teachers present a text to their students and ask them to consider its merits, a consideration that often occurs without the support of author biography, history, or even, initially, specific consideration of the context of the writing. In English classes, teachers and students look at a piece and generally discuss it, decide how and, in specific, where it is effective and well written, and then imagine the conditions—political, personal, historical, sociological—that inspired the writer to create this poem, short story, play, novel, or essay.

Imagine: A ninth-grade class reads "My Name," one of the brief sections from Sandra Cisneros' *House on Mango Street* (1984). While students know that when a work is published and presented in class it is likely to be considered worthwhile, they are often encouraged to discuss their reactions—both positive and negative—and, essentially, to assess general quality and to discuss why the selection is a strong piece of writing. In the case of "My Name," students would most likely conclude that it is short but effective and not only establishes the main character as a person but also gives some family background, cultural details, and a hint of what is to come in *Mango Street*. The humor of the piece might be a standout, as well as the professed individuality of the writer.

My Name

In English my name means hope. In Spanish it means too many letters. It means sadness, it means waiting. It is like the number nine. A muddy color. It is the Mexican records my father plays on Sunday mornings when he is shaving, songs like sobbing.

It was my great-grandmother's name and now it is mine. She was a horse woman too, born like me in the Chinese year of the horse—which is supposed to be bad luck if you're born female—but I think this is a Chinese lie because the Chinese, like the Mexicans, don't like their women strong.

My great-grandmother. I would've liked to have known her, a wild horse of a woman, so wild she wouldn't marry. Until my great-grandfather threw a sack over her head and carried her off. Just like that, as if she were a fancy chandelier. That's the way he did it.

And the story goes she never forgave him. She looked out the window her whole life, the way so many women sit their sadness on an elbow. I wonder if she made the best with what she got or was she sorry because she couldn't be all the things she wanted to be. Esperanza. I have inherited her name, but I don't want to inherit her place by the window.

At school they say my name funny as if the syllables were made out of tin and hurt the roof of your mouth. But in Spanish my name is made out of a softer something, like silver, not quite as thick as sister's name—Magdalena—which is uglier than mine. Magdalena who at least can come home and become Nenny. But I am always Esperanza.

I would like to baptize myself under a new name, a name more like the real me, the one nobody sees. Esperanza as Lisandra or Maritza or Zeze the X. Yes. Something like Zeze the X will do. (10–11)

In this ninth-grade class, beyond a general discussion, it would be routine for a teacher to ask students to explore specifically why they think the selection is an effective one; in answer, students might look at the use of vivid characters, the specific details, the figurative language. Essentially, then, students would consider what elements of craft this piece uses and how it fulfills these expectations of excellence.

Certainly in "My Name," many qualities of language and general appeal are present: Esperanza's great-grandmother is "a wild horse of a woman" and spent years in depression where she "looked out the window her whole life, the way so many women sit their sadness on an elbow." The pronunciation of Esperanza's name is made both poetic and a comment upon cultural differences: "At school they say my name funny as if the syllables were made out of tin and hurt the roof of your mouth." The end of the piece hints at how Esperanza would like to change: "I would like to baptize myself under a new name, a name more like the real me, the one nobody sees."

What rubric could be used to assess this piece? For instance, does "My Name" tell a fully developed narrative *(no)*; does it use poetic language *(absolutely)*; does it provide detail *(yes)*; does it give us a full character sketch of Esperanza *(yes* and *no)*. If we had to create a rubric that would fairly evaluate "My Name," what would it look like? Students might consider a sample rubric, using the headings *Narrative, Word choice, Use of detail,* and *General impression*. Pertinent questions related to each heading could prompt students to examine different parts of "My Name."

Sample Rubric for "My Name"

I. Narrative: *To what extent does this piece tell a complete story?*

II. Word choice: *To what extent does the writer use vivid or unusual words or phrases?*

III. Use of detail: *To what extent does the writer provide specifics to help make a point?*

IV. General impression: *At the end of this piece, to what extent do you feel you have a complete picture of "My Name"?*

Prompts for "My Name"

Finally, students might be asked to consider why and for whom the speaker wrote this piece—what, essentially, was the motivation or intent (or prompt)? If we had to write a prompt that might have generated something such as "My Name," what would we include in it? Let's look at some possibilities.

Is this a memory of the family? Certainly a father, a great-grandmother, a great-grandfather, and a sister are all mentioned. The connections are strong, as is the narrator's relation to these various people in her family group. If this is true, the prompt could be something like this:

Sample Prompt 1 for "My Name"

Write a brief memoir of your family and discuss the influences on you of your grandparents, parents, and siblings. Provide details.

Or, is this an effort to set the facts right? Surely Esperanza gives us her interpretation of her great-grandmother and great-grandfather's life; she critiques how her Anglo schoolmates pronounce her name as well as critiques her sister (at least through her less attractive name). If so, the prompt could be this:

Sample Prompt 2 for "My Name"

Sometimes people feel they are misunderstood. If you had to "set the record straight" about yourself, what one or two things would you want people to know about you? Be specific.

Is this a bid for a new life? It may be, for at the end of "My Name," Esperanza gives us a list of possible new names—is this whole piece a rationale for a new name and all that it might entail? If so, the prompt might be this:

Sample Prompt 3 for "My Name"

If you had the opportunity to give yourself a new name and a new identity, what would it be and why? What would be the reasons for this change?

Or is "My Name" more of a literal discussion of the name *Esperanza*, where it came from, how it is used, and why it is, at least to the speaker, less than ideal? If we approach the piece from that angle, we might conclude the following prompt is appropriate:

Sample Prompt 4 for "My Name"

Discuss your own first and/or middle name. To the best of your knowledge, what does this name or these names mean? Where do they come from, and what do you know about how your parents or guardians selected these names?

The point is: if we had to write a prompt that might have generated something such as "My Name," what would we include in it?

All of these considerations are similar to what teachers can ask students to do with writing models, working backward to consider general writing quality, a possible rubric, and, finally, a prompt. By considering what kinds of factors a writer might have had in mind, it may be clearer to students that writing can be truly purposeful, directive, and targeted. Further, the connection of prompts to rubrics can also be explored, although in most situations, the rubric is broad enough to accommodate a fairly wide range of prompts. To encourage further reflection, teachers could assign a writer's notebook and invite students to respond.

Using a Writer's Notebook

In this chapter and in subsequent ones we suggest topics that students can respond to in a notebook. These writer's notebook suggestions are an important strategy for teachers to use with students, as the topics can help them become more reflective regarding their own writing and more careful with what they choose to include in their writing. In addition, a writer's notebook can be an invaluable place to jot down ideas, phrases, quotations, interesting words, and other information that a writer may want to incorporate in a draft. Having students start a notebook early in the year and giving them credit for maintaining that notebook can help students feel a sense of ownership and pride, and it can encourage them to truly see themselves as what we want them to be: writers. Look, for instance, at the following writer's notebook suggestion, a question that may encourage students to think backward and understand more about writing.

Writer's Notebook

Select a piece of prose (essay, short story, novel) that you have recently read and enjoyed. Now imagine that it was written *in response* to a hypothetical prompt. What would that prompt contain; how would it read? Write out the prompt as if the author had responded to it with the essay, short story, or novel that you have selected. If you can, craft a second hypothetical (and also plausible) prompt.

And now let us move from literature to writing on demand.

Thinking Backward with Student-Written Models

For many students, the frustration and fear of responding to test-situated prompts is the sheer uncertainty of the enterprise: students are often unclear regarding what is required of them and what they should be focusing on in such an essay. It is, accordingly, vital to expose students to numbers of sample essays that try to meet the demands of a prompt and attempt to fulfill the expectations of an evaluative rubric. Literature is one thing—students expect that the writing in the anthology and in published books is what teachers consider the real thing, worthy of reading and critique. They may not always like what they read, but the unspoken assumption—assented to by most students, even the disaffected—is that the literature presented in class is something that someone thinks is good.

Not so with writing produced in a test situation. What constitutes an effective or acceptable response for a test may, for some, be far murkier. Accordingly, students must have chances to see, analyze, and discuss sample—if not always exemplary—pieces of peer-level work. They need, in class, to spend some time examining not just what could be improved but what makes a good response or good essay and how a good one effectively addresses a prompt and conforms to the criteria of an evaluative rubric. Certainly while many students are adept at pointing out (for some, even hunting out) writing weaknesses—identifying fragments, for instance, or citing a weak conclusion or insufficient detail—they may not have much practice in discussing what in specific contributes to the success of a strong piece of writing.

If students are to think backward and consider what makes a strong essay, they might start by looking at pieces of writing that are good, if not exemplary. Teachers can give students a number of essays that are either descriptive or persuasive (the dominant rhetorical modes required in most test situations) and ask them to read these in class, respond to them individually by writing in a journal, and then discuss openly—in either a large group, a small group, or both—what makes each piece effective. While it might be tempting to coach students into categories of evaluative classification—precise language, clear transitions, and unity of development—it is important that students have an initial opportunity to describe in their own words, *without using preset structures,* what makes a piece effective.

Writer's Notebook

Imagine that you are coaching a student who is younger than you and who is also having a lot of trouble writing successfully in school. Think about the writing you have done that has been fun for you—and which has gotten a good grade. What specific advice would you give this student about successful writing? What kinds of features should the student be sure to add to his or her writing or make sure he or she avoids? From your perspective, what can you tell the student about good writing?

After this general discussion, students can go back and specifically discuss the writing. Only then and using the characteristics that come from the discussion should they be invited to craft a rubric for the essay or response itself that would reflect its characteristics. The question is: If we were to devise a rubric that would capture the distinctive marks of the essay, what would it include?

Finally, students can go backward another step and create a possible prompt for which the essay might have been written. Our question to students is: What kind of question or prompt inspired or guided this essay?

Some Sample Models

Let's take a look at a number of essays from actual tenth graders who responded in class to a yet undisclosed prompt. (Please note: All student writing is reproduced as it was originally written and punctuated.) The setting was a practice for the state writing exam, and all of the essay samples were written at the same time and are from the same class. Again, in sequence, looking at two essays, students could consider a number of questions.

MINILESSON

Goal: To have students read two essays and discuss their general impression and their relative merit. To also have students speculate regarding the rubric and possible prompts that might have inspired these essays.

Talking Points:

- Rubrics can tell us much about what is expected for a successful piece of writing.

- Let's work backward and extract from a text what might be used on an accompanying rubric.

Sample Student Essay 1

ONLINE
1.2

Throughout my school career I feel the most valuable course I have taken is keyboarding/computer applications. Not only did I learn to type faster, but I was taught the correct way to type. I also gained general knowledge about the computer and some of its important programs. This course has greatly helped me in my high school career, but I guarantee it will help me in the future.

So far, I have been able to type my essays and reports quickly, which helps with time. Also, I've been able to produce amazing powerpoint presentations for school projects. This all benefits from the keyboarding/computer applications course I took. However, I also feel this course will benefit me in the future. Such as, I will know how to use databases and spreadsheets to help me organize important information, like tax payments or bills. Also, as time progresses computers are used more and more everyday. So, when applying for jobs or college, once they see I've taken a course in keyboarding/computer applications, that will be a positive factor, and might help me get the job or get into that college. I've also heard that college professors like for papers to be typed. This will also decrease my time writing papers in college.

Keyboarding/computer applications has definitely got to be the most valuable course I've taken. Not only has this course been a help to me now, but will also provide much help in the future. I'm very happy that I chose to take this course. After taking the course my knowledge of the computer grew. This is why I feel it is the most valuable.

Activity:

As a first step, encourage students to, for the moment, ignore length and usage issues and simply read and discuss the essay. (*Note:* Usage and spelling are reproduced as in the original.) Students can consider the following:

- What in general do you think is good about this essay? What kind of impressions or general points does it make?

- Looking at this essay, what in particular makes it a good essay? What particular aspects of this essay—such as structure, word choice, sentence variety—make it strong? If you were to create a rubric that could fairly score this essay, what would it contain?

- Going even further backward, what kind of prompt might have inspired this essay? What specific question or questions does it appear to be answering?

After a general discussion, students will certainly note that this writer presents his or her ideas directly and makes them clear throughout the essay. Students then might get specific: while there is a mechanical kind of restatement at the end *(This is why I feel it is the most valuable)*, this is a solid job and, essentially, gets the point across. It is well developed and clear, giving more than one or two reasons for the utility of a keyboarding and computer class, and features clear transitions *(also, such as, so)*, some interesting sentence construction *(not only did I learn; not only has this course)*, a definite introduction, and a conclusion.

As a second example, students might also look at the following essay:

ONLINE 1.3

Sample Student Essay 2

Through all the years that I have been in school, most of the courses I have taken have been the same. Math, Science, Social Studies, and English. It wasn't until 6th grade that I got freedom enough to choose my own courses.

In 6th grade, I choose to take a course called Orchestra. My grandfather had previously played the organ & the violin while he grew up. I wanted to impress him as much as I could, so I took that course. I didn't necessarily take it for him though, I wanted more options to things around me. Open the creativity I always knew I had inside me.

I have taken that course for more than five years now. I don't ever regret taking it. It's valuable because it lets me express my creativity and show that I understand the musical industry and the masterminds of the past.

Generally, students might agree that the brief piece of writing in Essay 2 sets up an idea and follows it. Specifically, despite the fragments, some punctuation problems, and occasional word misuse *(masterminds of the past)*, the writer makes a point and is more personal than the writer of Essay 1 regarding his or her own sense of self and connection to family. The writing links back to the creativity theme *(open the creativity I always knew I had inside me; lets me express my creativity)* and is expressive. It has some flavor to it *(I wanted to impress him as much as I could)*, and certainly shows more individuation—the example and approval of a grandfather—than Essay 1.

After students have generally and then specifically discussed these two essays and compared and contrasted tone, details, and content—a course that has given me skills that will get me into college and aid my schoolwork versus a course that has given me an opportunity to express my creativity—they might be invited to create a rubric that could be used to evaluate the two. Certainly, from the class discussion, it would emerge that both these papers are

- making an argument about the utility of a specific course;

- giving specific reasons to support that argument; and

- trying to appeal to the reader through logic and/or personal connection.

With regard to weaknesses in the papers, it might be helpful to include in the rubric criteria such as

- a conclusion that relates to the body of the paper as well as the introduction that sets the topic;

- the appropriate use of vocabulary; and

- correct usage.

These criteria could be organized and could then be used to score the two papers. A sample rubric such as the following might serve as a guide.

ONLINE
1.4

Sample Rubric

I. Argument with detail: *Does the writer make a point and provide specifics that illustrate that point?*

II. Voice (personal connection): *Does the writer "let us in"—can we tell that there is a real person behind this writing?*

III. Introduction and conclusion: *Is it clear from the beginning where this writer is going? Does the end provide a summary or final statement that seems to grow out of the whole piece?*

IV. Word choice and vocabulary: *Are the words appropriate to this piece? Are they used accurately?*

V. Usage: *Does the writer follow the rules regarding spelling, punctuation, capitalization, and so on?*

After establishing these requirements, students could also discuss weighting these five categories—they may wish to emphasize the argument and detail more than flavor in writing; usage, however, for some students, is perennially important. Here's a possible weighted rubric:

I.   Argument with detail (30%)

II. Voice (wit and personal connection) (20%)

III. Introduction and conclusion (20%)

IV. Word choice and vocabulary (15%)

V.   Usage (15%)

Students could use this rubric and score both papers; the weighting could be changed, obviously, but the rubric will show students how, in varying situations, different components can count more than others.

Assessment:
Finally, students could be asked to create a prompt that might encompass these two pieces. From the essays themselves, it would probably emerge that the prompt is asking the writer to make a case for an important course in school—what it was and why it was valuable. Students might create something such as the following:

Sample Prompt 1

Make an argument about something you learned in school that you think will help you later in life.

Sample Prompt 2

Discuss an unusual course or class you had in school that you especially enjoyed. What made it unusual and what specifically about it did you enjoy?

Sample Prompt 3

What is the most valuable course you have had in your school career? Be sure to tell why you feel it is important and give your reasons.

While Prompt 3 was the actual prompt used with these tenth-grade students, creating variations of the prompt based on slightly differing perceptions of the essays widens students' writing horizons and shows them how an essay can relate to and respond to a prompt.

Considering a Mix of Student-Written Essays

Once students have discussed two relatively successful essays, created a rubric, and come up with a prompt, they might benefit from quickly looking at other examples that are more of a mix and that might provide a more stark comparison and contrast. The following examples, though written by tenth-grade students in the same class as the previous two, are different from the preceding student essays largely in content, quality, and length. After reading them, students could, using the prompt and rubric they have established, rank and score the pieces.

Sample Student Essay 3

ONLINE
1.5

School is important for many reasons and goals. You learn things, you use your brain, you sharpen your social skills even enhance your weightlifting capacities through just stretching down to grab your back-pack. But it will also alert to people and things that you will despise once you get older. I found this out in middle school, in Mrs. Maddox's 5th period class. In this class, I would truly find the meaning of, "Help me!"

During this class, if she didn't give us homework the night before, then she pretended to have given us some and gave us a zero. If we needed to have a bodily function, then she just handed us a cup. If we were having trouble on a test, then she gave us a zero. The class in itself was a concentration camp and we were in the gas chamber. We learned what fear was, and that was about the extent of learning that we acquired in that deathtrap of a class. As the year drew to a close also, so did her threshold for sincereness. After the end of the year, only 3 kids were left in the class, she had consumed the others, but told the faculty that they died in a sad lab accident. Thank god I'm still alive to make words on this piece of tree.

After that class I learned a valuable lesson from the devil himself. I learned that a mean teacher doesn't make a good teacher. Strictness, which sounds the same, is the best thing, and a kind heart. A kind heart sure makes up for no heart. If someone finds Mrs. Maddox's heart, call me at 123–4876, thank you!

Students will most likely note the wit and hyperbole in Essay 3 but also the fact that it sets out its details well in the beginning and follows them through. There is also an overarching moral: being mean does not make a good teacher. One thing students might want to consider, however, is the possibility—a real one—that this student's unconventional take on school and occasional risqué language (*If we needed to have a bodily function, then she just handed us a cup*) might backfire. Otherwise-tolerant outside readers might find the comments about teachers unnecessary and offensive. Could that be reflected in the student's final score? It is certainly a possibility and should be discussed: Where do students think laudable creativity and risk taking might cross the boundary into foolhardiness? To what extent do students assume or believe in the broad-mindedness of their readers? To what extent is it possible for students to strike a middle ground here?

Here is another example.

ONLINE
1.6

Sample Student Essay 4

Throughout my extensive educational career contained within my feeble existence, a conclusion can be made pertaining to the most influencial educational seminar I have ever attended. Adamancy can be found in the desison that my eighth grade english class shaped my learning experience in the largest way. In attendance of this class my writing skills enhanced along with my once small vocabulary.

Students might point out that Essay 4 is not a particularly strong piece of writing and definitely not sufficiently developed. The vocabulary calls attention to itself and in some cases (*contained within my feeble existence;*

adamancy; enhanced) is misused. The very short piece also features odd constructions (*contained within my feeble existence;* equating a high school *course* with a *seminar*). The student is witty—yes, it is clear from this essay and its word choice that the writer's vocabulary has indeed been enlarged by English class—but further details are just not there. It is hard to figure out that eighth-grade English is the subject about which the student is writing in Essay 4, and, as a final critique, this three-sentence piece develops very little.

Here's another example:

Sample Student Essay 5

ONLINE 1.7

The most interesting class that I have ever taken was kindergarten. I chose this because it gave me the foundation that I needed for school.

I loved the years of kindergarten more than anything. Not having a care in the world, being able to nap, and not having severe consequences. I enjoyed having friends, the playground, and coloring. Those were the days when I didn't need a job, didn't have to worry about my grades or getting into college.

The greatest years and the best class I ever took was kindergarten. We take a lot of things for granit and we don't realize it until it's to late. One of the advantages of being older is the independence.

Students might like Essay 5; it has a sense of wit in that it cites kindergarten as an intellectual high point. The use of details in the second paragraph, listing what happened at that age as well as what the writer did not have to worry about *(not having severe consequences),* is effective. The conclusion is wistful *(we don't realize it until it's to late).* On the other hand, the last sentence *(one of the advantages of being older is the independence)* is a bomb shell: it undercuts the entire piece and begs for further development.

Sample Student Essay 6

ONLINE 1.8

Over the course of my many school years, I have absorbed ample amounts of knowledge to propel myself into the future of endless opportunity. However, there is one such course that widens my horizons when I go out into the world of diversity. This class is Spanish, and it affords me the ability to communicate to individuals from all different countries.

Length, as in some of the other pieces in this section, is a real issue here, but there are some useful sentence constructions *(absorbed . . . knowledge; propel myself into the future; affords me the ability)* and, despite the very brief nature of Essay 6, it has an introduction and a reason for the choice of Spanish as the most valuable course. Just how positively would students score this essay?

Here's a final example:

Sample Student Essay 7

From my sprouting years in elementary school to my present, drudging years of high school I have taken many courses; some that have interested me others not as much. My priviledged journey through school I have learned many skills and have discovered what kind of person I am. All of my courses have served their purpose though none like my photo class I am taking this year.

The first day of my photo class I was intimdated by all the curriculum and equipment the class required but I soon discovered the phenomenal world of photography. As the class unraveled, I adjusted and felt more and more comfortable "seeing photographically." Every class new knowledge was learned like how all the parts of the camera functioned and how their used.

Before long I was shooting assignments and learning all the processes involved in developing a roll of film. I was taught to always look for the fall of light on an object and to think of creative prospectives to capture. I saw that everyone in the class had their own unique touch for the photos they shot and I was discovering mine.

Great masters of photography like Ansel Adams and Robert Cappa have made me realize the marvelous pictures that can be taken with a camera.

Essay 7 is well developed despite some glaring word problems *(sprouting years; drudging years; as the class unraveled; creative prospectives)* and a reference *(Robert Cappa)* that misspells a famous photographer's last name *(Capa)*. It has a clear development, showing the writer's progress from the first class onward, and concludes with a relatively happy, even triumphant observation *(I saw that everyone in the class had their own unique touch for the photos they shot and I was discovering mine)*. As noted earlier, while the writer does not know the spelling of the famous photographers' names cited at the end of the essay, the attempt may well be appreciated and even rewarded in final scoring. Using this reference as a last single-sentence conclusion also shows some sense of drama and appropriate placement, although such a closing can also prove problematic because it introduces a whole new idea.

Writing on Demand: Practice and Evaluation

Once students have looked at real essay examples, both strong and not so strong, considered the construction of a rubric, and drafted a plausible prompt, they can compare and contrast essays through the rubric and have a better sense of what makes an effective response to a prompt. At this point students will be more ready to move forward, not backward, going now from prompt to writing to scoring, practicing writing to a specified prompt and then evaluating using a set rubric. Using a variety of prompts and opportunities to practice (interspersed with other class work), students will be better prepared for writing on demand. Further, they will become better writers, linking solid test preparation and good teaching.

After such preparation and practice, students can, in small groups or in pairs, score each other's papers and also benefit from a teacher's response and his or her discussion and scoring. Finally, if student-constructed rubrics do not contain the following heading areas, it might be good to present these to a class, as they represent, in the main, the qualities that are routinely assessed in rubrics:

Sample Standard Rubric

I. Introduction: *Is the topic clear from the beginning?*

II. Ideas and development: *Can you find the two or three major ideas, and are they explored in the essay?*

III. Organization: *Is there a sense of movement from the beginning to the middle to the end? Do the ideas progress?*

IV. Voice: *Can one hear the writer here?*

V. Word choice: *Are words used well, appropriately? Is there unnecessary repetition?*

VI. Sentence fluency: *Is there variation in sentence length, in the ways that sentences are started or shaped?*

VII. Conventions and usage: *Are words spelled correctly? Are punctuation and capitalization used correctly?*

Three Constants: The Rubric, the Audience, and the Purpose

Good writers are aware of a number of factors, and the consideration of rubric, audience, and purpose in test preparation can also underscore good writing and good writing instruction. (The rhetorical dimensions of these three factors are further explored in Chapters 3 and 6.) If the target writing-on-demand task is a state assessment or one required by the Advanced Placement exam, a wide range of published rubrics are available and can be used to guide teachers and students. Certainly being aware of the various categories of rubric concentration—conventions, organization, voice, and so on—is important, as is an understanding of the relative weight of those categories. (State assessments have been known to change the weight of emphases, and it is vital that teachers know if, in any given year, one trait is more heavily or less heavily weighted than in previous test administrations. See Chapters 6, 8, and 9 for more information.) Additionally, having students become comfortable with the rubric will help them, to an extent, guide their own writing and sense of emphasis.

Audience, however, is a definite constant. Students are less horrified, frankly, than most of their teachers that the audience for their writing will be an adult assessor with a clear agenda and a narrow focus. Getting students to understand the impersonality and even formality of this audience can be one of the most important things we do, and as Anthony Scimone reminds us, "A test may require them to take up a rhetorical position rather than communicate something they genuinely hold true. So what?" (2004, 15). So what indeed.

Finally, we need to remind students that in this case, their purpose is a clear one: pass or excel on the writing test. This may not be a time to show eccentricity, idiosyncrasies, or fragmentary brilliance (as in Essays 3 and 7), creating, essentially, an unnecessary distractor. This is writing for a specific, defined, and targeted purpose: to fulfill the rubric categories that are most valued and to demonstrate, in a confined space, that they can write and write effectively.

A Crucial Variable: The Prompt

Being able to read a prompt and to use it effectively is one of the great challenges of writing on demand. Certainly students must, in this scenario, have an idea of where they are going from the moment they begin to write: the generative principle of writing to learn is not, in this situation, wholly applicable. Scimone reminds us: "test conditions simply don't allow for the luxury of formulating tentative theories that might or might not hold up in the next sentence, and they seldom allow for enough time to reconstruct our opening positions" (2004, 14).

While Chapters 3 and 6 discuss prompts more extensively, students can, in their consideration of sample essays, have a more clear appreciation of how a skilled writer views a prompt and what sections or aspects of a prompt are important to address. And, looking over the range of twenty-some essays from this tenth-grade class, we see that four students prewrote before drafting, using the prompt to guide their thoughts. Two made fairly complicated webs, and two made lists. It is interesting that all four of the essays that showed some deliberate prewriting and planning were fairly long and, as a whole, better developed than those that did not show any sign of prewriting.

The Challenge of Time

Practice engenders confidence, and when students are able to quickly make notes on a prompt and prewrite and thus know where they are going in their writing, they are better prepared to use the time allotted—regardless of how long that time is. With practice and experience, time to draft will not be the same concern that it might be otherwise. And, if we are honest about most of our students' writing behaviors, secondary school students are indeed accustomed to writing within time constraints: they have done this for years on quizzes and tests and in creating short answers in response to class work. In addition, as evidence from one state (Virginia) writing test indicates, most students, when given the opportunity to take more time to work on their writing samples, do not avail themselves of the opportunity.

Writing on demand . . . is an artificial construct . . . it is not, however, an insurmountable task nor a mystery.

Key Points for Reflection

Writing on demand, as the epigraph at the beginning of this chapter claims, is an artificial construct. Despite that undeniable fact, it is not, however, an insurmountable task nor a mystery. Guided by their teachers, students regularly discuss literature using a structure that invites them to work and think backward; that same structure can be used to coach students and prepare them for writing on demand. With experience and practice, students can become comfortable addressing prompts in an effective manner and with an eye to a set evaluative rubric. Certainly there is a connection between test preparation and good writing instruction, and with our help, students will achieve success with both. The strategies they use to write efficiently and effectively and meet the needs of a predetermined topic can be used to advantage in many other academic and writing situations.

While success is never a foregone conclusion, by working backward and then practicing writing forward, students can acquire confidence and use specific strategies to meet the challenge of writing on demand. We believe:

- Writing on demand is neither an insurmountable task nor a mystery.

- Test preparation and good writing instruction are not incompatible.

- Working backward—and then working forward—can help students meet the challenge of writing on demand.

WORKS CITED

Atwell, Nancie. 1998. *In the Middle*. 2d ed. Portsmouth, NH: Heinemann.

Calkins, Lucy. 1994. *The Art of Teaching Writing*. Portsmouth, NH: Heinemann.

Cisneros, Sandra. 1984. "My Name." In *The House on Mango Street*. New York: Random House.

Emig, Janet. 1971. "The Composing Process of Twelfth Graders." In *NCTE Research Report No. 13*. Urbana, IL: NCTE.

Graves, Donald. 1983. *Writing: Teachers and Children at Work*. Portsmouth, NH: Heinemann.

Murray, Donald M. 1985. *A Writer Teaches Writing*. 2d ed. Boston: Houghton Mifflin.

Schwartz, Jeffrey. 2004. "Reflections of an AP Reader." *English Journal* 93 (4): 53–57.

Scimone, Anthony J. 2004. "The Trouble with Testing Is That It May Be Worth the Trouble." *English Leadership Quarterly* 26 (3): 14–15.

Processes of Writing

2

Writing is a lonely act that is never really performed alone.

—DONALD M. MURRAY

It seems impossible to talk about best practices and good writing instruction without including the *processes* writers use to craft effective prose—getting ideas, drafting, revising, editing, and considering evaluative criteria. While certain aspects of the best practices that go on in the process writing class cannot be carried over to most current testing situations—notably, extensive periods of time to compose and revise and the social dimension of working in peer response writing groups—we believe that most of what we call best practice, and processes of writing in particular, need not be in conflict with writing on demand. We recognize that this claim may seem unusual, even questionable, so in this chapter we will show that once students are comfortable and familiar with taking time to plan and get ideas and with taking time to reread their work and edit, they can use a writing process effectively on a writing test as well as in the classroom. We cannot transform an on-demand writing event into a full-blown writers workshop, but it is possible to use and use well a compressed, dense version of the writing process in a testing situation.

...it is possible to use and use well a compressed, dense version of the writing process in a testing situation.

Indeed, we are convinced that a process approach to writing should be integral: one of the best ways to help students develop as writers while simultaneously preparing them to face writing on demand is to make process writing a central part of teaching. We believe this because writing on demand can lead to a distorted focus on the *product* of writing, and everything we know about the ways actual writing works—as well as all the pedagogical research of the past forty years—tells us that total focus on the *product* of writing leads to inarticulate and terrified student writers. It also takes a great toll on teachers. Teachers can find balance by attending to the processes of writing, attention that will serve students well in the classroom and in testing situations.

To explain this point, we will take a brief look at history.

A Brief Look at the History of Writing Instruction

Almost one hundred years ago, a Kansas writing teacher wrote an article titled "Can Good Composition Teaching Be Done Under Present Conditions?" (Hopkins 1912). It was an intriguing title and, not surprisingly, the author, Edwin M. Hopkins, answered his own question in the one-word opening line: "No." Hopkins' discussion of why good composition teaching was difficult was the very first article published in the inaugural issue of *English Journal,* the flagship periodical of the newly formed National Council of Teachers of English. In Volume 1, Number 1 (January 1912), Edwin M. Hopkins discussed seriously—and even passionately—the state of early twentieth-century writing instruction in the United States.

As part of his discussion, Hopkins presented the results of a survey of writing instruction in American schools, research in which he had been seriously involved for some time. What is probably more memorable about Hopkins' 1912 piece, however, is his dramatic use of personal observations. Hopkins speculated that conscientious writing teachers, "worn out at an inhumanly rapid rate," would "resign, break down, perhaps become permanently invalided" (1) if conditions did not change. While his contemporary readers may not have realized it, Hopkins' almost melodramatic language was born less of academic inquiry than of bitter personal experience. As a young composition teacher, he had been hospitalized for exhaustion. He left teaching for some time to recuperate, and it was only when he could reduce his course load and the numbers of students whom he taught that he stabilized his emotional and physical health (Popken 2004). Hopkins returned to teaching, and over the remainder of his career he became a crusader of sorts for a reduced teaching load for writing instructors. Hopkins' 1923 *The Labor and Cost of the Teaching of English,* an extensive examination of the responses from almost one thousand secondary and college teachers across the United States, confirmed his beliefs, as the majority of the instructors agreed with Hopkins that good composition teaching was impossible at the time.

But what was it about student numbers in early twentieth-century American schools that made the teaching of writing so grueling? For one thing, the major focus for teachers was on the final draft, the product, of the student writer. In order, teachers felt, to improve the quality of student writing, it was essential that they spend significant time "marking" (meaning correcting) student papers, citing every error and making suggestions for stylistic changes. This kind of response took a tremendous amount of energy and became, for teachers of the time, the center of writing instruction. For even highly conscientious writing teachers in the early twentieth century, the attention to actually helping students get ideas, draft, and revise (and possibly use a teacher's marks and corrections to improve a draft) was never extensive. It was believed that students did not need this kind of help. Most instructors assumed that students could follow a series of steps in order to write well. The current wisdom was that, once given a topic, the student writer simply should decide what he or she wanted to write, organize it logically (most likely by putting the ideas in outline form), and then follow that outline to a successful final piece. In sum, teachers expected their students to get the idea, outline the idea, write from the outline, and then, as a last and final step, do some polishing.

If, however, for some reason the student's final draft was not successful, most writing teachers assumed it was because students just weren't following the procedure described previously. At any rate, the teacher's emphasis was on examining, marking, and fixing the final product: the extensive correction of papers, it was believed, would address all issues of writing deficiency. Using other writers—peers—to help with in-process drafting or with revision of drafts was not part of the procedure. While conferencing with the teacher was used in some writing classes in the early twentieth century, most student writers worked alone, wrote alone, revised alone, and dealt with the subsequent grade and teacher comments alone.

As always, some adaptable students wrote well under these circumstances. While numbers of students would indeed first write their drafts and *then* create an outline from what they had written (and then submit the outline to the teacher), the general format could be worked around. For many students, however, especially those who tried conscientiously to follow the step-by-step approach, the way they were told to write was not helpful. They never seemed to know exactly what to write *before* writing, and when the final product was found below standard, they were often surprised by the teacher's reaction. And for many students, the extensive marking of their papers was neither understood nor effectively implemented to the extent that they were able to make significant and lasting changes in their writing.

Writing Using a Traditional Model

In some classrooms today, the traditional model persists. In the traditional model of teaching writing, topics are wholly teacher determined and are relatively divorced from student experience and knowledge. In fact, in this model, writing topics tend to be fairly abstract and, for most middle schoolers and high schoolers, of little burning or immediate interest. There is also in this model limited attention to helping students get into a draft of writing, little attention to invention strategies or prewriting. As in years past, students are expected to come up with ideas on their own, and they may be asked to submit an outline of those ideas, which, as noted before, is expected to be complete and expected to be constructed *before* the submission of the final paper.

Because we know that many writers discover their topics as they write, this kind of assumption about what a writer knows before writing often leads to poor writing.

Another feature of the traditional model is limited time to write; most students are given a class period or a night to complete a final draft. Many times this writing is done wholly outside of class, which means that collaboration among students or sharing of drafts is rare and help from teachers is infrequent. In the traditional model, students write by themselves and figure out, by themselves, to what extent they can revise what they have written. Again, isolation is not helpful for many writers: the reactions and comments from readers are essential to understanding audience and to improving final drafts.

A further characteristic of the traditional model is the type of response. First, this response comes only from the teacher, and second, it is a response that is almost wholly summative, in that it results in a final grade with limited comments on content and extensive comments on organization and form. In most cases students are not aware of what evaluative criteria will be used to judge their final drafts and do not see or discuss rubrics that will be used with their writing. This kind of response is limited to one person and also does not invite students to change, revise, or write with an eye to what is specifically expected for the writing assignment.

The audience in the traditional model is always the teacher. Because no students see drafts, and the teacher alone reads and grades, the paper is written for him or her; sharing or publishing a work in an outside source or even within the classroom is rare. Not only is this limiting to student writers, but it puts a tremendous burden on the teacher.

Finally, in the traditional model of teaching writing, the structure of an assignment is often given to students in the form of a formula that they are to follow and from which they are not encouraged to vary or to move beyond. The five-paragraph theme and similar schemata are examples of this formulaic approach. While formula writing can be an important developmental step for many students, some are never encouraged to move beyond the formula.

Limitations of the Traditional Model

There are obvious flaws in the traditional model of teaching writing, some of which have been sketched here. Certainly, the traditional model of teaching writing can inadvertently make the practice and learning of writing unnecessarily difficult for many students. Again, while some students do function in a traditional model, for others, the whole learning-to-write process is an ordeal, especially when it follows closely the characteristics outlined previously. Some students never learn to write well or comfortably. And for teachers, upon whom the determination of what is good writing solely rests, the traditional model can be exhausting and difficult. Edwin M. Hopkins knew this, as do contemporary teachers. The teacher in the traditional model controls, determines, and judges all: he or she makes the assignment, sets up the relatively unvarying structure, and is the sole responder to and evaluator of the writer in a summative grade.

Finally, when the traditional model often demands that writing follow a formula, students can adhere to a cookbook approach only too well, producing, with the best of intentions, correct but lifeless prose.

What can we offer in the traditional model's place?

A Change in Thinking About Writing Instruction

It was in the 1950s that a movement challenged writing teachers' focus on the final writing product and on teachers marking that product thoroughly in the hope that it could be eventually improved. From a concern about the *way* people wrote, a theory about the process of writing emerged. This concern focused in particular on the getting of ideas (or invention), an interest that was heavily influenced by psychological theories of the time and by attention to how artists and other creative people worked. Composition theorist Sharon Crowley notes that aspects of this movement were seen as "antidotes to the sterility of current-traditional instruction" (1996, 66). Also, with unprecedented numbers of students coming into college writing classes after World War II, using the benefits of the G.I. Bill to further their education, techniques such as "peer workshops and small-group conferencing" (66) were viewed as pragmatic solutions to workload issues (Edwin M. Hopkins would have been thrilled). Confronted with a class of thirty or more students, a writing teacher could use the efficiency of small-group response rather than the time-consuming one-on-one conference. The workload of writing teachers was finally getting more attention, and new techniques such as using peer response were being accepted.

Looking at the Behavior of Writers

Added to this shift in emphasis came new research. In the late 1960s, composition teacher Janet Emig (1971) invited a reconsideration of the traditional way of teaching writing when she focused not on any conceptual schema but on the actual behavior of student writers as they wrote. Emig observed students as they drafted and revised and asked them questions, to which they responded, during their actual writing. What she found—again, based not on theory but on observation of behavior—was far removed from the "ideal" writing process that had governed writing instruction for most of the century. Students did not appear to get their ideas, outline them, write, and then revise but rather seemed to jump among activities, writing not in a linear, step-by-step manner but in more of a recursive pattern. The students Emig studied seemed to get their ideas as they wrote, and they revised their writing not at the end but throughout the process. As Frank Smith describes it, "Writing is not a matter of taking dictation from yourself; it is more like a conversation with a highly responsive and reflective other person" (1990, 27). This insight into writing behavior, accompanied with an understanding of the importance of invention—that writers needed to use techniques more like artists in their creative processes to find ideas—became the centerpiece of writing best practice as we currently know it. Crowley observes that this kind of concentration on "students' writing processes" (1996, 73) actually revolutionized the field of composition studies: how students *got there* was far more important than what they produced at the end. More important to teachers, however, the research also showed that how students got there was not consonant with much of the direction they were then receiving from their writing teachers.

A New Model of Teaching Writing

In *Learning by Teaching,* Donald M. Murray outlines what he calls "teaching writing as a process, not product":

> What is the process we should teach? It is the process of discovery through language. It is the process of exploration of what we know and what we feel about what we know through language. It is the process of using language to learn about our world, to evaluate what we learn about our world, to communicate what we learn about our world.
>
> Instead of teaching finished writing, we should teach unfinished writing, and glory in its unfinishedness. We work with language in action. We share with our students the continual excitement of choosing one word instead of another, of searching for the one true word . . . This process of discovery through language we call writing can be introduced to your classroom . . . as soon as you accept the full implications of teaching process, not product. (1982, 15)

In this model, the topic of the writing is one that students help determine and which is related to their interests and knowledge. Students are given an opportunity for and help with prewriting to give them ideas and a starting place. The time to write is more extensive than a class period or a night and takes place in and outside class. Students share their drafts with each other in peer groups and with the teacher in collaboration, and they receive response at the draft-writing stage.

A final draft receives a response, and if it needs work in areas, students can revise and resubmit the paper. This response is formative, in that it helps students change and refocus and possibly improve. The audience for this writing is not just the teacher but also other students. Widening the audience is achieved through collaboration in peer groups and also through the publication of student writing in anthologies, in class displays, and through schoolwide posting and distribution. Finally, the structure of the writing emerges from the topic; it is not predetermined by the teacher.

The following chart summarizes the differences between the two models (Christenbury 2000, 225):

	Traditional Model	**New Model**
Topic	teacher determined	teacher and student or student determined
Prewriting	limited or none	extensive
Time	limited	extensive
Help/collaboration	none	extensive
Response	from teacher only	from teacher and peers
	summative	formative and summative
Revision	limited	extensive
Audience	teacher only	teacher and others
Structure	provided by teacher	provided by student and nature of topic

Looking at this chart and considering the previous discussion, one may think the traditional model is a great fit with writing on demand, but it is not. To the contrary, the process model works far better because it discourages student dependence on the teacher for response and guidance and encourages students to be autonomous and effective. The kinds of skills that students learn when they pay attention to the processes of writing can be carried well into a testing situation, can help students wrestle with the demand of a prompt, and can help them write with an eye to what the rubric may be assessing.

Many teachers are aware of the processes of writing, and countless others have worked in summer institutes through the National Writing Project, where they have written and read research about the teaching of writing. Yet misperceptions and old habits persist in our often slow-to-change field. Even today, years after the research of Emig and others, many teachers (and, indeed, many writing textbooks) use terms such as *process writing* and *writing workshop* when what they are actually doing with their students is fairly traditional and product oriented.

Let's now look at the processes of writing and how these processes differ from traditional models of teaching writing.

Initiating the Processes of Writing: Invention

If teachers wish to help students write better, there are many aspects of the processes of writing to address. A vital part of successful writing is the getting of ideas. The most general or inclusive term for the discovery of knowledge is *heuristics,* but within composition studies we also use the terms *prewriting* and *invention*. Regardless of terms, however, for many students, serious writing anxiety begins right at the very onset: they contemplate a blank page or a blank screen and become apprehensive, wondering if they have—or will ever have—anything worthwhile to communicate. While not all students need guidance or work with prewriting or invention—for a lucky few, writing ideas seem to present themselves readily—most students will benefit from work with a variety of prewriting strategies. As teachers we can let our students practice a number of invention techniques to help them get into a topic, techniques that will give them confidence and which they can use in their writing in our classes or, in an abbreviated version, in a testing situation.

For many students, serious writing anxiety begins right at the very onset: they contemplate a blank page or a blank screen and become apprehensive.

The following is a brief set of descriptions for some basic prewriting or invention techniques. Some of the strategies can be combined (such as brainstorming and listing with looping or the five Ws), but being selective regarding the use of these strategies is important. Using numerous invention techniques for one piece of writing can exhaust students and be counterproductive. Further, as students are exposed to a range of strategies over a period of time, they will begin to self-select, using ones that work for them and discarding others. In addition, as indicated below, some strategies work really well with a large or small group (such as webbing or clustering) while others, like looping, must be done individually. Finally, some of the strategies are more applicable to certain topics than to others.

Invention Strategies: Ways to Get into Your Writing

Brainstorming: If students have an especially broad topic to address, brainstorming can help focus their ideas. They can consider the broad topic (such as challenges of growing up or economic pressures on college students) and as rapidly as possible, take a minute or two to jot down anything and everything they know about the subject, without selecting or censoring what they write: good brainstorming includes a wide range of words and phrases that relate, in some way, to the topic. Then they can take a brief break and review what they have written. Are there one or two items to pursue? Are there any related words or phrases? Are there any patterns? Is there something that sparks a new idea? They can use brainstorming to jump-start their writing. They can brainstorm by themselves, with buddies in a small group, or the whole class can consider a single topic and brainstorm together.

Listing: For more narrow writing topics (for example, reasons to go to college or three things all parents should know), listing can be focused and helpful, especially if students can put the list in categories (such as pros and cons regarding going to college or three things all parents should know from a parent's point of view and three things all parents should know from a son's or a daughter's point of view). As with brainstorming, they can take a minute or two to jot down their ideas in the categories they have listed. Then they can take a brief break and review what they have written. Does one list seem stronger than the other? Are there one or two items that they would like to pursue? Are there any related words or phrases? Do they see any patterns? Is there something they have written that sparks a new idea? They can use the list to jump-start their writing. Again, they can list by themselves, with buddies in a small group, or the whole class can consider a single topic and list together.

Listing and Forced Choice: Lists are more directed and focused than general brainstorming, and a list that relates directly to one aspect of an assignment (such as things that could be done to improve school cafeteria food) can be very helpful. After students have made a list that relates to their assignment, they can also use that list to focus and do a forced choice. They can look at the list they have generated and, if it is fairly long, choose five items from the list that seem most effective, most interesting, or most powerful (if the list is a short one, they may want to select just three items). They can circle those five (or three), look at the ones they have selected and, from them, pick one on which to focus. Circle it, and use that one item to begin their writing.

Students can list by themselves, with buddies in a small group, or the whole class can consider a single topic and list together. The selection of items in a forced choice should be individual, however; what one student chooses to focus on will most likely not be the same as what someone else chooses.

Webbing or Clustering: Many of us do not respond well to a list or a collection of words in columns; webs and clusters use circles and diagonals to

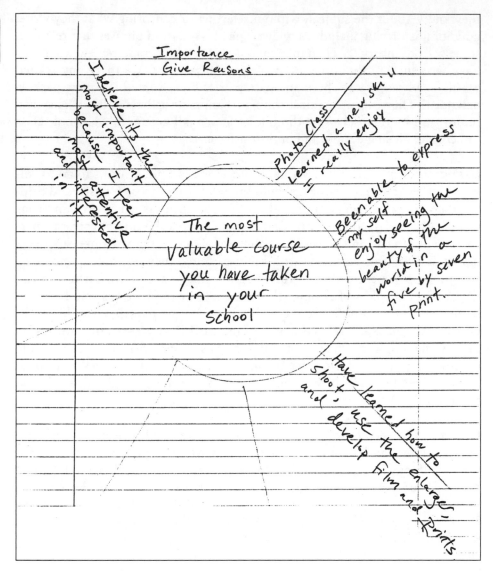

FIGURE 2.1

Student Clusters

highlight a topic and then surround it with pertinent words, phrases, and ideas. The format of webbing and clustering is thus different, but the idea—teasing out pertinent aspects of a topic—is very similar to the prewriting strategies listed previously.

Students can look at the two clusters that tenth-graders used for their prewriting in a testing situation (Figure 2.1) and consider what their web or cluster would look like if they had to write about their most important class.

Clustering and webbing can be done in small groups, but it is also very effective when done individually.

FIGURE 2.1 continued

Visualizing: Again, some do not respond well to word lists or columns; for those who are more visual and artistic, doodles, triangles, arrows, circles, and shapes can help with planning and prewriting. This is a very individual kind of invention strategy, but it should be noted that for some it is effective and important. When students doodle and draw, does it represent something particular to them? Can they use their drawings to represent or help plan their writing?

Freewriting: Used most notably by composition teacher Peter Elbow (1981), in particular to alleviate writing anxiety, freewriting is a brief (three- to five-minute) timed writing event in which students put their pen to the paper (or their fingers to the keyboard) and just write, write, write. The topic, of course, is the focus, but even if students find themselves writing the same word time and time again or something such as "This is stupid—I don't know what to write," they keep writing. They do not stop.

If students are using a computer, it can also be helpful to turn off the screen so that they are not looking at what they are writing while they write—the blank screen can be freeing.

Freewriting can, by its very physical act of continuing to write, generate ideas and fluency. It is an individual prewriting activity and, clearly, should be used selectively, at the beginning of writing or at a time when students become stalled and are running out of ideas.

Looping: The technique of looping, also from Peter Elbow, asks students to write in short, timed segments. They write for three to five minutes on a topic (such as what parents need to know) and then they stop. They make themselves (this seems odd, but it works) *reread what they have just written* and look for, in that brief segment, a phrase, a word, or even a whole sentence that seems the most important: Elbow calls it the "center of gravity." They can circle that word, phrase, or sentence. Then they are ready to start a second segment by *physically recopying their circled segment,* and then continue to write for three to five minutes. Then they stop and repeat the process.

This should be done individually and can help students explore the differing ramifications of a topic. No more than about three segments, by the way, are truly helpful—students will probably tire of looping if they do it for much longer.

Five Ws (Burke's Pentad):   For topics that need factual information, the journalist's five Ws (who, where, when, what, how) have been transformed by theorist Kenneth Burke ([1945] 1969) into a pentad that draws on drama (think of a scene with actors). As with looping, each segment is timed for three to five minutes, during which students, after they have a topic, attempt to answer the following questions in turn:

> *Action:* What is happening?
> *Agent:* Who is doing it?
> *Agency:* How is it being done?
> *Scene:* Where and when it is being done?
> *Purpose:* Why is it being done?

One really useful aspect of the pentad is that if they change the tense of any of the questions (e.g., What was happening? or What will be happening?) or use *should* or *ought* (Where and when ought or should it be done?), they can generate almost thirty questions and answers.

Burke's pentad can be done individually, with a small group, or with a large group. Again, it needs to be used in moderation, as answering all the questions can be counterproductive.

Cubing: If students imagine a cube (or make one for themselves out of a five-sided tissue box covered with colored paper), they can put on each side a command of sorts, which, like Burke's Pentad, can help them organize their thoughts on a complex topic. Again, taking no more than three to five minutes a segment, students can think of their topic and do the following in quick succession:

- Describe it.

- Compare it (to or with something else—your choice).

- Associate it (as above).

- Analyze it.

- Apply it.

- Argue for or against it.

This prewriting activity can be done individually or with a large group.

Once students have experienced these strategies, when they turn to any kind of writing—whether in class or in an on-demand situation—they can call upon these techniques and, using the prompts as cues, and ideas for what they want to say.

For more information on prompts and how to use them to cue writing, please see Chapter 3. There we discuss how students can look at a prompt and decide not only on a focus but on key concepts to include. Also, in Chapter 6, we explore the context of writing on demand and how students can use that context to guide their writing.

Using a Writer's Notebook

As noted in Chapter 1, a writer's notebook can help students become more reflective regarding their own writing and more careful with what they choose to include in the writing. In addition, a writer's notebook can be an invaluable place to jot down ideas, phrases, quotations, interesting words, or other information that a writer may want to incorporate in a draft. Having students use such a notebook can encourage pride and ownership and can encourage students to truly see themselves as what we want them to be: writers. The writer's notebook suggestion that follows invites students to understand more about how they get their ideas as writers.

Writer's Notebook

Many writers have standard techniques and strategies they use to get their ideas about what they want to write or to further their ideas as they are writing. Think about the last piece of writing you did and, if you can, try to recall the very beginning stages. What kinds of things did you do to help you get started? Did you write a list? Draw? Walk around? Talk to a friend? Read something related? Or did you just start to write?

In addition, can you recall if you got stuck or stumped during the writing? If so, what helped you get going again? Briefly describe it.

Finally, when you know you have to write something quickly, is there anything you customarily do to help you get ideas? Do you have any old reliable techniques? If so, outline them.

The Heart of the Process of Writing: Drafting

If we believe that writing is recursive, then drafting will have stops and starts. It will not be linear or even orderly, such as outlined here:

> *Step 1:* Get an idea.
> *Step 2:* Outline that idea. (Do not go back to step 1.)
> *Step 3:* Write. (Do not go back to step 2.)
> *Step 4:* Revise what is written. (Do not go back to step 3.)
> *Step 5:* Recopy. (Do not go back to step 4.) (Christenbury 2000)

Looking at how real writers write, we know that very few writers follow this pattern. What happens with real writers? After watching such writers write and asking them to talk about their writing, we think that the various "steps" in the process very often occur with amazing simultaneity. A writer might get an idea and start to put something down, which gives her another idea; while adding that idea, perhaps she realizes that something is not right with what she first wrote, and she crosses it out. She has, essentially, gotten an idea, written, gotten another idea, written, revised, even edited, all in a fairly unorderly way and sometimes virtually simultaneously. This pattern is far from being a step-to-step or linear procedure.

Every student will have his or her own drafting patterns, and allowing students to claim this kind of individuality can be important. With on-demand writing, however, it will be necessary for students to do something more focused and even deliberate, and they need to know that the recursive aspect of drafting, while a normal and acceptable part of writing, must be compressed quite a bit in a timed situation. (For more information on how to help students draft within a specified frame of time, please see Chapter 6.)

Drafting may be different in class assignments and in a testing situation, however. When students are familiar and comfortable with their individual drafting habits and patterns, they will be far better equipped to write something extensive and focused in a testing environment. Drafting will be an exercised muscle that is strong and that can be used, if not effortlessly, at least consistently, in any writing situation. When students understand their own drafting habits, they will be far better prepared for the pressures of writing on demand.

And one of the best ways to help students with drafting is to put a strong emphasis on invention. If students are comfortable getting ideas and returning to invention during their drafting, they are more likely to write quickly and to continue to write.

Making Writing Better: Revision, Editing, and Proofreading

Most students confuse the three activities of revision, editing, and proofreading. They are not interchangeable, but markedly different, and they represent very different levels of activity during the final draft of writing. As noted in Chapter 5, many students believe that the alteration of a single word or the correction of capitalization and punctuation is revision, but such is not the case. Students must look at the whole writing, not just at the word or sentence level. Revision is the major work of changing writing; editing and proofreading are last-stage polishing activities.

In general *revision* is best thought of as re-vision, re-looking, re-working of a piece of writing. This may include changing significant portions of the writing, such as rearranging sections, deleting sections, rewriting openings and closings, or even refocusing the entire piece. Revision can transform a piece of writing.

Editing, on the other hand, is a look at a revised piece of writing to review and change word order and sentence structure and to check usage issues. At this stage the major changes in the writing have been established; the changes made in editing are less intrusive and far less significant to the meaning of a final piece of writing.

Proofreading is a last look at a revised, edited piece, and it includes verification that all minor details of usage are addressed (such as capitalization, indentation of paragraphs, and sufficient spaces between title and body). It is a final polishing.

Most students who find writing difficult from the onset resist revision and hope that proofreading and some minor editing will be all that is needed to improve their hard-won first draft. For most students, however, revision is a vital activity to learn and practice. One of the most powerful ways to encourage students to revise their work is to use peer response writing groups (a section on establishing and maintaining those groups appears later in this chapter). On the other hand, there is also a real place for proofreading; many readers of writing tests cite adequate proofreading as one thing they look for when considering the quality of writing samples—while it is necessary to understand this last stage of correction in a broader context, proofreading is an important skill to use in writing-on-demand situations.

Teachers can help students make these distinctions by giving them drafts of papers and asking them to work with those drafts in different modes: revising, editing, and proofreading. If students can see and practice the difference between the major work of changing writing (revision) and the minor details of usage in proofreading, they will be far better equipped to improve their own writing both in the classroom and in a testing environment.

Evaluation and Multiple Rubrics

While publishing to a broad audience is often the end result of process writing, in writing on demand it is vital to remember that the audience is composed of test readers and evaluators. Accordingly, attention to specifics for writing assignments is vital because evaluators will be looking specifically and consistently for certain aspects and marks in the final writing product. How do we prepare students for this?

One crucial aspect of the processes of writing is the use of evaluation and multiple rubrics. Giving students rubrics for their writing—or asking them to help create rubrics, such as we did in Chapter 1, or to examine rubrics, as we will do in Chapter 8—will help students understand and participate in the evaluative process. When students prewrite, draft, and revise, they often are not clear about how a piece of writing might be judged, either by a teacher, by a peer, or, in a testing situation, by the anonymous reader and grader. Students can, as part of the processes of writing, learn that certain rubrics and certain grading emphases will result in different evaluations of the very same paper—something of which many are not fully aware. If, for instance, an assignment emphasizes voice, or organization, or narrative flair, the evaluative rubric should reflect that concentration. This kind of information is vital to students in their class writing and in a testing situation: once students understand the range of evaluation, they have a better chance to write to specification, as well as to keep some of their individuality. For more information on evaluation, the final step of the process of writing, see Chapters 4 and 8.

As a last note, while evaluation of final drafts is expected and important to improving student writing, grading rough drafts is not. Assigning a value to a work in progress is counterproductive; as most teachers know, many things can happen between a promising rough draft and a final draft. A high grade on a draft can encourage a student to stop working, and a low grade can so dishearten a writer that he or she ceases to work. Giving students credit for drafting is certainly something we want to do in our classes, but a grade on a draft, however tentative we may mean it to be, is often seen by students as a final judgment.

Responding, Evaluating, and Grading

Whether we use just rubrics or just comments or a combination, we give students feedback on their writing. There are different ways to react, and the distinction between responding, evaluating, and grading is important to note. The three activities are not necessarily mutually exclusive, but each differs somewhat from the others.

When we *respond* to students, we make an effort to talk to them, writer to writer, reader to writer; the primary issue is not the quality of the writing, as in good, better, best. A teacher's response to a student paper should encompass three things:

1. *Personally link to something the student has written.* A teacher could write: "Yes: I had a similar experience; that would anger me, too," or "That happened to a friend of mine."

2. *Tell the student what a reader might like about what he or she has written.* The experience of reading the paper can be important: pick one or two things the student does well and ask the student to think about them. A teacher could write: "Your introduction really grabs me—do you have any idea why that opening image is so powerful?" or "You are using parallel construction effectively here—do you see how?"

3. *Ask the student questions about the draft, questions that suggest changes.* A teacher could write: "Look at your title—Is that what this paper is really about? If not, what is it about?" or "Can you find where you could break this long section into two paragraphs?" or "What effect do you think this word has on what you are trying to say in this paragraph?" (Christenbury 2000)

When a teacher *evaluates* a paper, the emphasis should be on how well the paper is doing what it does, on how close the paper seems to come to what it is trying to do. That may mean more emphasis on Point 2 in the previous list and more direction on Point 3 (a teacher could make comments such as "I am lost in this section; what is it about?" or "Your paragraphs are so long, you are combining a number of points; can you break the section on page 2 into two—or three—paragraphs?"). Evaluation can also be a situation in which the teacher specifically compares one draft with another—how close does this version come to a model? Obviously, rubrics can be vital in evaluation, and teacher comments can accompany scores and percentages on a rubric.

To *grade* a paper requires a letter or numerical designation and some sort of final evaluative comment. As noted earlier, a rubric with percentages or points can help make this final grade explicit. We prefer single-letter grades and have never found the split grade of one letter for content and one for form (in a 50 percent/50 percent arrangement) to be successful. While many teachers like the split grade, as it seems to make a distinction between content and mechanics (surface errors), we have a hard time accepting that distinction. If surface errors diminish meaning—and they can—then content is really intertwined with form. How can these be separated? Is it really possible, if form is so related to content, for a paper to receive a B in content but a D in form (and thus average to a C)? One grade, either letter or numerical, seems more logical. And, again, many rubrics use points and percentages that can be readily translated into grades. Further, those rubrics often indicate that mechanics and usage should not constitute fully half of the final grade but something far more reasonable, such as 10 percent or 20 percent.

Rubrics are constants in on-demand writing; when students are accustomed to evaluative rubrics in classroom assignments, they will readily make the transition to the kind of evaluative requirements set out in on-demand writing. While on-demand writing does not receive a response, it does get evaluated and graded. We discuss ways to involve students in evaluation in Chapter 8.

What Are the Implications?

Considering the processes of writing and introducing our students to those processes are important. The implications for teachers are also serious: teachers need to help students get started and then give them time to use and develop their own patterns for working through drafting to a final (or somewhat final) version. In class students may be getting ideas on Wednesday and Thursday, writing on Friday and Sunday, and getting more ideas on Monday. If writing is truly recursive, teachers can create a schedule that allows for that recursiveness. This does not mean abandoning students and giving them three days to figure it out for themselves; teachers can help students during this time and use a workshop format. In a model that pays attention to process, however, teachers cannot completely confine writing behaviors to certain blocks of time because it doesn't work that way. Teachers who try to schedule writing processes are actually abusing the term—and not really helping their students. Giving students time over a period of days to write and prewrite and revise is more helpful than predetermining which writing step a group or individual will be involved in on any given day.

In an on-demand writing test, however, students know that the natural recursive nature of writing is compressed. Most writing-sample tests do not allow students the time to draft and change significantly. Therefore, planning writing through prewriting and reviewing writing at the end are vital tasks for successful on-demand writing. Once students have become comfortable using multiple days to write, they will also need to experience writing in a more confined space of time. The transition can be made: with serious attention to invention and an understanding of proofreading, students are better equipped to take the skills they have used in classroom writing and use them in a testing environment.

Writer's Notebook

Think about the last writing assignment you did for a class. Try to remember how you actually got ready to write, how the writing itself went, how much time it took, and what kind of revision or rewriting you did. Did you show the draft to a friend? Did you read the words aloud to yourself? Was it important that you use a pen, a pencil, or a word processor? What, in short, was your writing process for the last assignment you did?

Now imagine that you had to do the same kind of writing in a testing situation and had about thirty minutes. What kinds of things would you do differently? How do you think you could speed up or compress your getting of ideas, writing, polishing, and so on?

Peer Response Writing Groups: Principles and Procedures

Helping students with their writing is part of our task as teachers. Along with helping students get ideas, draft, and understand evaluation, we can also offer them powerful support in their revision, editing, and proofreading through writing groups. Peer response writing groups capitalize on the collaborative aspect of writing—as Donald Murray notes, "writing is a lonely act that is never performed alone" (1989, vii). Writing groups also help students see their work as broader than just between themselves and the teacher. The importance of this aspect of teaching writing cannot be overstated and the collaborative experience can also help students when they consider the broader audience in writing-on-demand situations.

An effective way to make assessment visible to students is to involve them in evaluating the writing of their classmates. Peer evaluation can occur at several stages during the process of writing, and it can take multiple forms. Just as it is always easier to see personality flaws in others rather than ourselves, so too is it easier to see problems in the writing of others. Experience with peer evaluation gives students tools they can eventually use to assess their own writing, both on writing tests as well as in other occasions for writing.

The times when peer evaluation can be valuable include

- during invention or prewriting, when students are generating possibilities for writing;

- during early drafting, when students are trying to find their central point;

- during later drafting, when students can attend to issues of language and audience;

- during revision, when students are dealing with syntax and word choice as well as issues like clarity; and

- during the final stages of editing, when students are polishing whole pieces of writing.

Clearly, students do not need to participate in peer evaluation at each stage, and frequently one stage blurs into or turns back on another. This list, however, suggests the many ways that students can sharpen their evaluative skills so that they can ultimately become more effective in assessing their own work when writing on demand. (Please see Chapter 4 for more discussion of the use of peer response writing groups in drafting and revision.)

The idea of peer response writing groups scares some teachers. There is, of course, the fear that students will get out of control in the groups, but an even greater fear is that students not only don't know what to do but will do nothing in their groups but share their own ignorance about writing. Students often share these fears. After all, isn't it the teacher's job to be the determiner of what is good writing?

These fears need not be realities. When the purposes and tasks of a peer response writing group are outlined to students, there is little real chance that a group will either get out of control or get lost. Some groups will be able to talk about drafts and take notes on their copies productively; other groups will need checklists and worksheets that they turn in with their drafts to encourage them to stay on task. Regardless of the use of checklists, peer response writing groups can work very effectively in middle school and high school. Once students are introduced to peer response writing groups, have modeled the behavior in a fishbowl kind of exercise, and have been given an accountability structure for what they do in their groups, peer response should work effectively.

Finally, peer response writing groups can engender confidence in students and more self-awareness, qualities that are important to successful writing on demand. Once students become familiar and comfortable with others looking at and questioning their writing, they will more likely be able to see, on their own, changes and adjustments that have to be made. They can internalize the attitude of the writing group.

Don't Peer Response Writing Groups Do the Teacher's Job?

But what about the concern that students in a peer response writing group are doing nothing more than sharing their ignorance and that response to writing is the teacher's job? The utility of the writing group is that it exposes students to the writing of others. A broad audience is important, in the classroom and in writing-on-demand situations. Gone is the isolation of one person writing his or her draft and never hearing or seeing what other students are doing. The writing of other students teaches; a draft presented in a peer response writing group may be significantly better or significantly worse than the work of the other members of the group. Nevertheless, in a peer response writing group, students get to read and consider a range of writing—one another's drafts. Often teachers wonder what effect it has on students to read and see only the polished, analyzed, credentialed work of the great, who we know can write: Annie Dillard, Lewis Thomas, Henry David Thoreau, Martin Luther King Jr. Letting students see and work with the writing of those like themselves, who are learning to write, can be a heartening experience.

Peer response writing groups also tap into the collaborative, each-one-teach-one aspect of learning.

Peer response writing groups also tap into the collaborative, each-one-teach-one aspect of learning. If a student gets lost reading another student's draft, if the point just seems to disappear, that student—the reader, not the writer—will need to figure out why and articulate it. By trying to help a peer, the person will have to put a name on the problem area and give some sort of advice about what to do. It makes all students in the group consider and grapple with issues of writing in an immediate way, which is far more active than responding in a large group to whatever the teacher asks students to look for and discuss. Students can become more independent, and a double learning can take place. If Brittany is motivated to help Jon with his writing, Brittany has to figure out what the issue is; by helping Jon, Brittany is helping herself.

Organizing Students in Peer Response Writing Groups

Any form of peer evaluation means thinking about organizing students into small groups. We have tried a variety of strategies and formats, and the following suggestions draw on our collective experience. Regardless of the approach, there are some fundamentals that will make any form of peer evaluation work well. These include the following:

• *Establish a climate of trust in the classroom.*

In our experience, students will never share their work with one another unless they feel that their English class is a place where put-downs are not tolerated, where everyone's contributions are valued, where confidences are respected. This is not something that can be established in one day or one week, but we have found that beginning the school year by working to make the classroom a safe space where students know they and the teacher will be expected to treat one another well develops a climate of trust. Using peer evaluation before such a climate is established leads, in our experience, to failure. If students don't know and respect one another, they will not be comfortable sharing their writing, and they will, intentionally or not, sabotage the work of peer evaluation.

• *Model processes of peer evaluation.*

Even if students feel comfortable with one another, it isn't enough to just divide them into small groups. If students don't have a clear idea of how peer evaluation works, they won't be able to provide useful feedback to one another. When we see student groups get off task in peer evaluation, it can nearly always be traced to the fact that they did not have adequate preparation. The best way to prepare students is to model evaluation for them. Teachers can begin by using anonymous student papers to do a workshop for the class. Showing students how the teacher responds to a piece of writing will give them strategies for assessing one another's writing.

Also, as described in more detail later, the *fishbowl* technique can give students a more immediate sense of how groups work. Teachers can put one small group of students in the center of the room and have them respond to a peer's writing while the rest of the class watches and takes notes. After the group is finished, participants and then observers can describe what happened, make suggestions for improvement, and note what worked well.

• *Develop a vocabulary for discussing writing.*

Part of the difficulty students encounter when they participate in peer response groups is that they don't have the language to describe what they see in one another's writing. We often hear students make vague and unhelpful comments like "That flows really well" or "I really like that" when they don't have terminology to talk about transitions or effective word choice. We have found that each class develops its own language to describe good writing, and teachers who give explicit attention to familiar terms and introduce others as needed find that students are more able to talk effectively about one another's writing.

The following evaluative terms can be especially helpful for students to use in responding to one another's writing:

- *introduction* or *lead*

- *transition* or *connection*

- *word-order problem* or *syntax problem*

- *word choice*

- *main idea* or *thesis*

- *wrap-up* or *conclusion*

- *audience*

Some of these terms, or at least the concepts they represent for writers, may be unfamiliar to students, and discussing each can help students expand their own critical understanding of writing. Alternatively, at schools that use a *common rubric,* whether from a state-mandated test or from their district, teachers can introduce students to the language of the rubric and encourage them to become familiar with the terms it uses. In still another variation on this idea, some teachers involve students in developing rubrics for the class or even for specific assignments, and terms to describe features of writing become part of the common language of the class.

- *Evaluate the evaluation.*

After students have had an opportunity to participate in peer response writing groups for a month or so, it is a good idea to ask them to evaluate their experience. In particular, they can provide useful feedback about the quality of the responses they have been getting from their peers. Teachers can learn a great deal from a short survey with prompts and questions like these:

- Describe a peer's comment that led you to change your writing.

- Describe a comment that focused on a sentence-level issue in your writing.

- Describe a comment that focused on the overall structure of your writing.

- What percentages of all comments focus on sentence-level issues?

Procedures for Implementing a Peer Response Writing Group

The composition of a writing group can be heterogeneous or homogenous; in other words, teachers can either mix writing ability or keep writers of the same ability in a single group. We have had the most success with heterogeneous groups of three or four members; we also always mix males and females and members of majority and minority racial or ethnic groups. We think diversity works well and prefer to use it in our classes.

There are many variations regarding forming peer response writing groups, but here is one way to put students into groups. We always ask each student for an ungraded writing sample a few days before we get into writing groups. We do some prewriting together, and we have students write about a personality characteristic of theirs or something that they are good at outside of school. It's an assignment that allows students to talk about something they know about and are interested in—themselves. We read these writing samples, looking at them with an overall general eye; it is holistic grading. While we respond to what students have written (students expect this, even with a sample), we do not give the papers a letter grade. Students get credit, of course, for having done the writing, but for our own purposes, we place the papers in stacks; one stack for the strong writers (1s); one stack for the middling writers (2s); and one stack for the writers who, at this point at least and within the context of this group, look like they will need work and help (3s). Whereas one writing sample is no sure indicator of writing ability, and this sort of 1-to-3 holistic scoring has limitations, the procedure gives us a handle on where the students might be at that moment in class.

Using this quick diagnosis, we then construct the peer response writing groups, mixing the 1s, 2s, and 3s as well as the males, females, and ethnic groups. So, for example, a single writing group of four might have, in ability, one 1, one 3, and two 2s; in gender, two females and two males; and in racial mix, three Caucasians and one African American. We do not, by the way, share the numerical designations of their writing samples with students until the end of the course. It is an initial diagnosis, based on a single piece of writing, and its function is only to allow the teacher to create intermediate groupings.

We have found that it is vital to talk with students about why peer response writing groups are important, giving them much the same argument outlined here. We assure them we will be circulating among the groups as they work. We review the questions in Online 2.1 (some of which are adapted from *Creating Writers,* by Vicki Spandel [2001]) during the following minilesson.

Goal: To familiarize students with principles of peer response writing groups and to give them practice working in a writing group.

Talking Points:

- In groups of three or four, you will have a class session to share one another's papers, suggest changes, and reinforce what you feel are the strongest parts of the shared papers.

- Every member of the group must participate in the revision and should, while being respectful of the others' writing, make a conscientious effort to help the others improve their drafts.

Time Suggestions:

group of three: fifteen minutes per paper
group of four: ten to twelve minutes per paper

Activities:

Acquaint students with the procedure for peer response groups:

1. One person should give copies of his or her rough draft to the members of the group. The person should then read the draft aloud to the group; there should be no preliminary apologies or explanations, just the reading.

2. The person should then pause for a few minutes to allow the group to consider the piece, look over the draft, make marks, and make notes.

3. The discussion of the draft should then start and include both negative and positive remarks. In all instances, the group should try to be specific about the paper. Comments such as "I don't like this paragraph" are not helpful; comments such as "In this sentence, this word seems too strong" and "This section seems out of place—could you move it closer to the beginning of the paper?" are more useful and will help an author in changing and revising a draft. (See below for questions students should consider during peer response.)

While the writer of the draft would do well to listen to suggestions and comments, the paper belongs to the writer, not the group. It is conceivable that the writer will listen to suggestions and hints and decide to accept only some of them in revision.

**ONLINE
2.1**

Questions to Consider for Peer Response Writing Groups

- *Ideas and content:* To what extent is the draft clear? Interesting? Convincing? Are details used well? Are main and secondary ideas balanced?

- *Organization:* Can a reader follow where the draft is going? Are there helpful transitions? Where can points be made clearer?

- *Voice:* Does this draft read as if it were written by a real person? Can you "hear" the voice of the writer? Is there flavor, honesty, humor here?

- *Word choice:* Are the writer's words fresh? Striking? Appropriate for the content?

- *Sentence fluency:* To what extent does the writing move the reader along? Are the sentences varied or do they all sound the same?

- *Conventions:* Are there areas where the writer needs to check spelling? Punctuation? Paragraphing? Capitalization? Do any of these errors interfere with the meaning of the draft?

After groups have finished this process, using a duplicated copy of an anonymous student draft, you can ask students to enact a fishbowl response group and role-play.

Four student volunteers sit at the front or in the center of the room and pretend they are the group discussing this draft; one student volunteers to be the author, and the others are members of the peer response writing group. The group follows the procedures outlined previously. The "author" begins by reading the draft aloud. The discussion then proceeds. The rest of the class watches in silence, noting not so much what is said about the draft but what kinds of remarks are made and by whom: who talks, who doesn't, how it goes. After about ten minutes of observation, you can stop the role-play and talk about what the class saw.

Then you can have four different student volunteers do another fishbowl with the same draft. Not surprisingly, the second group is always different from the first; they have the benefit of having watched the first fishbowl, and they usually have different ideas of their own and different ways of interacting. Again, you can discuss how the group went.

Assessment:

After you have taken a writing sample, grouped students, explained the purpose and intent of a peer response writing group, given students some written instructions, and conducted a number of fishbowl exercises, students should be comfortable beginning work in a writing group, and we should be able to observe that level of comfort. Once students have been through these activities, they should demonstrate effective work in a peer response writing group.

The Care and Feeding of Peer Response Writing Groups

Maintaining peer response writing groups is an ongoing process. Checklists and worksheets can be necessary to keep students on task—checklists that teachers discuss and briefly review—as well as teacher circulation among the groups. Groups can take a bit of time to bond, and they may have questions that need to be answered. To have students just get in groups and talk about one another's drafts is not possible for most; if we care about the process, we need, as outlined previously, to

- model the process step by step;

- reinforce the process; and

- monitor the process.

When students are asked to take on roles they do not understand and for which they are not prepared, chaos and upset can ensue.

How often groups are re-formed is a context issue; some teachers prefer groups that last for at least a semester, but a teacher may want to change groups more frequently. Personality conflicts between students, discipline issues, students whose writing skill changes so drastically that they would benefit from other peers, groups that for whatever reason are not productive or harmonious are all reasons to reconfigure writing groups. Teachers can sit in on the groups and will be able to sense what is working well and who is not; judgment is important in determining when and if a writing group needs a change. Using consistently the kind of survey questions noted on page 53 is also important: students will often be willing to anonymously write their concerns rather than discuss them openly with their group or with the whole class. Frankly, if the group is not meeting a student's needs, something should be altered.

Peer response writing groups are highly important to the processes of student writing and help students in the classroom and with writing on demand. When students truly hear the voices of their peer audience as they begin to write, these voices can be internalized for use in a situation of writing on demand.

Conferencing with Students

Besides groups, another activity that is helpful to students and part of the processes of writing is the brief conference. It may seem impossible to talk about a draft individually with each student in a class of thirty, but teachers can do it if the conferences are kept brief and are conducted while other writing and reading activities are going on. Let's imagine that students are working on their writing and a teacher is available, at a desk, for five-minute conferences with people who want to talk. The teacher could, conceivably, confer with seven or eight students and still have some time to circulate among the class or do some large-group instruction. Many students want the privacy—and the reassurance—of a conference. In *Learning by Teaching,* Donald M. Murray, discussing writing conferences, notes they should be short and frequent and limited to one concern at a time. He offers these conference guidelines for teachers:

- The student responds to the text or to the experience of producing it.

- The teacher listens to the student's response to the text and watches how it is presented.

- The teacher reads or listens to the text from the student's perspective.

- The teacher responds to the student's response. (1982, 163–64)

Practically, what does this mean? It might mean that a conference would start with questions that ask the writer how he or she views the draft (Murray's "text"). Murray offers the following typical questions a teacher might use in a writing conference, questions that students not only can become accustomed to but can use in writing-on-demand situations:

- What did you learn from this piece of writing?

- What do you intend to do in the next draft?

- What surprised you in the draft?

- Where is the piece of writing taking you?

- What do you like best in the piece of writing?

- What questions do you have for me? (159)

Other questions we use include

- What do you think of what you have written?

- How difficult was it to get this far?

- How easy was it to write about this subject?

- What do you want to work on?

- Where are the draft's strengths? Weaknesses?

- What can I help you with?

Notice that all of these questions, and the whole tenor of the conference itself, are focused not on the teacher making the draft better—or correcting it or improving it or criticizing it—but on making the writer look at his or her own work and selecting what he or she sees, or doesn't see, as an issue. A conference and the questions that accompany it allow students to focus on selected aspects of their writing, which will ultimately produce more learning than a list of corrections an instructor might hand a student in a conference setting. Students need to become comfortable with this kind of independence. Once they are accustomed to these kinds of questions, they can more effectively work with their own writing in an independent situation, such as a writing-on-demand test.

Writer's Notebook

Think about the more successful writing experiences you have had in school. What one paper (or papers) was the most satisfying to you? Why? Was it the grade? The topic? The process of getting the words down? The feeling after you had turned it in? Try to analyze why that writing assignment stands as one of your favorites. Be specific.

Key Points for Reflection

The traditional model of teaching writing is not helpful for many students, and what we have learned about the behavior of writers demands that we change our instruction accordingly. When students are familiar with the processes of writing, they will be more adept writers both in classroom settings and in testing situations. Students, given practice and encouragement, can learn to get ideas, plan their drafts, write, and then revise and proofread effectively. We believe:

- The processes of writing are adaptable to the classroom and to the testing environment.

- Invention, or prewriting, strategies can be varied and helpful and can be used in individual, small-group, and large-group settings. Choosing the right strategy for the right student writer and for the particular assignment is key to success.

- Drafting must be seen as recursive; students will stop and start as they write, getting ideas and revising as they write. Writing is rarely a linear, uninterrupted process.

- Once students have mastered a comfortable drafting process, they are more likely to be able to write quickly and effectively in an on-demand testing situation.

- Revising writing is more than cosmetic, changing a word or correcting punctuation; in class situations revision can be serious re-vision. In a testing situation, revision may need to be abbreviated because of time constraints and incorporated into the drafting itself; proofreading will also need attention.

- Peer response writing groups and conferencing with teachers and other writers are excellent tools to use in the writing classroom, and the strategies learned in those activities can be transferred to writing on demand.

WORKS CITED

Burke, Kenneth. [1945] 1969. *A Grammar of Motives*. Berkeley: University of California Press.

Christenbury, Leila. 2000. *Making the Journey: Being and Becoming a Teacher of English Language Arts*. 2d ed. Portsmouth, NH: Heinemann.

Crowley, Sharon. 1996. "Around 1971: Current-Traditional Rhetoric and Process Models of Composing." In *Composition in the Twenty-First Century: Crisis and Change*, ed. Lynn Z. Bloom, Donald A. Daiker, and Edward M. White (64–74). Carbondale: Southern Illinois University Press.

Elbow, Peter. 1981. *Writing with Power: Techniques for Mastering the Writing Process*. New York: Oxford University Press.

Emig, Janet. 1971. "The Composing Process of Twelfth Graders." In *NCTE Research Report No. 13.* Urbana, IL: NCTE.

Hopkins, Edwin M. 1912. "Can Good Composition Teaching Be Done Under Present Circumstances?" *English Journal* 1 (1): 1–8.

————. 1923. *The Labor and Cost of the Teaching of English in Colleges and Secondary Schools with Especial Reference to English Composition.* Chicago: NCTE.

Murray, Donald M. 1982. *Learning by Teaching: Selected Articles on Writing and Teaching.* Portsmouth, NH: Boynton/Cook.

————. 1989. *Expecting the Unexpected: Teaching Myself—and Others—to Read and Write.* Portsmouth, NH: Boynton/Cook.

Popken, Randall. 2004. "Edwin Hopkins and the Costly Labor of Composition Teaching." *College Composition and Communication* 55 (4): 618–41.

Smith, Frank. 1990. "Myths of Writing." In *Rhetoric and Composition: A Sourcebook for Teachers and Writers,* 3d ed., ed. Richard L. Graves. Portsmouth, NH: Heinemann.

Spandel, Vicki. 2001. *Creating Writers Through Six-Trait Writing Assessment and Instruction.* 3d ed. New York: Longman.

The Rhetoric of Prompts and Assignments

3

Histories make men wise; poets, witty; the mathematics, sub-tle; natural philosophy, deep; moral, grave; logic and rhetoric, able to contend.

—FRANCIS BACON

Rhetoric is a term often used dismissively to imply that nothing was said, as in "That senator's speech was just a bunch of rhetoric." Or it is used to describe language that seems manipulative and full of flourishes but lacking substance. In other cases, *rhetoric* is described as an ancient art that has nothing to do with the present. Thus, for many people, *rhetoric* means several equally inaccurate things—everything from empty language to an ancient and useless art. Despite the bad press that the term *rhetoric* gets, we think rhetoric is valuable for writing teachers, especially when preparing students for writing on demand.

Rhetoric as Heritage

One reason we value rhetoric is it provides much of the foundation for our work as teachers of writing. Many of the terms and processes common in writing classrooms have their origin in Aristotle's *Rhetoric* or in studies of rhetoric written subsequently. When Aristotle wrote his *Rhetoric* in 350 B.C.E., the Greeks had been using rhetorical practices for some time. Aristotle simply developed a way to describe what speakers of his age were already doing. Similarly, rhetoric gives us a language to describe many of the best practices in writing instruction. For example, *prewriting,* a term familiar to composition teachers, is a version of what Aristotle called *invention.* In Aristotle's terms, invention was the process of discovering all the possible arguments. Today, when teachers ask students to map, freewrite, or brainstorm to begin generating ideas for a piece of writing, they are asking them to enact a variation of Aristotle's invention.

A number of the familiar paper genres commonly assigned in today's writing classes owe something to Aristotle's description of rhetoric. Assignments that ask students to *compare and contrast,* consider *cause and effect,* or create a *definition* draw upon Aristotle's commonplaces, or widely accepted ways of developing an argument. Students who know how to use strategies like these are at a great advantage in all writing, including writing on demand.

Even the familiar five-paragraph theme can be traced to classical rhetoric, which described the parts of an argument this way:

> *Exordium:* This is the introduction, which gives the topic, captures the reader's interest, makes an effort to gain the trust of the reader, and presents the thesis.
>
> *Narratio:* In this section, the writer seeks to maintain the reader's trust by giving background on the topic using objective facts, definitions, summaries, and so on.
>
> *Confirmatio:* The writer gives reasons to believe the thesis.
>
> *Refutatio:* The writer seeks to refute the opposing arguments.
>
> *Peroratio:* This is the conclusion. It summarizes the main points and may include a call to action. In addition, Aristotle said the peroratio should leave the reader in agreement with the writer and out of agreement with the opponent.

Many of the terms and processes common in writing classrooms have their origin in Aristotle's Rhetoric *or in studies of rhetoric written subsequently.*

If teachers have ever wondered why a five-paragraph essay requires students to restate their main points or why this familiar form asks students to define their terms in the paragraph after the introduction, they can see how these requirements resemble Aristotle's description of how a good argument should be planned.

Each age, from Aristotle's time to the present, has defined and used rhetoric for its own purposes. Philosophers and rhetoricians have contended with one another, stylists and grammarians have contributed to and departed from rhetoric, and rhetoric has occupied various roles in relation to education. In the United States, European models contributed to the ways rhetoric has been used in teaching writing. During the nineteenth century, for example, the work of Alexander Bain, a Scottish rhetorician, helped shape rhetorical education in this country. His 1866 text, *English Composition and Rhetoric,* described what we know today as the four modes—exposition, narration, description, and argument. John Genung, a professor of rhetoric at Amherst College, published a text titled *Practical Elements of Rhetoric* (1885) that institutionalized the four modes into composition instruction. Although the value assigned to them has shifted across time, the four modes still contribute to the way we talk about writing instruction today:

Exposition: The aim of exposition is to inform the audience.

Description: Essays written in this mode are designed to characterize something.

Narration: A narrative essay tells a story.

Argumentation: An argumentative essay seeks to persuade the *audience* to the position promoted.

As rhetoric drew away from other disciplines like psychology and philosophy during the last few decades of the nineteenth century, the modes gained prominence in writing instruction. As twentieth-century rhetoricians became more interested in other fields and writing teachers gave more attention to writers' purposes, however, the modes came under attack. For example, Albert Kitzhaber, a professor of rhetoric at the University of Oregon during the middle decades of the twentieth century, wrote this about the modes: "They represent an unrealistic view of the writing process, a view that assumes writing is done by formula and in a social vacuum. They turn the attention of both teacher and student toward an academic exercise instead of toward a meaningful act of communication in a social context" (1953, 220–21). Yet, despite the criticism heaped upon them, the modes remain part of the vocabulary of composition teachers, and this piece of our rhetorical heritage takes on particular significance in the context of writing on demand. Many writing-on-demand prompts reference the modes, and students will be more comfortable responding to those prompts if they know the conventions of the mode called for.

In the twentieth century, rhetoric continued to grow and change, and writing teachers adopted new approaches, including Kenneth Burke's dramatistic pentad ([1945] 1969), discussed in Chapter 2, which offers another way to generate ideas for writing, and Chaim Perelman's concept of identification, which provides new ways of thinking about the relationship between writer and audience (1982). Another twentieth-century theorist whose work contributes to today's teaching of writing is Stephen Toulmin, who developed a model for substantiating claims made by writers (2003). Toulmin begins from the position that the goal of every argument is to establish a claim and then support the claim through warrants with backing and qualifiers. He explains that arguments usually include qualifiers that indicate the scope or degree of the assertions, and he urges that writers acknowledge the rebuttals or counter-arguments that could be mounted in response to their claims. Students who become familiar with Toulmin's approach to argument find it easy to respond to many types of writing prompts, and they do especially well on prompts and assignments that call for argument.

Rhetoric for Contending

In addition to creating historical grounding for composition studies and making our heritage more comprehensible, rhetoric offers a way for writers to, as Francis Bacon put it, "contend." Writing an exordium, using the modes of discourse, employing strategies like comparison and contrast, considering the audience, understanding the dynamics of a given situation, and developing warrants for claims are just some of the ways that rhetoric can help students respond to the challenges of writing; they need not be intimidated by difficult assignments or complicated prompts on writing tests. Rhetoric provides tools for unpacking and responding to invitations to write, or prompts, as they are called.

Rhetoric offers a way for writers to . . . "contend."

We don't know why the directives that appear in writing tests are called *prompts.* It may be because it is a word used by psychologists, and standardized writing tests draw upon psychological norms. It may be because nineteenth-century rhetoricians began using the word. Whatever the reason, the term seems an apt one, especially when we consider the origin of the word as "something said or suggested to incite to action, or to help the memory." It goes back to 1597, when J. Payne wrote in the *Royal Exchange,* "Common dronckards and carnall lyvers . . . esteme themselves as honest and as truly religiouse as the best, and bothe by a subtill prompt of the divill." When students confront prompts on writing tests, they often feel as if they are facing something constructed by a devil. Rhetoric can give them tools to contend confidently with the challenges presented by prompts.

Here, for example, is a prompt that students may find challenging because of the number of questions it poses.

> You are completing a job application. As part of the application process, your potential employer requires a writing sample explaining the expression "Experience is the best teacher" and telling how it applies to you or someone you know.
> Write what you will present to your potential employer.
> Thinking about the following will help you focus and plan your writing.
> - What might the expression "Experience is the best teacher" mean?
> - What are some experiences you have had (or someone you know has had) that taught you an important lesson?
> - What did you learn and why was it valuable? (Delaware Grade 10 Assessment 2001)

The following chart shows how a rhetorical approach can be used to understand and begin to generate ideas for responding to this prompt. The chart can be used to analyze other prompts.

ONLINE 3.1

Rhetorical Analysis of Prompt

Prompt	Central Claim/Topic	Audience	Purpose/Mode	Strategies	Role
1	Experience is the best teacher.	potential employer	exposition	examples cause and effect	applicant

---

Writer's Notebook

Use the blank chart (Online 3.1) available on our companion website *www.heinemann.com/writingondemand* to do a similar analysis of other prompts. Can you determine topic, audience, and so on? To what extent does a chart like this help you address and respond to the prompt or prompts?

Five Prompt Analysis Questions

As the chart above shows, rhetoric offers resources that students can call upon to understand and respond to assignments in their classes as well as in writing prompts. Filling in the cells of such a chart requires students to answer a number of questions, and answering such questions will guide students to become close readers of prompts. Of course, prompts vary radically in the types and amount of information they provide to students about the kind of writing expected, so it may not be possible to answer every question for each prompt or assignment. However, learning to ask and answer a series of questions about the claim or topic, audience, purpose or mode, strategies, and role enables students to discern what is required of them and generate ideas for meeting that requirement.

We offer the prompt analysis questions below as a sturdy support or scaffold for student writers. Each of the five questions can be amplified by additional questions that may or may not be appropriate in every case. These rhetorically based questions recur throughout this chapter and the rest of the book because we have found them particularly useful for students who want to understand prompts and assignments. The additional questions will not be repeated in every case, so you may want to make copies of the full set (see Online 3.2) so students can refer to them.

Five Prompt Analysis Questions

ONLINE
3.2

1. What is the central claim or *topic* called for?

   Do I have choices to make with regard to this claim or topic? Will I need to focus the claim or topic in order to write a good essay? What arguments can I make for this claim? What do I know about this topic?

2. Who is the intended *audience?*

   If named specifically, what do I know about this particular audience? If the audience is implied or not identified, what can I infer about it? In either event, how might the expectations of this audience affect my choices as a writer?

3. What is the *purpose* or *mode* for the writing task?

   Is the purpose stated or must it be inferred? What is this writing supposed to accomplish (besides fulfilling the demands of the prompt or assignment)? What does the goal of this writing suggest about the mode (narration, exposition, description, argument) or combination of modes that I should consider in responding?

4. What *strategies* will be most effective?

   What does the purpose or mode suggest about possible strategies? Of the strategies I am comfortable using—like examples, definitions, analysis, classification, cause and effect, compare and contrast—which will be most effective here? Are there any strategies, such as number of examples or type of support, that are specified as required?

5. What is my *role* as a writer in achieving the purpose?

   Have I been assigned a specific role, like *applicant* or *representative?* If I have not been assigned a specific role, what does the prompt or assignment tell me about the level of expertise I should demonstrate, the stance I should assume, or the approach I should take?

In presenting these questions to students, teachers will probably want to explain terms like *claim*, distinguishing it from *topic* and acknowledging that an argument rests on a claim, though to some extent all writing can be described as an argument. At the same time, some prompts specify a particular topic (like the role of experience in learning) on which the claim needs to be based. Students may also need some explanation of the relationship between *purpose* and *mode*. The purpose designated by the prompt—to explain, to describe, to argue, and so on—will usually dictate the mode of writing to be used. At the same time that teachers explain the modes, it is a good idea to indicate that the modes frequently blur into one another since it's very difficult to write an explanation without some description or an argument without some explanation. This is also a good time to remind students of rhetorical *strategies* like compare and contrast, cause and effect, example, definition, and so on. Another term that may be unfamiliar to students is *stance,* and teachers can use physical terms like *crouch, loom,* or *cower* to suggest how writers take on different positions in relation to their audience and topic.

In the following pages we will show how writers can use prompt analysis to engage a wide variety of prompts and assignments. Through this process students can shift away from seeing prompts and assignments as designed to confound them. Instead, they can see prompts and assignments as language with which they can engage and ultimately succeed.

Expository Prompts

As we described earlier, exposition is the mode concerned with explaining something. Here is a sample expository prompt:

> Choices shapes our lives in many ways. Write an essay explaining how one choice shaped your life in a positive way.

How can teachers help students understand the expectations of this prompt? Here's a suggested approach.

MINILESSON

Goal: To help students learn to analyze a prompt in preparation for writing in response to it.

Talking Points:

- Rhetoric gives us a way to understand the relationships among audience, topic, and writer.

- Looking at a prompt rhetorically can help writers develop a successful response to it.

- A series of rhetorically based questions can help writers analyze a prompt.

- Rhetoric also offers strategies for responding to a prompt, strategies like compare and contrast, cause and effect, examples, definitions, and so on.

Activities:

Write the prompt on the board. Tell students that you will be analyzing the prompt together. Use the prompt analysis questions, and if students have difficulty responding, you might turn to the possible student answers we've included.

1. What is the central *claim* or *topic* being called for?
    The topic is *one* choice. A challenge of this prompt will be deciding upon a single choice to write about. It will be important to select a compelling choice because the claim of the writing will be based on this choice.

2. Who is the intended *audience?*
    The prompt doesn't specify any audience, so I'll have to imagine one. Since my readers will be adults and maybe teachers, I imagine they would like to read something original and interesting. I assume my audience will expect a relatively formal style and details to support my claims.

3. What is the *purpose* or *mode* for this writing task?
    The word *how* tells me that I will need to explain, and the direction to focus on the positive influence of the choice shapes my purpose. I will have to keep this in mind as I select the one choice.

4. What *strategies* will be most effective?
    Because I'll be explaining one choice I've made, I'll need to use examples. I could also use classification or definition to show why this choice was so positive.

5. What is my *role* in achieving the purpose?
    Because I'm writing about my own experience, I will be taking on the role of expert.

At this point you may want to ask students if they have other questions or comments about the prompt. This would be a good time to discuss the issues they raise.

Assessment:
Ask the class to brainstorm a process that a student might follow in writing the essay:

- List possible choices.

- Select one choice based on the following criteria:
    It was positive.
    It changed a life.

- Ask questions to generate material:
    What happened when I made the choice?

Why was the choice positive?

How did the choice change a life?

How clear is the connection between the choice and changing a life?

What would my reader find interesting about this choice?

What strategies will I use and why?

Will I write about my own choice or someone else's?

What are the implications of this choice?

This minilesson not only helps students understand the expectations of the prompt but also shows them a way to get started in answering the prompt. We believe that rhetorical analysis can help students write better. That is, everything they learn in the analysis of a prompt or any assignment should lead to a better understanding of the writing requirements and build confidence in being able to meet those requirements.

Rhetorical analysis can help students write better.

But what happens when there is very little to analyze? Here's another expository prompt for a tenth-grade writing assessment that doesn't give as many explicit cues as the previous example:

Tell your classmates about a responsibility you have been given.

Understandably, students feel lost when they see a prompt like this (and so might teachers when faced with preparing students to respond to such a prompt). Very little explicit information is given, and students may not feel motivated to share information about a responsibility. This is a situation ripe for a good case of writer's block, but working through the prompt analysis may help students see some footholds in what originally seemed a blank, smooth wall.

1. What is the central *claim* or *topic* called for?
    This prompt doesn't specify any claim to be made, and the topic is *responsibility*. I know what the word means, but I am left with many choices.

2. Who is the intended *audience*?
    My classmates are the audience, so I can assume that I know a lot about this audience.

3. What is the *purpose* or *mode* for the writing task?
    The verb *tell* suggests explanation, and it will probably also require

some descriptions. Because *tell* is such a vague word, I could try to come up with some more precise verbs. Here's a list:

_____ your classmates about a responsibility you have been given.

inform	describe
instruct	complain about
warn	reveal
notify	convey
advise	show
explain	

One way to choose from among these verbs is to think about what would work best with my audience of classmates. Another parameter is to think about what would work best with the specific responsibility chosen.

4. What *strategies* will be most effective?
   This prompt doesn't indicate who gave the responsibility, so one of the things I need to think about is what difference it makes if the responsibility is given by, say, my teacher, my boss, or my mom. Deciding on that will help me decide what strategies to use, but in any event, I'll need to explain and describe. Another thing that isn't clear is the kind of responsibility. Here are some possible adjectives to describe it:

   Tell your classmates about a _____ responsibility you have been given.

   onerous
   fantastic
   unmanageable
   exciting
   annoying
   uplifting

Each of these would suggest a different way of explaining and describing the responsibility.

5. What is my *role* in achieving the purpose?
   Each of the different verb choices would put me in a slightly different role. For example, if I chose the verb *instruct,* I would put myself in the position of teacher, and I would have to sound like some kind of expert. If I chose *complain about,* I would be putting myself in a

more childish role, whining to my friends. In a similar way, the adjectives I apply to *responsibility* will contribute to my role. For example, if I use *fantastic,* I'll be taking up an enthusiastic role, but if I use *annoying,* I'll be taking a more negative stance.

After a class has worked through the analysis of prompts, teachers can ask them to construct four different variations on the prompt and brainstorm ways to develop each. Here is an example of four:

1. Complain to your classmates about an onerous responsibility your father gave you.

• driving younger sister to ice-skating practice at 5 A.M. each day

• sweeping out the garage every Saturday morning

• waking up your older brother for his college class

2. Reveal an uplifting responsibility your Scout leader gave you.

• organizing the annual canned food drive

• choosing the location for the annual banquet

• assisting with the meetings of younger Scouts

3. Warn your classmates about an unmanageable responsibility your boss gave you.

• cleaning up after the store closes on school nights

• telling another employee that he or she needs to dress more appropriately

4. Describe to your classmates an exciting opportunity your teacher gave you.

• leading a discussion on the next chapter of the novel

• creating a short video about class rules

• redecorating the bulletin board with student work

At this point, students should have many ideas about how to approach a prompt that provides little information. The prompt analysis questions can help them analyze and amplify the prompt and also move them in the direction of generating material for their essays.

> **Writer's Notebook**
>
> Select one of the four variations above and write a response to it. Share with a classmate: how different or similar are your responses?

Persuasive Prompts

As we discussed in the introduction to this chapter, the mode of argument, or persuasion, has its own conventions. It is useful to be aware of these conventions when approaching a prompt like the following:

Prompt 1

ONLINE
3.3

Recent funding cuts have been made to the school district. To cope with the problem, your school board has plans to eliminate all sports and music programs. Some members of the community have questioned the board's controversial proposal.

Write a letter to the editor arguing your point of view on the proposal. Be sure to support your position with reasons, examples, facts, and/or other evidence. Readers should feel convinced to take your position seriously.

Close examination of the language of this prompt reveals several key terms. Words like *controversial, support,* and *convinced* all suggest the need to make an argument, to persuade readers. Students are left with the choice of whether to support or oppose the proposal, but regardless of their choice, they will need to provide support for their claims, as the directive to provide *reasons, examples, facts, and/or other evidence* suggests.

Teachers can have students work through the prompt analysis questions as a way of unpacking this prompt. Student responses that might stimulate discussion are included with each question.

1. What is the *central claim* or *topic* called for?
    Because this prompt requires a persuasive essay, I will have to make a definite claim about the pros and cons of eliminating sports and music programs. Once I've decided on a position, I'll need to consider how I can make the best arguments for it. I'll need warrants for my claim.

2. Who is the intended *audience?*
   Since a great variety of people read letters to the editor, I have to assume a general audience. I also have to assume that some members of my audience won't know much about high school sports and music.

3. What is the *purpose* or *mode* for this writing task?
   My main purpose is to persuade the reader to agree with my claim about the budget cuts. I'll be writing an argument and will need to make it convincing.

4. What *strategies* will be most effective?
   Analysis or classification will be useful as I organize the reasons for or against cutting the sports and music programs. I don't want to just throw a bunch of ideas out without organizing them.

5. What is my *role* in achieving the purpose?
   Once I've decided on my claim, I'll have to become an advocate for it, emphasizing all the points in favor of my position.

After students have worked through the prompt analysis questions, brainstormed some possible approaches to this prompt, and written a draft, they will have a new strategy for taking ownership of prompts by transforming them into topics they can write about. One of the challenges of writing in response to any prompt is figuring out how to transform it into something one can write about, or how to own it.

Teachers might explain to students that taking ownership of an assignment, whether one given in class or one included in a writing test, is an essential skill for student writers. In the process of making an assignment their own, they also choose a focus for the essay, identify an audience, and take a step toward establishing tone. Exercises like this one should help demystify prompts and help students see them as opportunities to take ownership of their writing.

Other prompts include more directions for students, and the challenge in these cases is to use the instructions in a productive way. Here, for example, is a prompt that gives students several directives:

ONLINE 3.4

Prompt 2

Change is generally considered either an improvement or a change for the worse. Most people resist changes because they feel the old ways are working, so changes are not necessary.

Write a persuasive paper presenting one change you feel is needed. Discuss a change that relates to your school, your community, the state, or the world. Include examples and evidence to support why the change is needed. You should do the following:

1. Take a few minutes to plan your paper by making notes.
2. Choose *one* change you think is needed.
3. Give specific reasons that explain why this change is needed.
4. Organize your ideas carefully.
5. Check that you have correct sentences, punctuation, and spelling.

You'll have forty minutes to write this essay.

Before turning to the prompt analysis questions, teachers might have students examine this prompt, noting how it differs from the others we have considered so far and thinking about what guidance they could draw from it. Among other points to discuss are the following. The directive to begin by making notes suggests the importance of prewriting in test situations, and it is worth taking some time to assure students that the most successful responses to writing on demand always include a considerable portion of planning and/or prewriting. Directives 2–5 can be read as an outline for a reader's assessment of the response, so students can use these to determine the criteria that will be used to evaluate their writing. Directive 5, with its explicit reference to sentences, punctuation, and spelling, suggests the need for students to pay close attention to the conventions of written English. It also suggests the importance of sentence structure (see Chapter 7 for a detailed discussion of sentences).

The prompt analysis questions provide a good way to conclude the examination of this prompt. We've included some of the points teachers might want to emphasize with each question.

1. What is the *central claim* or *topic* called for?
   One is a key word in the prompt. I should make a claim for only one change and not introduce several. Because I can write about my school, community, state, or world, I have many choices for a topic, and it may be difficult to figure out where to focus.

2. Who is the intended *audience?*
   Although no audience is specified, I think it makes sense to address an audience related to the area where I focus my topic—the principal of the school, the mayor of the community, the governor of the state, and so on.

3. What is the *purpose* or *mode* for this writing task?
   Because my purpose is to argue for one change, I'll be making an argument, but I would probably use narrative or description to lay out the situation I want to change.

4. What *strategies* will be most effective?
   Comparison and contrast might be useful if I try to explain the difference my change will make. Of course, I'll need examples, and definition may also be necessary.

5. What is my *role* in achieving the purpose?
   Because I'll be proposing a change and people don't always like change, I'll need to take on the role of expert, and a persuasive one at that.

Other prompts offer still more information, and in these cases students face the challenge of needing to read quickly and identify the information that is vital to their success. The following example gives teachers an opportunity to talk with students about how to make sense of a prompt that includes a great deal of information.

ONLINE
3.5

Prompt 3

Read the following writing prompt:

As part of an exhibit on inventions, the Delaware Museum is sponsoring a writing contest for high school sophomores on notable inventions and their impact on history.

Write an essay for this contest identifying the invention you consider notable and how it has impacted the world in either a positive or a negative way.

Answering the following questions will help you focus and plan your writing.
- Think of the many inventions throughout the history of the world.

- Think about the effect these inventions have had on our world.

- Is there one invention you think is better than the others?

- Is there one invention you would get rid of?

- Choose one invention to write about.

After you have planned your response, begin to write. Proofread your finished paper to check for complete sentences, correct punctuation, and spelling.

The *Writer's Checklist* below may help you plan, write, and revise your response.

Ideas and Organization

_____ Focus on your audience and your purpose for writing.
_____ Develop a clear opinion about the topic.
_____ Support your opinion with ideas, explanations, and examples.
_____ Present your ideas in the order that best supports your opinion.

Sentence Fluency

_____ Use sentences that vary in structure and length.
_____ Make your sentences flow smoothly.

Voice and Word Choice

_____ Use language that sounds natural.
_____ Use specific and accurate words.
_____ Write to your audience.

Conventions

_____ Capitalize, spell, and punctuate correctly.
_____ Make sure others can read your handwriting.

Because the prompt includes so many details, students may be tempted to skip all of it and just begin writing. We have seen students do this frequently, so it will be important to emphasize the need to read and plan. In discussion, teachers might point out to students that the directions include important clues for writers. The specification of a contest, for example, suggests that students should begin their prewriting by thinking about how judges associated with a museum might regard inventions. Another significant detail appears in the term *identifying*. This word suggests that choosing the invention or topic is an important part of the writing task, and the list of questions to consider reinforces this point. There is no language here to tell students anything about the form their essay should take, but clearly it needs to be persuasive in order to convince readers that a particular invention has made a significant impact on the world.

In analyzing the list of directions, it is worth talking about the fact that they appear in chronological order, suggesting how student writers should use their time. This list can also serve to reinforce the point that successful writing on demand requires planning, and it is, as Chapter 6 suggests, worthwhile to pause for prewriting before beginning to write the response. The writer's checklist can also seem overwhelming to students who are anxious to begin working on their response to the prompt. Teachers can suggest that they scan the list to get an overall sense of what it covers and then return to examine each of the items under headings like *Conventions* and *Sentence Fluency.* Alternatively, if there is an equivalent writer's checklist that is a constant, teachers can go over it during class time so that students will not have to use exam time to read and understand it.

*Learning how to gener-
ate ideas for writing
and to move directly
from analysis to
prewriting will help
students face the chal-
lenge of prompts.*

Prewriting After Analysis

The rhetorically based prompt analysis questions give students strategies for analyzing prompts and assignments to understand more fully what is required. In the process, they also begin to generate ideas for their papers, and, as Robert Frost has said, the key to writing is the having of ideas. Learning how to generate ideas for writing and to move directly from analysis to prewriting will help students face the challenge of prompts. Teachers can help students with this progression by using the following prompt.

**ONLINE
3.6**

Prompt 4

Writing situation: A major teen magazine has voted your city as one of the ten worst places in the country for teens to live. What is your point of view?

Directions for writing task: Write an essay either supporting or opposing the teen magazine's designation of your city. Use facts, examples, and other evidence to support your point of view.

A first step with this prompt would be to analyze it using the prompt analysis questions, noting the need for a persuasive essay about your city addressed to an audience of other teens from around the country that uses examples and facts. After working through the questions, it would be useful to practice some prewriting strategies with students. For example, to help students both generate material and organize their essays, model the use of two-column notes using this prompt. Here is an example of what this might look like.

Two-Column Notes Using Prompt

ONLINE 3.7

Claim: Our town is an excellent place for teens to live.

Key Points in Argument	Support for Key Points
1. The weather makes this a year-round place for teens to enjoy sports.	A. Because the first snow flies in October and doesn't melt until March, our teens get the most days on the slopes to snowboard. B. Cool weather makes the hockey season extra long, and we have more teams per capita than any other city. C. Every two years we have the Arctic Winter Games, which allows us to compete in a plethora of winter sports, like speed skating, snowshoeing, cross-country skiing, hockey, and curling with athletes from Canada and the Yukon.
2. The low crime rate makes life more positive and less stressful for teens.	A. Students don't have to lock their cars in the parking lot. B. It is safe to walk anywhere in the city, even in the dark. C. Because there is little crime, there is an atmosphere of trust among teens and between adults and teens.
3. Teens get an Alaska Permanent Fund Dividend check every year.	A. The permanent fund check ranges from $300 to $1,300 dollars and helps teens pay for things they normally couldn't afford, like car insurance, family vacations, and computers. B. There is a special fund for investing the dividend checks that can be used to pay for college. C. No taxes and free money—what other city in the country has benefits like this?

After you have modeled how writers can generate ideas for an essay in support of the idea that their city is a good place for teens, you could engage students in generating ideas for the opposite position. Use the blank chart available in Online 3.7, on the companion website.

It is useful to prepare both sides of the argument so students can take into consideration objections from the side opposite to the one they are arguing. Obviously, this will take a great deal of class time, but the critical-thinking skills that students will be developing are part of what we know to be best practice in the English classroom, not mere test prep. After all, the rhetorical tradition inherited from the Classical period prizes the ability to look at both sides of an issue, and perspective taking is key for any developing writer. Interrogating prompts will help students approach any writing task more confidently, whether it is the next assignment in class, a job application, or a college essay.

Interrogating prompts will help students approach any writing task more confidently, whether it is the next assignment in class, a job application, or a college essay.

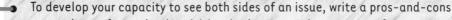

Writer's Notebook

To develop your capacity to see both sides of an issue, write a pros-and-cons essay about after-school activities. In the pro section, try to craft arguments that support these activities and offer as many reasons as possible. In the con section, oppose these activities, again using substantial support.

Literary Persuasive Prompts

Many state writing tests have prompts that reflect the literary influence in their curricula. Here is one such example:

Writing Assignment

Often in works of literature there are characters—other than the main character—whose presence in the work is essential.

From a work of literature you have read in or out of school, select a character, other than the main character, who plays a key role. In a well-developed composition, identify the character and explain why this character is important.

Once again, the prompt analysis questions introduced earlier in this chapter are useful in doing a rhetorical analysis of this prompt.

1. What is the *central claim* or *topic* called for?
   The topic is a literary character who is not the main character, and choosing a character to write about is one of the key parts of responding to this prompt because the character needs to be significant enough so that the student writer can argue for the character's

importance to the narrative and yet explain why the character is not significant enough to be a main character.

2. Who is the intended *audience?*
   The audience is not stated in the prompt, so students should work with the default audience: the grader of the exam. Knowing that test graders are often retired English teachers who are well read, students should realize that an extensive amount of summary about the literary work from which their character is drawn is not necessary.

3. What is the *purpose* or *mode* for the writing task?
   The primary purpose, of course, is to demonstrate the importance of a secondary character to a work of literature. Secondary purposes include showing familiarity with recognized literary texts, an ability to write about literary characters, and a capacity to be persuasive.

4. What *strategies* will be most effective?
   Students will need to include examples to support their claims about their character. They may also need to include a definition of *importance* to make their point.

5. What is my *role* in achieving the purpose?
   To persuasively present evidence that proves that the secondary character is important, students should take on the role of expert on this character.

Although the subject matter is literary, the process of analysis remains the same. Students still need to think about the various dimensions of what the prompt requires.

Narrative Prompts

Another genre that appears in some writing tests is the narrative. One narrative writing task begins with a picture that serves as a prompt for a story. The prompt accompanying the picture reads as follows:

Writing Task A

Visual images are compelling, and some would say they are especially so in the media-rich world in which we live. View this image carefully and then construct a narrative based on what you see and what you imagine.

This prompt does not specify an audience, but it does provide information about how student writers should proceed in responding to it. First, of course, students need to view the picture closely; then they need to engage their imaginations to develop a story. In our increasingly visually oriented world, preparing students to look at images is valuable for many reasons, including the fact that it will prepare them for prompts and assignments that are visually oriented. One way to begin preparing students is to photocopy a color transparency of a thought-provoking visual image or use an image from one of the transparency sets that come in the teacher materials for your textbook company. Ask the students the following questions for discussion:

ONLINE 3.8

Five Questions About Images

1. What setting do you see? Describe the time and place of the setting. Use all five senses to describe the setting. Even though this is a visual image, try to turn up the volume on your other senses.
2. What characters do you see? Describe the characters. How are the characters feeling? What names fit the characters?
3. What is the relationship between the characters?
4. What is the predominant mood of the picture?
5. What is the conflict in the picture? If there is no conflict happening at this moment, imagine a conflict that just happened or one that is to come. How could the conflict be resolved?

These questions help students create a setting, characters, and a problem, the most elemental building blocks for a story. Even students who do not consider themselves creative writers can create a satisfying story with these elements. However, it may not be immediately apparent to students how this discussion can be formed into a story, so here is a way of making that process visible to students.

1. Record student responses to the five image questions during discussion.

2. Type up each sentence, then make six copies of the sentences.

3. Cut the sentences into strips and put each set into an envelope.

4. At the next class, hand out the envelopes to small groups.

5. Ask each group to arrange the bits to form a story and to think about the process they are going through as they make decisions.

FIGURE 3.1

Visual writing prompt

6. Next, have each group explain why they chose the bits that they did and what kind of mental process they went through to make those decisions. As the groups are sharing, students will realize that many different kinds of stories can be made from the same image. They will also have an idea of how to move from generating observations to organizing their material. This can also lead to a discussion of what kinds of story structure students found most satisfying.

This exercise will be most fruitful if teachers model it first for students. The photo in Figure 3.1 provides a sample image. Here are the image questions along with possible responses.

1. What setting do you see? Describe the time and place of the setting. Use all five senses to describe the setting.

   The setting is a forest in the autumn. There are high-bush cranberry bushes and black spruce trees. The ground is covered with golden leaves. The tart smell of rotting cranberries hangs in the crisp, clean air. The leaves make a crackling sound as the boy steps on them and the bright sun stings his eyes. He has a sour taste in his mouth from the berries he has been eating.

2. What characters do you see? Describe the characters. How are the characters feeling? What names fit the characters?

   There is one character in the picture—a small blond boy, about five years old. He is wearing a short-sleeved shirt and jeans. He holds one hand up and his fingers are clutched around something. He has a wide smile on his face. He is happy. He pushes out his chest as if he is proud of what he has in his hand. He seems content. I will call him Samuel.

3. What is the relationship between the characters?

   The boy is the only one in the picture, but he is not alone. He is smiling at someone, maybe his mother or father, who is taking the picture, or maybe a brother or sister or friend.

4. What is the predominant mood of the picture?

   Peace, contentment.

5. What is the conflict in the picture? If there is no conflict happening at this moment, imagine a conflict that just happened or one that is to come. How could the conflict be resolved?

   The boy is having too much fun picking berries, kicking up leaves, and seeing the familiar woods from the perspective of a new season. The high-bush cranberry bushes are far apart, and his desire to eat more berries draws him farther and farther from his father, who is more preoccupied with taking photographs of his son than actually spending time with him. After spending several minutes learning to use the close-up function on his new digital camera to take a picture of an especially bright amanita mushroom, the father looks up for Samuel. Samuel is nowhere in sight. He calls for Samuel, but his voice echoes hollowly in the woods. He then remembers that a grizzly bear has recently been spotted in the neighborhood. He thinks he hears a cry, but it turns out to be a raven flying overhead, almost mocking his confusion.

After working through the observations generated by the five questions about images, teachers might talk with students about point of view. From whose point of view might the story be told? Samuel's? The father's? An omniscient narrator's? How could the author resolve the conflict? What would be the best way to interest others in the story?

Analysis of a picture using the five questions about images not only helps generate ideas for responding to a prompt that requires narrative but also reinforces student knowledge about the basic elements of a story.

Writing in Response to Quotation Prompts

Some prompts ask students to respond to quotations without providing a clear indication of what mode or genre of writing is expected. Here is an example of the unelaborated quotation prompt:

> Respond to one of the following quotations:
> "Hitch your wagon to a star."—Ralph Waldo Emerson
> "I never let schooling interfere with my education."—Mark Twain

Even though this prompt provides very few rhetorical cues, the prompt analysis questions can still be helpful in preparing students to respond. You might have students work in small groups to generate answers to the questions to help them begin to envision multiple possible responses to such a prompt. We include possible answers that you could share with students.

1. What is the *central claim* or *topic* called for?
   The word *response* makes it sound as if I could write anything that comes into my mind, but I don't think that would be a good idea.

2. Who is the intended *audience?*
   No audience is specified, but I know that adult evaluators will be reading, so I assume I need to be relatively formal and structured in my response.

3. What is the *purpose* or *mode* for this writing task?
   There is no mode or purpose specified, but I could imagine writing an argument agreeing or disagreeing with one of the quotes, or I could write a narrative that shows how one is or isn't true.

4. What *strategies* will be most effective?
   No matter what mode I use, I'll need to include plenty of details, explanations, and examples.

5. What is my *role* in achieving the purpose?
   The assigned role of responder leaves me plenty of freedom to take up any stance I like.

Here is a quotation prompt that includes more scaffolding:

You are completing a job application. As part of the application process, your potential employer requires a writing sample explaining the expression "Experience is the best teacher" and telling how it applies to you or someone you know. Write what you will present to your potential employer.

Thinking about the following will help you focus and plan your writing:

- What might the expression "Experience is the best teacher" mean?
- What are some experiences you have had (or someone you know has had) that taught you an important lesson?
- What did you learn and why was it valuable?

While this prompt in response to a quotation provides more information for the student, sometimes this support can have the opposite of the intended effect. For example, providing a list of questions might make a student think he or she just needs to answer the questions in the order asked to fulfill the writing task. We've seen students labor through a list of questions, thinking that they were doing what was expected of them. It is important for students to look at how the questions are introduced: "Thinking about the following will help you focus and plan your writing." Students are not asked to *answer* the questions, but to *think about* them.

Once again, answering the prompt analysis questions can help students analyze the prompt. Among other things, this exercise will help them think about the topic of experience, and this can be important since students have such a wide range of experience. Some students have never held a job and feel they don't really have any experiences yet. Others are more confident in this area. Sometimes high school students don't recognize their experiences as such because they are not validated by the larger society. The prompt analysis questions will also aid students in generating ideas about what a potential employer might expect, how job seekers might best present themselves, and the strategies that will make this presentation memorable.

Prompts *and* Assignments

Although this chapter has focused on prompts that appear in various writing tests, we want to underscore the fact that the process of analysis transfers easily to any writing assignment. Once students are comfortable using a rhetorically based probe like the prompt analysis questions to unpack the expectations built into prompts, they will be able to use those skills with assignments as well. Many of the assignments students encounter will resemble the various types of prompts discussed here. Assignments will ask students to make explanations and arguments, tell stories and describe things; they will ask students to make decisions about what to include and exclude, to decide on claims and offer warrants; some assignments will be filled with questions and suggestions to the writer and others will be as spare as a single quoted line.

Whether faced with a lack of information in a writing task or bombarded with bulleted lists of requirements and suggestions, students must be able to think critically about the prompts and assignments they encounter. Strategies of rhetorical analysis can help students understand what is expected of them regardless of the context in which the writing task appears. Slowing down the rapid calculations that fluent writers make as they respond to various tasks helps make the process clear to students who find writing mysterious and, therefore, intimidating. The prompt analysis questions instill confidence by showing students how to break the code, and with confidence comes success. In our experience, students who initially welcome the assistance offered by the prompt analysis questions eventually incorporate task analysis into their thinking and don't need the questions anymore. They, like all the scaffolding we provide our students, can eventually be removed.

Whether faced with a lack of information or bombarded with bulleted lists of requirements, students must be able to think critically about prompts.

Using the Five Key Questions About Prompts to Create Assignments

One of the things we have learned from our own experience with using rhetorically based questions to examine prompts and assignments with our students is that rhetorical analysis can be a useful tool for the *creation* of assignments. We have come to understand that the typical student question "What do you want?" usually indicates that we have not done an adequate job of making the topic or claim, audience, purpose or mode, strategies, and role clear enough for students to know how to proceed in their responses. Accordingly, we often use the prompt analysis questions as a lens through which to examine the assignments we give our students.

We no longer feel comfortable giving students assignments like "Write about an important experience" or "Describe your room." Producing assignments that can stand up to rhetorical questions takes longer, but we get fewer questions from perplexed students. Better yet, we see improved student writing when we craft our assignments carefully. And in a world where concerns about plagiarism abound, we find that students cannot buy or download essays that respond to carefully crafted rhetorically based assignments.

Key Points for Reflection

One of the strengths English/language arts teachers bring to the classroom is an ability to read and comprehend texts, and this is a skill students need in order to understand what is expected of them in responding to prompts and assignments. Whether they are writing for a timed test or an assignment that stretches over several weeks, students can't do their best work unless they understand fully what they should do.

Rhetoric, a long-standing part of the tradition of writing instruction, offers resources that students can call upon to unpack prompts and assignments. It prepares them to contend in the world of writing. Regardless of the type of writing task or the amount of detail provided, the process of asking and answering rhetorically based questions like those included in our prompt analysis questions—focusing on topic or claim, audience, purpose or mode, strategies, and role—enables students to discern what is required of them.

Continued analysis of many different types of prompts and/or assignments to determine what they require will prepare students for whatever writing tasks come their way. We believe:

- Understanding how the history of rhetoric has shaped writing instruction will help us understand some of the traditions in our field.

- Learning to do a rhetorical analysis of prompts can assist students in writing tests.

- The rhetorically based prompt analysis questions can help students understand not only the demands of prompts but also challenging assignments in the classes they attend.

- Classroom instruction that fosters rhetorical analysis of prompts and assignments will prepare students for success in writing and in writing on demand.

WORKS CITED

Burke, Kenneth. [1945] 1969. *A Grammar of Motives*. Berkeley: University of California Press.

Kitzhaber, Albert. 1953. Rhetoric in American Colleges 1850–1900. Ph.D. diss., University of Washington.

Perelman, Chaim. 1982. *The Realm of Rhetoric*. South Bend, IN: University of Notre Dame Press.

Toulmin, Stephen. 2003. *The Uses of Argument*. New York: Cambridge University Press.

Making Assessment Visible

4

Whadja get?
She gave me a B–.
I got a 72 on that paper.
I did OK.

School hallways are full of comments like those above. As students shuffle from one class to another, they regularly compare notes about the grades they receive for their writing. Most students see assessment as something that is done to them, something over which they have no control. For a number of them, assessment is an arbitrary, even capricious, process that is inaccessible and invisible. We have found that one of the most effective ways to prepare students for writing on demand and to improve their abilities as writers is to make assessment a visible and regular part of their classroom experiences. If students understand and practice various forms of assessment, they will be much more able to do their best work on high-stakes tests of writing. They will also become better writers by understanding how readers and evaluators think.

To prepare students for writing on demand and to improve their abilities as writers ... make assessment a visible and regular part of their classroom experiences.

Introducing Terms

Teachers typically use a number of terms commonly included in discussions of assessment, but these are not words students usually know. The first step toward making assessment more visible to students is to help them become familiar with its language. Students who become familiar with the terms used in testing are often able to move toward more and better thinking about their own ways of learning as they develop writing skills. The chart below includes a number of terms that students can benefit from understanding.

ONLINE
4.1

Common Assessment Terms

Term	Definition	Example
Achievement test	Measures learning already accomplished in writing	• state-mandated writing test • Advanced Placement test
Analytic evaluation	Writing assessment that is conducted by trained readers who focus on specific features of writing such as ideas, organization, word choice, sentence fluency, and presentation	• some large-scale writing tests
Aptitude test	Measures capacity or ability to learn	• Scholastic Assessment Test (SAT)
Assessment	Gathering information to determine what learning has occurred	• can include everything from informal comments on a draft to a score on a state writing test
Constructed response	Students create responses (write) in response to task	• test that requires an extended piece of writing
Criterion-based assessment	Writing assessment that focuses on specific features (criteria) identified in advance (see *analytic evaluation*)	• many school districts' assessments • some large-scale tests
Formative assessment	• Occurs during writing process • Provides feedback that can be used in further writing • Does not result in grade or score • Often called *informal assessment*	• comments from peer response group • teacher response to journal entries
High-stakes test	A single test that controls a life-shaping event like passing to the next grade or graduating from high school	• district-mandated test • state-mandated test

Term	Definition	Example
Holistic evaluation	Writing assessment that is conducted by trained readers who focus on overall quality, not becoming concerned about any one aspect of the writing	• some state-mandated tests • some states use a variation called a *focused holistic evaluation* that concentrates on a few features of writing
Performance assessment	Test that requires students to perform a task rather than select answers from a ready-made list (see *constructed response*). In the case of writing, performance assessment means actually writing rather than identifying features in a prepared text	• many large-scale writing tests
Rubric	A guide for evaluating writing that lists features to be considered along with qualitative dimensions of each so that distinctions can be made among pieces of writing (see *scoring guide*)	• many teachers • many schools
Scoring guide	A predetermined list of features and qualities of each to be used in assigning a score to a piece of writing (see *rubric*)	• many teachers • many school districts • some large-scale tests
Selected response	Students select answers from choices given	• multiple-choice grammar test • true/false test
Summative assessment	• Occurs when writing is completed • Results in final grade or score	• letter grade given to a piece of polished writing • score on state achievement test

Students who learn about terms like these will understand more about the various kinds of evaluations they are likely to face. In the schools we know, students have already begun to pick up some of the terminology that permeates the current climate of high-stakes testing. Hallway conversations include sentences like "She's just teaching to the test" and "My score is in the top 10 percent on that test." We've also encountered students who have expressed anger and frustration at the number of tests they have to take, and we've found that such students can become less hostile if they understand more about various forms of evaluation as well as the larger context into which high-stakes tests fit.

Analyzing Test Items

Once students understand the difference between selected-response and constructed-response test items, it can be valuable to look at a few of each in order to understand them better. In suggesting this, we don't mean simply having students take practice tests so they can become familiar with the genre of standardized tests. Rather, we believe that students can learn from examining what skills are required to answer different types of test questions. When students look closely at the processes they go through to answer questions, the literacy skills they need to develop become evident.

Selected-Response Items

Most writing tests emphasize constructed responses, asking students to produce texts, but there are also some selected-response test items that fall under the heading of composition. Some of these items focus on relatively uncomplicated features, like parts of speech, as this one does:

> Identify the correct part of speech for the underlined word in the following sentence.
> When its brakes failed, the car rolled <u>quickly</u> down the hill.
>   a. adjective
>   b. noun
>   c. adverb
>   d. gerund

Most students do not have too much difficulty identifying *quickly* as an adverb. Because this is a relatively easy—even transparent—question, students are usually able to describe the thinking they did to decide on an answer. Other selected-response items, like those used on the AP Literature and Composition test, can be more challenging. Consider this:

Selected Response Question

ONLINE 4.2

Directions: Rephrase the following according to the directions given, and choose the response that best corresponds to the necessary changes to the original sentence. Keep the meaning of the sentence as close to the original as possible, maintaining natural phrasing, the requirements of standard written English, and logical and concise construction.

1. Subsequent references to the man are absent; this has always been considered puzzling and conspicuous.

    Begin with *The absence*

    a. the man has always
    b. references have always
    c. puzzling has always
    d. the man considered
    e. the man puzzled

The rephrased sentence would read: *The absence of subsequent references to the man has always been considered puzzling and conspicuous,* and the correct answer to this item is, of course, Option *a.* Students who answer a test item like this can then write an explanation of how they arrived at the answer.

Writer's Notebook

Make notes on your thinking as you try to figure out the answer to the previous test item. After selecting an answer, write an explanation of how you were thinking as you decided on the answer.

Students can usually provide a rather detailed explanation of how they arrived at an answer to a selected-response item. If they have difficulty creating a narrative, they can simply make a list of steps they went through. Here is an example of what a student might produce:

My Thinking

I read through the sentence and then looked at *The absence.* In my mind I tried to think how the sentence would go if *The absence* came first. Then I scanned the possible answers and eliminated *d* and *e*. I tried to imagine the rest of the sentence and decided *The absence* would have to be followed by *of subsequent references to the man*. Then I realized that *this* wouldn't belong in the sentence anymore and I could get rid of the semicolon. I looked at the rest of the sentence and realized that it could stay the same because *The absence* had become the subject of the sentence and the verb *has* would agree with it.

Putting the rest of the sentence together helped me eliminate *b* and *c,* so then I knew that *a* was the answer.

The term *metacognition* is often used to describe an explanation like this, when students focus on how they think. Doing such an exercise can help students understand more about assessment because it shows them how they think through the various options presented by selected-response items on writing tests. This metacognition or metaprocessing will make them more aware of how items like this are constructed and how they might respond to them, and comparing accounts like these with their peers' responses will help them see alternative ways of approaching test items.

After students have written and compared some accounts of the ways they think when they are answering selected-response items on writing tests, they will be ready to take this process to the next level by figuring out what literacy skills they need in order to do the thinking that items on a given writing test require. This process heightens students' metacognition because they begin to think about the skills and knowledge they draw on as they write. We find that students can begin to identify their own literacy skills if they look at each cognitive move in turn. For example, the account about the "absence" sentence begins by describing a process of reading and then moves on to describe a mental rearrangement of the sentence. Students typically do best when they analyze a peer's account of thinking processes. This exercise helps them simultaneously do better on tests and become better learners because they gain insight into what it takes to be successful on writing tests. Here, for example, is a list of the literacy skills necessary to do the thinking described in "My Thinking":

Abilities Necessary to Answer Question 1

- read and comprehend written passages

- rearrange components of a sentence

- identify wrong answers

- recognize correct subject-verb agreement

Once students have identified skills necessary for answering items successfully, they can become more intentional about developing these skills. Recognizing, for example, that it is useful to know how to do a mental rearrangement of sentences can make them more receptive to doing sentence-combining exercises (see Chapter 7). Similarly, knowing that they need to be able to identify and use subject-verb agreement can make them much more attentive to minilessons on various aspects of grammar.

Constructed-Response Items

The most common form of writing test, of course, asks students to actually write rather than to identify features in sentences written by others. Accordingly, students will benefit from spending the greatest proportion of time analyzing these items. The process, however, is the same as for selected-response items. Students make notes as they write, recording the decisions they made and the way they arrived at these decisions. When they have finished composing, they write an account of the thinking that produced the writing. Many teachers ask students to practice writing with the prompts that appear in constructed-response items, and we think that can be productive, especially when combined with a metaprocessing analysis of how the writing is actually accomplished. Just as is the case with selected-response items, students can learn to identify skills necessary to succeed with the writing, and they typically become more receptive to learning those skills when teachers focus on them in class. Here is a prompt that appeared in a writing test:

> *Writing situation:* The principal of your school has been asked to discuss with a parent group the effect watching TV has on your grades and on your friends' grades.
>
> *Directions for writing:* Think about the effect watching TV has on your grades and your friends' grades. Now write to convince your principal to accept your point of view on the effect watching TV has on grades.

Here is what one student, Don, wrote in response to the prompt. Before he wrote this response, he was asked to make notes about his thinking processes during writing and to plan on writing an account of that thinking after he finished:

> I believe that television could affect a student's grades if the student watches too much television. If you were to watch television while you did your schoolwork it would definitely take longer and lower your quality of work.

Personally I do not watch much TV. When I watch TV, often I watch game shows such as Jeopardy or Lingo. I think shows like this are actually helping you learn, so shows that teach should be encouraged.

Watching television while you study would affect your grades, though, even if you are not watching it but are around a television because you would lose concentration on your work. For example, when I was writing a paper for English class the TV was on, and I was constantly losing my train of thought.

Looking at my grades compared to someone who watches more TV *could* differ, but a comparison of grades of someone who doesn't *do* work with a television in front of them to someone who watches TV while working *would* differ.

Overall, I think watching TV doesn't affect most students' grades, but it could if the right of watching TV is abused or if students try to do schoolwork while watching TV. Parents should monitor their children on how and how much they watch TV.

When asked to write about his thinking process as he wrote this piece, Don produced the following. He said that he didn't really need to keep notes about his thinking because he could remember what he had been thinking by looking at what he had written:

I read the question over a couple of times and then thought about how much TV I watch and how my grades compare with other kids. I decided that I don't watch enough to affect my grades. I also thought about the *kind* of TV I watch, and it seemed like game shows could be described as educational. I started writing and got through the first couple of paragraphs. Then I thought some more about the relationship between watching TV and grades, and I remembered a time when I was writing something and the TV was on. Even though I wasn't really watching it, it was difficult to concentrate on my writing. That made me think about how watching TV while you're studying is more of a problem than watching TV—unless you watch a whole lot. So that's what I decided to write about.

I just realized that I didn't actually address the principal.

Moving from Don's account of his own writing to a discussion of the skills necessary to produce this piece of writing led to the following list:

Abilities Necessary for Responding to the Writing Prompt

- read and comprehend question

- call on extracurricular knowledge (of TV programs and viewing habits)

- consider relationships (between grades and TV viewing)

- develop a thesis or main point

- address an audience

As is true for looking at the thinking that produces answers to selected-response items, an examination of the account of thinking that accompanies writing enables students to identify the literacy skills they need to respond to a specific prompt. Developing a list like this and eliciting student suggestions about how to incorporate these skills into classroom learning can help students become much better learners at the same time that they prepare to perform successfully on writing tests.

Another thing students learn from this exercise is that they follow a slightly different process with each writing task, and in turn, the literacy skills they need vary from one task to another. While some processes extend across tasks, others do not. The question about the relationship between television viewing and grades requires students to draw on extracurricular background knowledge, whereas a question about whether a specified amount of homework should be required asks students to make judgments about an aspect of their own education. Understanding the different knowledge and skills required by various questions helps students become better readers of—and responders to—any writing prompt or assignment.

Peer Evaluation

Another effective way to make assessment visible to students is to involve them in evaluating the writing of their classmates. Chapter 2 explains ways to establish and sustain peer response writing groups. Here we discuss the various ways these writing groups can serve the project of assessment. Peer evaluation can occur at several stages during the process of writing, and it can take multiple forms. Just as it is always easier to see personality flaws in others rather than ourselves, so too is it easier to see problems in the writing of others. Experience with peer evaluation gives students tools they can eventually use to assess their own writing, both on writing tests as well as other occasions for writing.

Peer evaluation can occur at several stages during the process of writing, and it can take multiple forms.

The times when peer evaluation can be valuable include the following stages:

- during invention or prewriting, when students are generating possibilities for writing;

- during early drafting, when students are trying to find their central point;

- during later drafting, when students can attend to issues of language and audience;

- during revision, when students are making global changes to enhance clarity; and

- during the final stages of editing and proofreading, when students are polishing whole pieces of writing.

Clearly, students do not need to participate in peer evaluation at each stage, and frequently one stage blurs into or turns back on another. This list, however, suggests the many ways that students can sharpen their evaluative skills so that they can ultimately become more effective in assessing their own work when writing on demand. Showing students how the teacher responds to a piece of writing will give them strategies for assessing one another's writing.

Evaluating Plans and Ideas

Early in the writing process, students can benefit from assessment of their tentative ideas and plans. We have found it effective to have students meet in pairs and share ideas in order to get feedback from another student. Each, in turn, explains a general plan for writing, including the topic, the main points, and sources of information. In response, we instruct the partner to do the following:

- Decide whether the topic is too broad or too narrow and offer suggestions for focusing or expanding it.

- Brainstorm at least two details that can be included in the main points.

- Suggest a way to develop the writing.

Talking through issues like these helps students develop the capacity to generate ideas for writing. At the same time, this kind of evaluation helps students think about the overall shape of writing and consider ways of evaluating the general pattern of a given composition.

Because writing prompts and assignments vary in complexity, a writing group focusing on plans and ideas is also an ideal space for unpacking and discussing how one might respond. The following prompt, taken from an Advanced Placement test, is fairly complicated, and we have found that students need to spend some time figuring out how they might respond to it.

Advanced Placement Prompt

ONLINE
4.3

Time: 40 Minutes

Examine the following passage by Edgar Allan Poe. Then write an essay that defines and discusses the effect of the selection on the reader. Pay particular attention to how the writer uses syntax, diction, imagery, tone, and argument to produce that effect.

For the most wild yet most homely narrative which I am about to pen, I neither expect nor solicit belief. Mad indeed would I be to expect it, in a case where my very senses reject their own evidence. Yet, mad am I not—and very surely do I not dream. But tomorrow I die, and today I would unburden my soul. My immediate purpose is to place before the world, plainly, succinctly, and without comment, a series of mere household events. In their consequences, these events have terrified—even tortured—have destroyed me. Yet I will not attempt to expound them. To me, they have presented little but horror—to many they will seem less terrible than baroque. Hereafter, perhaps, some intellect may be found which will reduce my phantasm to the commonplace—some intellect more calm, more logical, and far less excitable than my own, which will perceive, in the circumstances I detail with awe, nothing more than an ordinary succession of very natural causes and effects.

An exercise that works well with a prompt like this one is to ask writing groups to meet and develop plans for writing. Then individual students write an introductory paragraph for what could become an essay response and meet again in writing groups to critique one another's introductions, using the language of the prompt to guide their discussion.

Evaluating an Early Draft

When students have completed a first draft, they may have written only a few sentences or paragraphs. Still, this can be an excellent time to meet with a group of peers who will share what they have produced. At this stage in the writing process, emphasis still belongs on generating ideas, and discussion with peers can help students learn to evaluate their own plans more effectively. When students are evaluating an early draft, we ask them to do the following:

- Read aloud everything you have written, even if sentences aren't complete. Don't explain what you *meant* to say, just read what's on the paper.

- Ask group members to summarize in one sentence what they heard.

- Based on group response, ask three questions about your draft and write down the responses of each group member.

The process of summarizing someone else's draft will help students develop analytical skills that are essential to becoming better evaluators of their own writing. Asking questions about the responses to their drafts helps authors learn to look at their own work from a slightly distanced perspective, and that ability is key to assessing their own writing.

One of the points of discussion—and sometimes debate—in teacher talk about writing groups is whether group participants should have copies of the text or simply listen to the author read aloud. We have found both procedures effective, but at an early stage such as this, we prefer oral reading because it prevents students from focusing on surface features like spelling and punctuation when what the student author really needs is attention to the overall ideas and shape of the piece. There is plenty of time to turn to surface features when writing is more fully developed.

Evaluating a Later Draft

Once students have found a direction for their writing and have produced several fully developed paragraphs, they are ready to participate in a writing group that attends to issues of language and audience. Of course, attention to audience should begin in the earliest stages of invention and/or prewriting so that the draft includes appropriate material. As Don's account about writing in response to the prompt on television and school grades shows, however, it's often not possible for students to think explicitly about audience when they are concentrating on what to say. Still, the difference between writing to a school principal and to, say, a friend about watching TV would lead to different arguments. Concerns about grades, educational programs, and ability to concentrate on homework would probably be more convincing to a principal than discussions of funny sitcoms, ways to use TV in homework, or comments about the pleasures of watching ESPN.

As soon as students start thinking about audience, they will also begin to focus more closely on their own language. They can start to consider words and phrases in terms of the person who will be reading them. Here, then, is a process that can help students in peer response writing groups evaluate and revise writing at this stage.

- Before the author starts reading a draft to the group, he or she explains who the audience is.

- Group members list three to five traits they associate with this audience.

- As the author reads the draft aloud, group members note places where the language of the draft is especially well suited to the audience.

- Group members share their notes with the author.

By focusing exclusively on the relationship between audience and language, students develop another evaluative skill. This will help improve their writing in general because it will enhance their rhetorical awareness, making them think explicitly about the potential readers of their work. At the same time it will help them meet the challenges of writing on demand because it gives them another lens through which to look at their own writing.

Evaluating for Final Revisions

When students have been working on a piece of writing for some time, it is often difficult for them to look at their own texts with any objectivity. Indeed, we find the same is true for ourselves. After working on multiple drafts, we can no longer remember which sentences are on the paper and which are simply inside our heads. When we read the text over, we find ourselves mentally filling in explanations that aren't actually included in the writing. We imagine transitions where none exist, and unless we read aloud, it's easy to skip over clunky phrasing. These things happen because we read with our brains, not our eyes, and brains fill in what should be on the page and ignore the things that shouldn't be there.

Peer response writing groups can provide valuable feedback on drafts, giving students ideas for polishing their work and helping them learn to evaluate complete selections of writing. This is a time when we favor circulating the written text to group participants, but it's valuable for authors to read the selection aloud while group members follow along on the written copy because some problems with language are much easier to hear than see. When students read their drafts aloud to one another, they find questions like the following particularly helpful.

- How would you summarize this selection?

- Which phrases strike you as particularly effective?

- What language sticks out as awkward?

- When you get to the end, what questions remain?

Students who answer these questions develop their ability to assess whole pieces of writing, and students who receive answers to these questions get a broader perspective on how readers may respond to their writing. Our students are often surprised by what their peers see as the essence of something they have written, and they begin to realize that things they understand completely may not be clear to others. This increased capacity to take the perspective of others, to consider their audience, serves them well as writers and as test takers.

Evaluating for Polish

If noticing problems in overall structure and wording is difficult for student authors, proofreading the final version is *extremely* difficult. Reading the text aloud is one way to find errors because silent readers of their own texts nearly always miss errors. Students can learn to become better proofreaders of their own writing by proofreading the writing of their peers. Pairs of students can exchange papers and proofread one another's work. One objection to this practice is that students may not always be able to recognize errors or know how to fix them. In our experience, we have found that there are usually a few "grammar nerds" and "spelling champs" in our classes, and serving as consultants for their peers gives them an opportunity to shine. Identifying students who can serve as resources for proofreaders and encouraging readers to pause and ask when they have questions help them all learn more about the mechanics of language in an authentic way.

When proofread papers are returned to the original authors, students can do a final exercise that will strengthen their ability to evaluate their own work. In addition to correcting the errors, they can analyze them to determine what kinds of mistakes they make most frequently. The following chart will help them with this process by asking them to categorize and quantify their errors.

ONLINE 4.4   # Error Chart

Total number of errors identified by proofreader:

Error	*Type/Example*	*How Many*
Spelling	Misplaced internal vowel: *wierd* for *weird*	
Spelling	Prefix/suffix: *scarfs* for *scarves*	
Spelling	Pronunciation/structural: *waring* for *wearing*	
Wrong Word	*Are* for *our* or *where* for *were* or *it's* for *its*	
Punctuation	Comma	

Total number of errors identified by proofreader:

Error	Type/Example	How Many
Punctuation	Colon or semicolon or hyphen	
Capitalization	Proper name, sentence beginning	
Usage	Subject-verb agreement: *he don't* for *he doesn't*	
Unintentional Sentence Fragment	*Running down the street* for *the thief was running down the street*	
Incorrect Modifier	*The horse ran quick* for *The horse ran quickly* or *He took the joke literal* for *He took the joke literally*	
Run-on Sentence	*Mary was noisy at first, now she's settled down* for *Mary was noisy at first, but now she's settled down*	
Unclear Pronoun Reference	*Joe called Frank when he got home* for *When he got home, Joe called Frank*	
Misused Preposition	*We divided the reward between the four of us* for *We divided the reward among the four of us*	
Other	Fill in example:	

Filling out this chart and looking at the number of errors in each category gives students a very clear idea of the areas where they are most likely to make errors. This knowledge can help them focus their energies for improvement, and it can also serve as a guide for a quick scan of texts produced for writing on demand.

Self-Evaluation

The various processes of peer evaluation serve as the best preparation for self-evaluation because as students learn to identify problems in the writing of others, they are developing skills that they can use in their own writing. In addition, it is useful for student writers to imagine themselves in the position of an evaluator and have a few processes they can go through to evaluate their own writing. The following list is a good point of departure.

...as students learn to identify problems in the writing of others, they are developing skills that they can use in their own writing.

ONLINE
4.5

Self-Evaluation Suggestions

- Make an outline of your piece of writing. Include major and minor headings. If you have difficulty finding information to fit into each category, look again at transitions and connecting ideas in your writing.

- Imagine the audience specified by the prompt or assignment, if there is one. List at least five things that would matter to this person, and try to imagine thinking the way he or she does. With that mindset, reread your writing, asking whether it addresses the concerns of this audience.

- Read your work aloud. This will slow you down enough to catch errors that would be difficult to see during silent reading. In a test environment, simply whisper to yourself. Since you won't have time to recopy your work, this is a quick way to make sure you eliminate glaring problems.

- Recall the kinds of errors that you have made on other pieces of writing and scan your work for these.

Rubrics

Rubrics, or the list of criteria that will be considered in evaluating writing, offer another way to make assessment visible to students. Some schools use a common rubric so that students will consistently be evaluated on the same terms. Other schools use the state rubric so that teachers and students alike will become familiar with its terms. Such rubrics are usually quite general, based on criteria like these:

- explores topic fully and thoughtfully

- shows depth and complexity of thought

- demonstrates clear and coherent organization

- includes full detail and development

- exhibits control of conventions of language

Students can benefit a great deal from examining such rubrics because they can begin to see that assessment is based upon qualities that can be named and demonstrated. In schools that do not use a common rubric, teachers can introduce students to the previous example or develop one in collaboration with students.

After students have become familiar with a generic rubric like the one above or something similar that is used by the school, they can benefit from an opportunity to use it. The following prompt and student writing could be used to give students an opportunity to apply the rubric.

Prompt and Student Response

ONLINE 4.6

Assignment: Write an essay about the course you have found most valuable. Explain why it was important to you and be sure to include examples to support your claims.

Student Response: I think one of my most important courses was Business Marketing. I like that class because you do a lot of fun things there. Like the other day we talked about people who making money and I learned something from that. Sometimes it is boring and most of people sleep, and sometimes we learn a lot of stuff.

I got a job because of that corse. I love my job as computer operator in Saunders Retirement Managing. I use a lot of strategies that I learned. My boss is kind sometimes and other days he is mad. But business is coming along good. We got at least 10 people to invest already. The market is coming up every day.

I hope a lot of people attend that class. It will help you in life without you knowing it. And you learn about partnership and how to start a business.

Regardless of what items their rubric includes, students will probably agree that this sample student text is not an excellent piece of writing. The process of using a rubric to evaluate a text like this one will prepare students to be more careful and critical readers of rubrics. Accordingly, they will benefit from examining a state rubric like the one below.

Sample State Rubric

ONLINE 4.7

Focus. Focus refers to how clearly the paper presents and maintains a main idea, theme, or unifying point.

- Papers receiving lower and middle scores may contain information that is loosely related, extraneous, or both.

- Papers receiving higher scores demonstrate a consistent awareness of the topic and avoid loosely related or extraneous information.

Organization. Organization refers to the structure or plan of development (beginning, middle, and end) and the relationship of one point to another. Organization refers to the use of transitional devices (terms, phrases, and variations in sentence structure) to signal (1) the relationship of the supporting ideas to the main idea, theme, or unifying point and (2) the connections between and among sentences.

- Papers receiving lower scores may lack transitional devices and summary or concluding statements.

- Papers receiving higher scores use transitional devices (signals of the text plan or structure) and developed conclusions.

Support. Support refers to the quality of details used to explain, clarify, or define. The quality of the support depends on word choice, specificity, depth, credibility, and thoroughness.

- Papers receiving lower and middle scores may contain support that is a bare list of events or reasons, support that is extended by a detail, or both.

- Papers receiving higher scores provide elaborated examples and fully developed illustrations, and the relationship between the supporting ideas and the topic is clear.

Conventions. Conventions refer to the punctuation, capitalization, spelling, and sentence structure. These conventions are basic writing skills included in Florida's *Sunshine State Standards.*

- Papers receiving lower and middle scores may contain some or many errors in punctuation, capitalization, spelling, and sentence structure and may have little variation in sentence structure.

- Papers receiving higher scores follow, with few exceptions, the conventions of punctuation, capitalization, and spelling and use a variety of sentence structures to present ideas.

Looking at rubrics developed by others has clear value, but an even more valuable exercise asks students to develop a rubric themselves.

Examining the details included with each of the features of this rubric will give students a clearer sense of how terms like *organization* and *support* might be applied by evaluators. This examination will also sharpen students' general sense of what constitutes high-quality writing.

Looking at rubrics developed by others has clear value, but an even more valuable exercise asks students to develop a rubric themselves. Many rubrics are generic and can be applied to nearly any piece of writing, regardless of the assignment or genre. While these rubrics are useful, they operate at a higher level of generality than do those designed for specific assignments. Accordingly, we find it effective to involve students in the process of developing a more specific rubric that addresses a specific assignment.

Goal: To show students how to develop a rubric for a specific assignment.

Talking Points:

- Some rubrics are very general and can be used with any piece of writing.

- Other rubrics are developed for specific assignments.

- Developing a rubric for a specific assignment can enhance your understanding of an assessment.

Activity:

Copy the assignment and sample response below onto an overhead transparency. Show students just the assignment at first and invite discussion of what an evaluator might look for in a response to this assignment.

Sample Assignment and Response

ONLINE
4.8

Assignment: A committee at your school is considering changes in the curriculum. To help with their planning, they have asked students to write to them explaining which course they have found most valuable.

My Most Valuable Course

The most valuable course I have taken in my school carrer is Spanish. Many people choose to take foreign languages just to graduate with an advanced diploma, but I take the course because it is fun and educational. The most upcoming foreign language is Spanish, and the Hispanic population is dominating. An advanced Spanish language study can possibly help me get along in the future.

In the 8th grade, I started my first year of a foreign language. Since I had started early, I was ahead of most of my class. I decided to take a two-year Spanish 1 class to help me understand the fundamental of the Spanish language. My first class was Spanish 1A, followed by 1B in my 8th grade year. I was very interested in the Spanish culture, and language. I decided to take Spanish 2 Honors in my 9th grade year. The second year of a language is always the hardest, so I studied very hard to be successful, and the studying paid off. I then moved on to Spanish 3 Honors in my current, 10th grade year. To end my high school years, I plan to take Spanish 4 and 5 and soon hope to speak fluent Spanish. Once I graduate from high school I will go off to college, and hopefully major in Spanish. In my future carrer, I hope to move to a Spanish speaking country and become a doctor.

Spanish has made an early impact on my life, and hopefully will apply to my future. If I do not stick with my Doctor plan, I would still love to be a Spanish interpretor. As the Hispanic race rises, so does the need of fluent Spanish speakers, and I hope I can help out.

To help students think about what features would contribute to a successful response, engage them in a conversation about what they would expect an evaluator to look for. Some of the following questions might aid discussion:

- What information about your course will help a committee member understand its value to you?

- How can you demonstrate what the course has taught you?

- Are there ways to compare this course with others you have taken?

- Why would you argue for keeping this course in the curriculum?

Keep a running list of the features identified by students, and after they have discussed the assignment for a while, show them the sample response and continue the discussion in light of this response.

Assessment:
Help students come to some agreement about which features should be included in the rubric and write one on which everyone can agree.

This minilesson can be extended by having students write in response to the assignment in Online 4.7, exchange papers, and use the rubric to evaluate one another's final drafts. This extension will help them understand assessment more fully and, in turn, will enable them to perform better when writing on demand as well as in many other contexts of writing.

Key Points for Reflection

Much of the anxiety students feel when approaching writing tests comes from not knowing how they will be evaluated. Of course, students feel this anxiety when they are asked to do almost any writing assignment because assessment usually feels frightening and mysterious to them. Even when they know a teacher well, they often lack any clear sense of how she arrives at grades for the writing that she assigns. This feeling is multiplied many times over with a writing test because students have no way to know who will be evaluating their work—although they always know that it will be an authoritative adult who has expertise in English—so even the modest security provided by a day-to-day relationship with a teacher/grader is absent.

Giving students opportunities to explore various kinds of assignments and questions and to look inside the process of evaluation will help relieve some of their anxiety about writing tests, leading them to perform better. At the same time, this enhanced perspective on assessment will also enable them to become better writers because the analysis required to evaluate peers' work, reconsider their own writing, and create rubrics will develop their capacity to anticipate and address the concerns of their readers, whether classroom teachers or external evaluators. We believe:

- Assessment needs to be more visible to student writers.

- Examining questions and/or rubrics from writing tests will strengthen students' understanding of assessment.

- Peer evaluation of writing will lead to better self-evaluation.

- Developing and using rubrics for a specific assignment will sharpen students' analytical skills.

5 Reading for Writing

It is fit for the beginner and learner to study others and the best. For the mind and memory are more sharply exercised in comprehending another man's things than our own; and such as accustom themselves and are familiar with the best authors shall ever and anon find somewhat of them in themselves.

—BEN JONSON

Ben Jonson wrote the above stylistic advice in the mid-seventeenth century, some 360 years ago, and as venerable as Jonson's words may seem, his advice is one of the longest established—and possibly most traditional—methods of teaching writing. In this method, teachers present to students exemplary models and ask them, in turn, to both analyze what the models say or do and then try to imitate them. While at first glance this may seem an outdated, even patronizing way to teach writing, it is actually one of the most valuable methods teachers have to show students good writing and to encourage them to make that good writing their own. Certainly we don't want consideration of models as our sole method of helping students improve their writing, but it can be really powerful. The key, of course, is moving beyond *examining* exemplary models to *using* the models as tools to improve writing. While discussing great literature, nonfiction or fiction, is a staple of the English language arts class, this use of exemplary writing is for a specific purpose, not an end in itself.

That said, it might seem appealing to simply ask students to read a great deal of exemplary writing and then to write. Not so easy. The transfer from reading good writing to creating good writing is, first, not automatic. Second, students are in many cases accustomed to assessing what is *wrong* about writing; assessing what is *right* about writing may not come quite so easily. We often encourage students to ferret out unnecessary repetition, to critique a weak opening, to find the logical flaw in the development of a piece. But what about the flip side of this? What makes a piece of good writing good?

Surely our students occasionally enjoy, agree with, even remember certain pieces they read. But why? Why does something work so well that it just seems right, effective, almost perfect? Most readers at any age hardly notice, and our job as teachers is to ask students to examine and assess what makes a strong piece of writing strong.

The key, of course, is moving beyond examining exemplary models to using the models as tools to improve writing.

Thus a vital step is to ask students to look at an effective piece of writing and to note in particular what makes it successful and why. When students are aware of the strength of a piece of writing, they have a better chance at replicating some form of that strength in their own work. And it is important to note that exemplary writing need not be writing that comes only from professional or otherwise sanctioned or even exalted sources. Solid writing from peers can be similarly useful and can, in addition, have the effect of not overwhelming students or implying to them that their prose need be the equal of veteran adult award winners to be acceptable and well done. Someone in second period may have solid writing talents even though she is not headed toward a Pulitzer prize.

The examination and unpacking of writing we are advocating is *close reading*, a kind of analysis that many students find unfamiliar. Yet, when students learn to employ close reading and to note how words and phrases and sentences and paragraphs make a strong piece of writing, and how openings and closings are effective, they will have a clearer idea of how to proceed in their own work.

Writer's Notebook

Try to recall something you read recently outside of school that you really liked or on which you spent some time reading. Name its title and list what kept you interested (Subject? Memorable writing? Effective opening? Strong conclusion?). Now do the opposite: try to recall something you picked up and then did not finish. What made this piece of writing *uninteresting* to you (Subject? Writing style? Vocabulary?)? If you cannot recall something you read recently outside of school, browse through some materials from your classroom or library media center and try to answer the same questions.

The Art of Close Reading

Once students learn to look at a piece of writing with a keen eye, they will never lose the skill. Although they may not choose to exercise it with all their reading—it would slow them down immensely as well as interfere with the overall meaning and sense of a piece of prose—the ability to notice how a piece of writing works, why it has the effect it does, is, once acquired, not easily lost.

From our experience, it is best, once the principles are established, to teach close reading inductively. It takes a bit of time, but simply telling students that parallelism is operative or the use of assonance strings the concepts together or the verbs are powerful and well placed will not be sufficient. Students who are interested in close reading will listen attentively, but it will not be easy for them to replicate the process independently. And obviously, the range of good writing is such that there are few immediate and reliable triggers for specific or standard patterns; writing devices and techniques are a kaleidoscope, and students must be able to find their way into the passages.

There are literally thousands of excellent examples of prose that you can present to your students or, even better, that they can present to the class as a large group or in a small group. The key is starting with a general impression of merit or impact or interest and then moving, specifically and precisely, to *how* that impression is conveyed. Sometimes it may be obvious that the piece works because of some sort of large and readily identifiable unit. It might be a generally effective paragraph, a dramatic style of writing, or an opening topic or subject that intrigues. Sometimes, however, the effect may be achieved or enhanced by something smaller or more subtle—a sentence, a phrase, or even a word. The key is to stop, in a way, being a reader, and to instead read as a writer: good writers have skill and, like basketball players, have moves that are effective. We begin with broad questions that only later will become more narrow and more specific. We ask our students: What are a writer's moves and how do they work? We are asking, essentially, How does the writer achieve his or her effects? What is the art?

We might start by asking students to offer general impressions:

- What is the writer trying to say? What is the sense? To what extent does the way this is written make you care about that sense?

- What catches your eye or makes you notice this passage or any other? Look at big things but also at smaller units (such as word choice, length of sentences, sentence structure).

- What would happen if this part or section or word were changed? What would you substitute and why? Can you see any difference in the possible alteration? Why then do you think the writer chose that specific pattern of sentence or word? What work does the sentence or word seem to do in the passage?

When students get into the habit of not just consuming prose but actually unpacking its craft—when they read for writing—then they are more able to replicate this in their own work. And, in sequence, we can invite students to move from general impressions to more specific features, looking at different aspects of exemplary writing. We start, logically, with openings.

Openings

One of the most crucial aspects of effective writing, and one that is particularly important in successful on-demand writing, is the opening. At the onset the writer needs to capture attention for the subject, establish a theme and a tone, and indicate in some way what is to follow. Thus in the opening, a skillful writer states the general topic, communicates an attitude, and forecasts or indicates where the piece will go.

Returning to the tenth-grade student essays used in Chapter 1, the following three opening sentences, while not brilliant, do communicate their general subject and, in some cases, forecast what might follow in subsequent sentences:

School is important for many reasons and goals.
Throughout my school career I feel the most valuable course I have
   taken is keyboard/computer applications.
The most interesting class that I have ever taken was kindergarten.

Another student opening sentence takes a bit more time but effectively sets up its subsequent subject:

Through all the years that I have been in school, most of the courses I have taken have been the same. Math, Science, Social Studies, and English. It wasn't until 6th grade that I got freedom enough to choose my own courses. In 6th grade I chose to take . . .

Turning to the skillful writing of professionals, it can often be easier to see openings that are not only intriguing but which state the general subject, communicate an attitude, and forecast where the piece will go. In one deceptively plain yet highly effective sentence, Joan Didion's opening to her essay "Goodbye to All That" does all of that:

It is easy to see the beginnings of things, and harder to see the ends. (1980a, 317)

Along with the truth of what Didion writes (and the extent to which this one sentence could be the whole point of the essay that follows), students might also look at this opening sentence and consider the general issues outlined earlier:

- interest of the opening (To what extent does it make you curious to read more? How does it capture your attention?)

- attitude of writer (What appears to be the tone of the writer? How can you tell?)

- ideas in the opening (What is the major point or points? How is it narrowed or refined? Where do you think this is going?)

Once students have considered these broad questions, as a second stage of the discussion, students might also look at the specific craft of the opening sentence itself, considering the following items in particular:

- sentence structure (What is noticeable about the way the opening's sentences—or, in this case, sentence—are written? Do you see a pattern?)

- word choice (Are there unusual words in this opening? If not unusual, what words might be considered highly appropriate?)

Students could specifically consider the following:

- how this opening sentence operates as a balance scale, thus:

it is easy	it is harder
see the beginnings	see the ends

- how the opening sentence might be affected if Didion had chosen to repeat the entire verb, rather than make it understood, thus:

    It is easy to see the beginnings of things, and it is harder to see the ends.

- How the opening might have been affected if Didion had chosen to use *but* instead of *and*:

    It is easy to see the beginnings of things, but it is harder to see the ends.

    or

    It is easy to see the beginnings of things but harder to see the ends.

Putting these different sentences on an overhead or on the board helps students look at them as a whole and consider distinctions. While all students may not see the differences immediately, they will notice that something changes with each single sentence variation. This is the beginning of close reading and may show students that they know—instinctively as readers and writers—more than they might assume about sentence structure and word choice. Certainly the issue is choices, and if students are asked about rewriting the entire opening, looking at word choice, sentence structure, and sentence sense, they can consider what they might change and why. What would be gained? Lost? Significantly altered?

A way to do this is to play with versions of a fill-in-the-blank model that uses Didion's structure but which could also be applied to something students might want to write. They could experiment with the blanks and then compare what they have not only with each other but against the original model.

The following versions offer increasingly less support for students:

a. It is easy to see the _____, and harder to see the
   _____.

b. It is easy to _____ the _____, and harder to _____ the
   _____.

c. It is _____ to _____ the _____, and _____ to _____ the
   _____.

Students can use these models, compare them, and discuss.

Let's turn to another famous one-sentence opening, from George Orwell's "Shooting an Elephant" (1980, 128). Again, the title is intriguing, but equally so is the first line:

> In Moulmein, in lower Burma, I was hated by large numbers of people—the only time in my life that I have been important enough for this to happen to me.

What Orwell does here is reversal, a surprise that some students instinctively will notice. The verb *hate* is one not to be dismissed easily, but Orwell turns the entire sad commentary on its head by noting that the hatred came because it was "the only time in my life that I have been important enough." This is not the mirror image of words and structure that Didion uses, but an intriguing, provocative opening that also, like Didion, tells the reader what "Shooting an Elephant" will probably contain: not only descriptions of the hatred but descriptions of the role of the author in this one place and time. Surely most of us would never naturally link *hatred* and *importance*; Orwell, with these two words, gives us a political, hierarchical link. In this context at least, important people are hated.

Additionally, Orwell uses a powerful piece of punctuation, a dash, which not only interrupts the flow of the sentence (so different from the smooth balance of clauses that Didion uses) but also indicates that what will follow is something very strong or even startling. Asking students what they notice about punctuation can be helpful here. Orwell's dash helps make a point and make it early on.

Again, we can ask students about these factors:

- the interest of the opening (To what extent does it make you curious to read more? How does it capture your attention?)

- the attitude of the writer (What appears to be the tone of the writer? How can you tell?)

- the ideas in the opening (What is the major point or points? How is it narrowed or refined? Where do you think this is going?)

As a second stage of the discussion, students might also look at the craft of the sentence itself, considering the following in particular:

- sentence structure (What is noticeable about the way the opening's sentences—or, in this case, sentence—are written?)

Finally, we could also do a fill-in-the-blank with the Orwell sentence and, again, offer decreasing levels of support:

   a. In _____, I was _____ by large numbers of people— the only time in my life that I have been _____ for this to happen to me.

   b. In _____, I was _____ by _____—the only time in my life that I have been _____ for this to happen to me.

   c. In _____, I was _____ by _____—the only time in _____ that I have been _____for this to happen to me.

As with the Didion sentence, students could fill in these blanks and discuss the differences and choices. By experimenting with fill-in-the-blank exercises, students see that innovative structures can add to an effective opening.

Despite their contrasting elements (subject, when they were written, author, sentence structure, etc.), what these two effective one-sentence openings have in common is the establishment of the subject, the communication of attitude or tone, and a forecast of what is to come. All of this is achieved through a certain craft: mirror imaging of phrases in the case of Didion and reversal of expectations with Orwell. The three aspects of an effective opening—

   stating the subject,
   communicating an attitude,
   forecasting of what is to come,

—are all-important for our students to remember when they create their own openings.

Goal: To give students an opportunity to compare and contrast essay openings and to specifically note qualities or characteristics of those openings.

Talking Points:

- Good essays have effective beginnings.

- Three aspects of an effective beginning involve the clarification of subject matter, the establishment of tone (or attitude), and an indication of where the essay might be headed.

Activity:

Look at the following single-sentence openings and decide what might make each one effective (hint: it is different for every one). To what extent does each one *state its subject, communicate an attitude,* and *forecast what is to come?*

Single-Sentence Openings

ONLINE
5.1

1. I remember, to start with, that day in Sacramento, in a California now nearly thirty years past, when I first entered a classroom—able to understand about fifty stray English words. ("Aria: A Memoir of a Bilingual Childhood," Richard Rodriquez 1982, 522)

2. When Ulysses S. Grant and Robert E. Lee met in the parlor of a modest house in Appomattox Court House, Virginia, on April 9, 1865 to work out the terms for the surrender of Lee's Army of Northern Virginia, a great chapter in American life came to a close, and a great new chapter began. ("Grant and Lee: A Study in Contrasts," Bruce Catton 1982, 180)

3. Anyone interested in the future of American commerce should take a drive sometime to my neighborhood gas station. ("They Also Wait Who Stand and Serve Themselves," Andrew Ward 1982, 89)

4. Five score years ago, a great American, in whose symbolic shadow we stand, signed the Emancipation Proclamation. ("I Have a Dream," Martin Luther King Jr. 1982, 451)

Assessment:

To what extent did students identify and compare the three aspects of these four openings?

Once students have considered one-sentence openings, they may be more comfortable and ready to look at longer opening passages. Even the most skillful of writers cannot always create an effective (or even interesting) opening in a single sentence, and sometimes it takes a cluster to establish the tone and make the point. The following minilesson encourages students to look at longer openings.

MINILESSON

Goal: To give students an opportunity to apply their knowledge of the characteristics and qualities of essay openings.

Talking Points:

- Effective openings do more than establish subject, present an attitude, and forecast what is to come.

- Effective openings can also use an identifiable strategy to capture reader interest (such as present facts, tell a story, give background information, use a pertinent quotation).

Activity:

Look at the following paragraph openings and assess the effectiveness of subject, attitude, and forecast. You have more information to work with (i.e., the passages are longer), and accordingly you may have a clearer idea of where the writer is going. What do you notice about the five examples? Which of these do any or a number of the following:

- state the idea and show the writer's attitude

- present startling facts about the subject

- tell a story about the subject

- give background information that will illustrate the subject or show its importance

- begin with a quotation

Multiple-Sentence Openings

**ONLINE
5.2**

1. It is a bright summer day in 1947. My father, a fat, funny man with beautiful eyes and a subversive wit, is trying to decide which of his eight children he will take with him to the county fair. ("Beauty: When the Other Dancer Is the Self," Alice Walker 1993, 675)

2. I sometimes think of what it means that in their heyday—in 1830, say—the Kiowas owned more horses *per capita* than any other tribe on the Great Plains, that the Plains Indian culture, the last culture to evolve in North America, is also known as "the horse culture" and the "the centaur culture," that the Kiowas tell the story of a horse that died of shame after its owner committed an act of cowardice, that I am a Kiowa, that therefore there is in me, as there is in the Tartars, an old, sacred notion of the horse. I believe that at some point in my racial life, this notion must needs be expressed in order that I may be true to my nature. ("My Horse and I," N. Scott Momaday 1993, 427)

3. It is now theoretically possible to recreate an identical creature from any animal or plant, from the DNA contained in the nucleus of any somatic cell. A single plant root-tip cell can be teased and seduced into conceiving a perfect copy of the whole plant; a frog's intestinal epithelial cell possesses the complete instructions needed for a new, same frog. If the technology were further advanced, you could do this with a human being, and there are now startled predictions all over the place that this will in fact be done, someday, in order to provide a version of immortality for carefully selected, especially valuable people. ("On Cloning a Human Being," Lewis Thomas 1993, 589)

4. The first thing people remember about failing at math is that it felt like sudden death. Whether the incident occurred while learning "word problems" in sixth grade, copying with equations in high school, or first confronting calculus and statistics in college, failure came suddenly and in a very frightening way. ("Who's Afraid of Math, and Why?" Sheila Tobias 1982, 343)

5. "The greatest contribution to civilization in this century may well be air conditioning—and America leads the way." So wrote British Scholar-Politician S. F. Markham 32 years ago when a modern cooling system was still an exotic luxury. In a century that has yielded such treasures as the electric knife, spray-on deodorant and disposable diapers, anybody might question whether air conditioning is the supreme gift. There is not a whiff of doubt, however, that America is far out front in its use. ("The Great American Cooling Machine," Frank Trippett 1982, 123)

Assessment:

To what extent did consideration of these more extensive openings give students a sense of the range of good openings and expand their writing repertoire? Is there a sense that students now, when confronted with a prompt, can create a single-sentence or multisentence opening that is effective and interesting?

Writer's Notebook

Choose a topic with which you are comfortable. You might choose something with which you are really familiar or about which you have a strong opinion (such as the legal driving age, the role of computer games in your life, the corruption of professional sports, tattoos and body piercings, or what it means to hook up). Play with writing different openings about that topic. Look at the following list and try to use at least three different types of openings:

• state an idea and show your attitude

• present startling facts about the subject

• tell a story about the subject

• give background information that will illustrate the subject or show its importance

• begin with a quotation

   Now reread your openings. Which do you like better and why? Which seem to be easier to follow with more sentences and elaboration? Why? Share these openings with a friend or a classmate and ask him or her to comment on which of the openings he or she responded to. What in particular caught your reader's attention?

Closings

Students know that effective essay closings summarize what has gone on before and give the reader a sense of a satisfying end. In that sense, closings are far easier to write than openings. The ground has already been covered, and all that is needed is some sort of restatement. But students also need to know that truly effective closings give the reader a bit extra; they offer something more than *just* restatement or summary. And from a teacher's perspective, helping students look at conclusions or closings is a bit more complicated than helping them look at openings. Out of context, closings often do not make sense—or reveal their craft; students must read or consider the entire piece that precedes it to really see the value of the closing. Thus a writer's cunning, creative, or skillful conclusion may be lost if it is presented as a decontextualized single sentence or even multiple set of sentences.

> *But students also need to know that truly effective closings give the reader a bit extra; they offer something more than just restatement or summary.*

For example, the conclusion to James Baldwin's "Stranger in the Village," a discussion of an African American man's brief residence in a Swiss village where no black man had ever been seen, is global and ringing, especially after one has read the entire piece. Baldwin moves from one village to the world and declares that the universe is unalterably changed. But presenting to students, by itself, Baldwin's one-sentence ending may not be as impressive as, in context, it absolutely is.

> This world is white no longer, and it will never be white again. (1993b, 77)

As a second example, an essay that talks about being a teenager, "Ducks vs. Hard Rocks," by Deairich Hunter, divides teens into two opposing groups and uses a fine conclusion that does far more than summarize. Hunter has hinted at this in her essay, but it is only at the end that she expands "Ducks" into the entire issue of being young:

> Maybe the only people left with hope are the only people who can make a difference—teens like me. We . . . must learn to care. As a fifteen-year-old, I'm not sure I can handle all that. Just growing up seems hard enough. (1982, 70)

In context, this conclusion is strong and opens out a new idea from the essay, but just reading it as it stands alone, students would be hard-pressed to understand that.

As a final example, in "Naftale," by Gertrude Reiss, the writer asks her father to tell her about his life, and the incidents are recounted without interpretation and comment. It is only through the one-sentence conclusion that the reader understands the whole essay:

> Until I asked my father to tell me about his life, I never knew he was a happy man. (1997, 52)

This conclusion opens up the entire essay and reveals, in essence, the point of the stories, making it far more than a mere restatement.

What is the solution? It would appear that it is best to show students whole pieces—or at least the last third or half of the piece—so they can get the sense of the power of a conclusion. Otherwise the craft and the thought will not be apparent.

Effective Closings

Effective closings, as noted at the beginning of this section, need to do more than restate. Let's look at some student examples first for ending sentences (the whole essays are replicated in Chapter 1). Consider the closing sentences for these tenth-grade essays that discuss the most valuable course ever taken in school:

1. This is why I feel it is the most valuable.

2. In attendance of this class my writing skills enhanced along with my once small vocabulary.

These two closing sentences are clunker sentences, sentences that fail to conclude the piece other than to simply say, in essence, "Bye—got to go now." Such unimaginative closings do little to strengthen, extend, or reconceptualize what came before.

As a different issue, some of the student essays discussed in Chapter 1 use closings that are not imaginative—bad enough—and which do something different and equally problematic. These closings introduce in the conclusion new and unexpected elements. These new elements are not only out of place but, ultimately, confusing. One such student essay on photography and its importance concludes with a wholly new reference and thought:

1. Great masters of photography like Ansel Adams and Robert Cappa have made me realize the marvelous pictures that can be taken with a camera.

Another essay, which cited kindergarten as a great class and used a bit of nostalgia for that carefree time, concluded:

2. We take a lot of things for granit and we don't realize it until it's to late. One of the advantages of being older is the independence.

A final essay, on the importance of music, noted:

3. It's valuable because it lets me express my creativity and show that I understand the musical industry and the masterminds of the past.

In the first conclusion, the writer is mentioning examples of photographers to whom he has never alluded before. In the second example, the advantages of being older are never discussed, never even mentioned, until this last sentence. In the third, like the first, the writer mentions new reasons for taking music (understanding the industry and appreciating classic musicians), which have never been explored or even cited until the conclusion. While all of these ideas may be important, they have not been previously developed at all and are simply stuck at the end to conclude—and confuse—the piece. In these three examples, there is no effective conclusion.

So what kind of things should a good conclusion do? There are a number of options:

- restate or summarize the major points

- offer a final, clincher point

- emphasize one particular insight

- cite the broad significance or deeper implications of the main points

- make a prediction

- recommend how the information can be applied

- be creative: tell a pertinent story, ask a question, or cite an authority

Certainly the first option is the most tempting: as mentioned before, the groundwork for this kind of conclusion has been laid in the essay itself, and all the writer needs to do is recapture the major points. The other kinds of conclusions, however, can be very effective, and students can experiment with all of them to broaden their repertoire.

Let's imagine a brief sample essay on the most valuable course taken in school. Can students do any of the above with the essay? It might be fun to try to change the concluding paragraph to make it more effective.

Other kinds of conclusions . . . can be very effective, and students can experiment . . . to broaden their repertoire.

MINILESSON

Goal: To encourage students to try on different ways to conclude an essay.

Talking Points:

- Summary is not the only way to conclude an essay.

- Other strategies (clincher point; broad implications; prediction; application; creativity) can be equally or more effective.

Activity:
Look at the following student essay and in particular at the conclusion (the very last paragraph, which begins with *Overall*). If you wanted to change this conclusion (which is a summary of the two major ideas: English prepares you

for successful work on the SATs and prepares you for a good job), which of the following could you use? Using one or two of the following strategies, re-write the conclusion.

- Offer a final, clincher point.

- Emphasize one particular insight.

- Cite the broad significance or deeper implications of your points.

- Make a prediction.

- Recommend how the information can be applied.

- Be creative: tell a pertinent story, ask a question, or cite an authority.

ONLINE 5.3

Writing a New Conclusion

English is the most valuable course taken throughout every grade level. You learn not only many, many subjects needed on the SATs, but also skills needed to perform well in life.

One of the main reasons English is such a benefit is for the SATs. SATs are so important to your future because they decide which college you will go to, which decides what kind of job you will have and how well off you will be in life. You get the basic knowledge needed for this test all through your years of English classes.

Another reason English is an important course is because it teaches you to have a great vocabulary. The better your vocabulary, the more high class you will seem. When being interviewed for a job position in any area, the better one speaks about him or herself, the more eligible you will seem for the job.

Overall, English will help you succeed in life. It can give you the basic knowledge for SATS and the skills needed to have a successful life.

Rewritten Conclusion 1

_____

_____

_____

Rewritten Conclusion 2

_____

_____

_____

Share your conclusions with a partner. What other ideas do you get about different conclusions?

_____

Assessment:
To what extent are the rewritten conclusions effective? How many of the different approaches did the students attempt and use?

→ **Writer's Notebook**
→
→ Pick a piece of short writing with which you are familiar and, as in the mini-
→ lesson you have done in class, rewrite the conclusion. After you have created
→ your new conclusion, cite two things about your closing that, from your per-
→ spective, improve the original or change its tone and/or subject.

Looking at Words

Mark Twain once said that the difference between the best word and a good word is the difference between lightning and a lightning bug. Many students would agree and, in fact, the search for the best word consumes many younger writers. While words and vocabulary are indeed important, a caution is in order: many students honestly believe that an entire piece of writing can be unified or clarified by the glue of a single correct or right word. Few teachers who have worked with student writing have not heard the lament that if only the student could find the right word, the entire essay would be somehow fixed. As Nancy Sommers (1980) reminds us, the first line of defense for many inexpert writers is the alteration of the smallest unit, the word. And certainly this is not entirely a student's fault: the concentration that many high-stakes tests place upon vocabulary and the use of thesauruses with their emphasis on an expanded vocabulary give many students the mistaken impression that strong writing is characterized, first and foremost, by exotic vocabulary, by the silver bullet of the single, just-right word. Despite Jonathan Swift's contention that "proper words in proper places, makes the true definition of a style" ([1720] 1980, 349), good writing is far more complex than demonstrating a strong command of vocabulary. While the alteration of words can certainly strengthen a piece, consistent concentration on single words is misplaced and distracting, especially in the pressured atmosphere of timed conditions.

Good writing is far more complex than demonstrating a strong command of vocabulary.

Still, word choice is indeed part of effective writing, and when students can notice words that do the work in the right place, their close reading can help them, in turn, select and use words that actually work well in their writing.

(For further discussion of vocabulary, see Chapter 7, including the chart that lists words that are often confused.)

Let's return to the opening of the Alice Walker essay and consider her choice of words:

> It is a bright summer day in 1947. My father, a fat, funny man with beautiful eyes and a subversive wit, is trying to decide which of his eight children he will take with him to the county fair. (1993, 675)

We can ask students to look at this opening and select words that do more than just tell. Certainly our students would come up with a number of them: *bright, fat, funny* (as a unit); *beautiful eyes; subversive wit.* None of these words is by itself exotic, but within the opening, the words paint a picture of a person and an incident; they are powerful and work well. Again, we might try a fill-in-the-blank exercise as students look at Walker's choices and try to create their own alternatives. The following are, as before, in decreasing level of support:

a. It is a _____ summer day in 1947. My father, a _____, funny man with beautiful eyes and a _____ wit, is trying to decide which of his eight children he will take with him to the county fair.

b. It is a _____ day in 1947. My father, a _____, _____ man with _____ and _____, is trying to decide which of his eight children he will take with him to the county fair.

c. It is a _____. My father, a _____, _____ man with _____, is trying to decide
   _____.

Students can compare and discuss these.

Students also need to know that word choice can dictate the tone of a piece and unify the ideas. For example, look at the repetition of the verb *kill* in the following excerpt from "Little Fish, Big Fish," a pointed and angry editorial about driving by Ted West:

> I have in mind a certain kind of idiot. Here are some clues. He (or she or it) hates cars yet depends on them abjectly and with fear in his heart . . . He believes that cars kill people. That speed kills people. That everyone who doesn't drive the way he drives kills people. That doing anything he hasn't done before, or isn't already doing right now, kills people . . . he believes that if one isn't very careful, one will arrive at one's destination ahead of schedule—which kills people. (2001, 10)

Can students find similar examples of single words that convey strong emotion?

Writer's Notebook

Start keeping a list of unusual or interesting words you like or words that you do not use and would like to use in the future. Put these in your writer's notebook. If you can, recopy the original sentence in which the word appears so that you will have a sense of how it is used.

One thing that students need to remember to avoid is using words that are too complicated for the context of the writing or words of which students are not sure (either in meaning or in form). This kind of word use—or misuse—can actually call attention to the writing in a negative way, and students don't want to pen such examples as these tenth-grade student ones (misused words are in italics):

1. From my *sprouting* years in elementary school to my present, *drudging* years of high school, I have taken many courses.

2. *Adamancy* can be found in the decision that my eight grade English class helped my learning experience in the largest way. *In attendance* of this class my writing skills *enhanced* along with my once small vocabulary.

As a game, students might want to pick a word from a grab bag (you can prepare these on slips of paper and put them in a bag) and play with the creation of multiple synonyms for the word. (This can be done with the thesaurus feature on a computer.) Verbs and adjectives are probably the most fruitful for this game. Such a list might include the following:

- Verbs (and synonyms)
  work (labor, endeavor, try)
  know (understand, comprehend, realize)
  believe (hold, contend, maintain)

- Adjectives (and synonyms)
  important (useful, significant, crucial)
  interesting (intriguing, fascinating, unusual)
  negative (damaging, destructive, dangerous)

- Nouns (and synonyms)
  person (individual, citizen, human being)
  talent (flair, bent, ability)

Looking at Sentence Units, Single Sentences, and Paragraphs

Once students have considered openings, closings, and word choice, they might want to look at sentences and how they are put together. This may also include larger units—paragraphs—where students can see the differing patterns that writers use to achieve their effects.

First, consider what phrase within the following sentence stands out, and what George Orwell, in "Shooting an Elephant," achieves:

> I was sub-divisional police officer of the town, and in an aimless, petty kind of way anti-European feeling was very bitter. (1980, 128)

Certainly students will note *aimless, petty kind of way,* and, possibly, the power of the single word *bitter.*

Along with unusual phrases, sometimes writers like stringing together sentences, as in "On Morality," where the sentences mirror the tedium of the time writer Joan Didion was spending:

> As it happens I am in Death Valley, in a room at the Enterprise Motel and Trailer Park, and it is July, and it is hot. (1980b, 313)

While we often counsel students not to string clauses together with *and,* in the Didion example, just that kind of pattern is effective and memorable, especially at the end of the sentence *(and it is July, and it is hot).*

Contrast the Didion example with what James Baldwin does with his sentence length in the following excerpt from "Autobiographical Notes"; the first two sentences are short, simple, and direct, followed by a third, longer sentence that expands his point and intensifies the drama. The mixing of sentence length is dramatic and important:

> I was born in Harlem thirty-one years ago. I began plotting novels at about the time I learned to read. The story of my childhood is the usual bleak fantasy, and we can dismiss it with the restrained observation that I certainly would not consider living it again. (1993a, 63)

This kind of alternative rhythm (eight words in Sentence 1; twelve words in Sentence 2; twenty-eight words in Sentence 3) can be very effective, and Baldwin uses it to draw us in.

While most students will not be able, nor would they want, to replicate the very long (almost one-hundred-word) sentence from Henry David Thoreau's "Where I Lived and What I Lived For," it is useful to examine how he puts his elements together in this one long sentence and, as noted earlier, to examine his word choice:

> I wanted to live deep and suck out all the marrow of life, to live so sturdily and Spartan-like as to put to rout all that was not life, to cut a broad swath and shave close, to drive life into a corner, and reduce it to its lowest terms, and, if it proved to be mean, why then to get the whole and genuine meanness of it, and publish its meanness to the world; or if it were sublime, to know it by experience, and be able to give a true account of it in my next excursion. (1993, 617)

Students can note in this passage alliteration, assonance, strong verbs, imagery, and effective word choice. They could also work with breaking up this sentence into smaller units. How many sentences might they create and how do those multiple sentences compare with the original?

Finally, students might wish to look at paragraphs and consider how the sentences link together and, further, what other features regarding word choice and phrasing are noticeable. Contemporary journalism is a good source for effective paragraphs, as is evident from the following *Automobile* magazine description by David E. Davis Jr. in "Geneva Redux," an account of a European automobile show:

> Geneva is a wonderful automobile show. It is of manageable size—you can cover the whole thing in a single day. It usually coincides with the arrival of spring in that part of Switzerland, and that contributes heavily to its charm. The onset of spring and a new selling season make the automotive community optimistic and good-humored, and its members are thus more accessible, more willing to waste their valuable time chatting with the several thousand automotive journalists who throng the place. (2004, 44)

Students might want to look at how the four sentences in this excerpt relate to each other in subject, how long the sentences are (like the Baldwin excerpt, the sentences are longer at the end of the passage), and how the phrasing works (such as *contributes heavily to its charm*). They might also consider the possible presence of a cliché even in this solid piece of writing *(waste their valuable time)* and look at word choice *(onset, throng)*.

MINILESSON

Goal: To encourage students to look at a piece of writing and to notice and examine specificities of content, language, tone, and sentence structure.

Talking Points:

- Most of us read opinion pieces and, if they are effective, are inspired, in turn, to respond with our own opinion.

- All opinions, however, are not equal: some are presented more effectively than others.

- This opinion piece has certain features that are worth noticing.

Activity:

Read the following paragraph from a *Newsweek* essay on the Iraqi war. Make notes on the questions and share them with a partner. To what extent do the two of you agree? Disagree?

- What is the writer's point? Where is it located in the passage? How does the writer set up that point?

- What kind of language or word choice does the writer use? Does that language give you a sense of attitude or tone? If so, what is it?

- Do certain words have more than one meaning in the passage? How do you know?

- Where do you think this passage is headed?

- If you had to choose the most complicated sentence in this passage, which one would it be? Why?

**ONLINE
5.4**

Considering a Passage from *Newsweek*

There were many reasons that Americans believed Saddam Hussein had weapons of mass destruction. There was bad reporting and bad intelligence. But I suspect that many people believed the assertion because he was a bad man. And it was easy to conclude that a bad man will do bad things, even if there is insufficient evidence for one bad thing in particular. ("Personality, not Policy," Anna Quindlen 2004)

Now look at a passage from *Flight Journal* magazine. Again, make notes on the same questions and share them with a partner. To what extent do you two agree? Disagree?

Considering a Passage from *Flight Journal*

ONLINE
5.5

1971: The Vietnam War was in progress; the microprocessor made its debut; Apollo 14 and 15 astronauts explored the moon; and the swing-wing F-14 Tomcat prototype took to the skies. Since then, the Tomcat has evolved into one of the most venerated and versatile fighters ever made. Thirty years into its existence, it is more lethal than it was ever anticipated to be, and now, it's about to be retired. ("Top Gun Icon Retires," Ted Carlson 2004)

Assessment:
How specific were student examples? To what extent did students note differences between these two very dissimilar passages?

Rhetorical Grammar

Beyond looking at passages and their components, as we have done in this chapter, it is also helpful to have students explicitly consider certain devices that they can use as part of their writing. While grammatical terms are not completely necessary in order to do this successfully, mastery of those terms and what they represent can help students understand certain stylistic constructions and be able not only to recognize and name them but to use them in their own writing. Thus rhetorical grammar is not the memorization of the parts of speech or the ability to identify a direct object or a subjunctive verb. It is, as linguist Martha Kolln (2003) calls it, a linguistic grammar, grammar in the service of rhetoric. Further, it is also not the ability, as writing teacher Laura R. Micciche notes, to merely "teach correctness divorced from content and situation . . . [a grammar that is] error driven and disciplinary" (2004, 720). It is larger than that and can, when taught and practiced, give students, especially those for whom extensive reading is not part of their life, a more broad repertoire of ways to express their ideas (see also the useful *Writer's Grammar,* by C. Beth Burch [2003]).

Taking it even further, Micciche believes that "the chief reason for teaching rhetorical grammar in writing classes is that doing so is central to teaching thinking . . . The grammatical choices we make—including pronoun use, active or passive verb constructions, and sentence patterns—represent relations between writers and the world they live in" (2004, 719). This is an even stronger reason to use rhetorical grammar.

Recognizing and Practicing Rhetorical Strategies

While too much attention to the techniques discussed here can be stultifying, giving students a vocabulary so that they can both name and then use these kinds of strategies can be helpful. A working definition is useful, but we think, beyond that, it is important that students see an example of the strategy. Again, students read for writing: when students can identify some of the following and understand their utility, they are more likely to be able to use the strategies in their own writing.

Weak Versus Strong Verbs

Students need to know that active verbs are strong and will always be more effective than passive ones, which can be seen as weak (see Chapter 7 for further discussion). Thus, *I threw the ball* is more effective than *The ball was thrown by me.*

Beyond structure (active versus passive), word choice is also important with verbs. For instance, *hurl* is more vivid than *throw*. Students need to be able to identify verbs and verb forms and to determine if they are weak or strong; if they are weak, how can they be changed?

The following passage from Samuel G. Freedman's *Small Victories* uses strong verbs to paint a portrait of an empty school building:

> The high school sits empty and silent in the late afternoon, a breeze nudging litter down the streets outside, for the commencement is being held eighty blocks farther north in Manhattan, at Hunter College. (1990, 8)

Parallelism

Word structures that are the same can help link ideas, and parallelism can be used effectively with verbs, subjects, prepositional phrases, and clauses. Look at the parallelism in the following passage from *Brief Intervals of Horrible Sanity,* by Elizabeth Gold:

> We are having a meeting. It is so strange that in the midst of all this Charter-applying, Teacher-developing, Standard-raising, Voice-expressing, Computer-destroying, Ninth-Grade disciplining, Guava pastry-eating . . . we still have time—we *always* have time—for the true purpose of school, which is, I have found out, to have meetings. (2003, 177)

Antithesis

Antithesis adds drama to writing, and placing opposing concepts close together, such as in the famous opening line of Charles Dickens' *Tale of Two Cities*, creates a memorable effect:

> It was the best of times, it was the worst of times. ([1859] 1936)

Another example, used earlier in this chapter, is the beginning lines of Joan Didion's "Goodbye to All That":

> It is easy to see the beginnings of things, and harder to see the ends. (1980a, 317)

Assonance and Alliteration

Assonance is a repetition of internal vowels (such as the *o* sound in *only, know, along,* and *boring* in the following example). Alliteration is the repetition of initial consonants (such as the *m* sound in *merrily marching* in the following example from Ellen Goodman's "Steering Clear of the One True Course").

> The only adults I know who are still merrily marching along their one true course are boring, insensitive or lucky. (1982, 435)

Incremental Repetition and Multiple Repetition (Anaphora)

While many students are taught to vary words in their writing, repetition can be used skillfully. Multiple repetition often becomes incremental, reinforcing an idea and, in context, also deepening and changing the meaning of the original word (see the use of *bad* in Anna Quindlen's "Personality, not Policy"):

> There were many reasons that Americans believed Saddam Hussein had weapons of mass destruction. There was bad reporting and bad intelligence. But I suspect that many people believed the assertion because he was a bad man. And it was easy to conclude that a bad man will do bad things, even if there is insufficient evidence for one bad thing in particular. (2004)

Key Points for Reflection

Many older writers have absorbed a range of vocabulary words and a wide repertoire of effective sentence structures from their reading; after years of consuming good writing, they have internalized both words and structures. For students facing on-demand writing, though, teachers need to accelerate the process a bit and invite them to explicitly use their reading to inform and expand their writing. Close reading of good writing—consideration of openings, closings, word choices, and sentence and paragraph structures—can help students understand what makes writing effective. Further, students can then imitate the kinds of strategies they recognize in good writing. In particular, we believe:

- The ability to notice the detail of how a piece of writing works, why it has the effect it does, is, once acquired, not easily lost.

- Effective writing is characterized by openings that state a subject, communicate an attitude, and forecast what is to come.

- Effective writing is characterized by closings that do more than merely summarize.

- Word choice is important to good writing, although a single word cannot mend or fix an otherwise weak or disorganized piece of prose.

- Attention to sentence units and to paragraphs can strengthen writing and make it logical and powerful.

- Rhetorical grammar can give students nomenclature and tools to shape and refine their writing.

- Close reading can sharpen writing skills, skills that transcend the concerns of on-demand writing.

WORKS CITED

Baldwin, James. 1993a. "Autobiographical Notes." In *In Depth: Essayists for Our Time,* 2d ed., ed. Carl Klaus, Chris Anderson, and Rebecca Faery (63–67). Fort Worth, TX: Harcourt Brace.

———. 1993b. "Stranger in the Village." In *In Depth: Essayists for Our Time,* 2d ed., ed. Carl Klaus, Chris Anderson, and Rebecca Faery (68–78). Fort Worth, TX: Harcourt Brace.

Burch, C. Beth. 2003. *A Writer's Grammar.* New York: Longman.

Carlson, Ted. 2004. "Top Gun Icon Retires." *Flight Journal* 9 (4): 28.

Catton, Bruce. 1982. "Grant and Lee: A Study in Contrasts." In *The Norton Sampler,* 2d ed., ed. Thomas Cooley (180–86). New York: W. W. Norton.

Davis, David E., Jr. 2004. "Geneva Redux." *Automobile* (June): 44.

Dickens, Charles. [1859] 1936. *A Tale of Two Cities.* New York: Signet Classic.

Didion, Joan. 1980a. "Goodbye to All That." In *Eight Modern Essayists*, 3d ed., ed. William Smart (317–27). New York: St. Martin's.

———. 1980b. "On Morality." In *Eight Modern Essayists*, 3d ed., ed. William Smart (313–17). New York: St. Martin's.

Freedman, Samuel G. 1990. *Small Victories: The Real World of a Teacher, Her Students, and Their High School*. New York: HarperCollins.

Gold, Elizabeth. 2003. *Brief Intervals of Horrible Sanity: One Season in a Progressive School*. New York: Penguin.

Goodman, Ellen. 1982. "Steering Clear of the One True Course." In *The Bedford Reader*, ed. X. J. Kennedy and Dorothy M. Kennedy (433–36). New York: St. Martin's.

Hunter, Deairich. 1982. "Ducks vs. Hard Rocks." In *The Norton Sampler*, 2d ed., ed. Thomas Cooley (68–72). New York: W. W. Norton.

King, Martin Luther, Jr. 1982. "I Have a Dream." In *The Bedford Reader*, ed. X. J. Kennedy and Dorothy M. Kennedy (451–57). New York: St. Martin's.

Kolln, Martha. 2003. *Rhetorical Grammar: Grammatical Choices, Rhetorical Effects*. 4th ed. New York: Longman.

Micciche, Laura R. 2004. "Making a Case for Rhetorical Grammar." *College Composition and Communication* 55 (4): 716–37.

Momaday, N. Scott. 1993. "My Horse and I." In *In Depth: Essayists for Our Time*, 2d ed., ed. Carl Klaus, Chris Anderson, and Rebecca Faery (427–31). Fort Worth, TX: Harcourt Brace.

Orwell, George. 1980. "Shooting an Elephant." In *Eight Modern Essayists*, 3d ed., ed. William Smart (128–35). New York: St. Martin's.

Quindlen, Anna. 2004. "Personality, not Policy." *Newsweek* CXLIII (25): 78.

Reiss, Gertrude. 1997. "Naftale." In *The Perceptive I: A Personal Reader and Writer*, ed. Edmund J. Farrell and James E. Miller Jr. (49–53). Lincolnwood, IL: NTC.

Rodriquez, Richard. 1982. "Aria: A Memoir of a Bilingual Childhood." In *The Bedford Reader*, ed. by X. J. Kennedy and Dorothy M. Kennedy (522–44). New York: St. Martin's.

Sommers, Nancy I. 1980. "Revision Strategies of Student Writers and Experienced Writers." *College Composition and Communication* 31: 378–88.

Swift, Jonathan. [9 January 1720] 1980. "A Letter to a Young Gentleman Lately Entered into Holy Orders by a Person of Quality." In *Eight Modern Essayists,* 3d ed., ed. William Smart (348–53). New York: St. Martin's.

Thomas, Lewis. 1993. "On Cloning a Human Being." In *In Depth: Essayists for Our Time,* 2d ed., ed. Carl Klaus, Chris Anderson, and Rebecca Faery (589–92). Fort Worth, TX: Harcourt Brace.

Thoreau, Henry David. 1993. "Where I Lived and What I Lived For." In *In Depth: Essayists for Our Time,* 2d ed., ed. Carl Klaus, Chris Anderson, and Rebecca Faery (613–22). Fort Worth, TX: Harcourt Brace.

Tobias, Sheila. 1982. "Who's Afraid of Math, and Why?" In *The Bedford Reader,* ed. X. J. Kennedy and Dorothy M. Kennedy (343–51). New York: St. Martin's.

Trippett, Frank. 1982. "The Great American Cooling Machine." In *The Norton Sampler,* 2d ed., ed. Thomas Cooley (123–29). New York: W. W. Norton.

Walker, Alice. 1993. "Beauty: When the Other Dancer Is the Self." In *In Depth: Essayists for Our Time,* 2d ed., ed. Carl Klaus, Chris Anderson, and Rebecca Faery (675–81). Fort Worth, TX: Harcourt Brace.

Ward, Andrew. 1982. "They Also Wait Who Stand and Serve Themselves." In *The Bedford Reader,* ed. X. J. Kennedy and Dorothy M. Kennedy (89–95). New York: St. Martin's.

West, Ted. 2001. "Motor Mouth: Little Fish, Big Fish." *Sports Car International,* 17 (4): 10.

Contexts: What to Expect When You're Expecting to Write

6

I felt the prompt was so general it was difficult to write about.

—CHRIS MARTIN

I really like the open-ended question, but I'm not sure how they were grading it. Like I think I built a really good argument, but what if I went off the topic? You know how, like, the analysis of a passage question kind of, like, gives you a thesis? Well, this doesn't have that.

—BAILEY GAUTHIER

I don't know if most kids keep a journal, but I have since sixth grade, and I feel my journal really helped me on the exam to, like, experiment with different styles.

—LYNN AMELIO

I think, if you just can write well, you can do well on this test.

—DEVON SNYDER

Students' comments about their experiences with writing on demand can teach us how they make sense of the prompts that ask them to write. As their comments reveal, some students felt they were better prepared for writing tests than others, and the differences weren't always a consequence of student ability alone. Prompts for writing vary, just as student writing does. While we agree with Devon Snyder that good writers can do well on tests, we also believe that teachers can help students learn strategies for reading and writing that will help them do well on tests and when writing for other occasions too.

Once students know what to expect when they're expected to write, much of the fear of the process evaporates, and they are able to present strong and effective prose. From our perspective as teachers, developing students' skills for analyzing the prompt environment, as well as prompts themselves, is crucial. This chapter suggests ways to help students negotiate the prompt environment, or the context within which the prompt appears. What is this context? Actually, test makers provide a variety of cues, checklists, requirements, writing aids, and time limits that surround prompts, and this context can inform how a student approaches a prompt. Accordingly, we explore these features to help teach students how to make the most of them. Context is important for all writers, and it is especially crucial for writing on demand because of what is at stake in most writing tests.

Context is important for all writers, and it is especially crucial for writing on demand.

Context Analysis: Strategies for Analyzing the Prompt Environment

We believe that demystifying the process of approaching a writing test by examining the prompt environment helps students succeed, and it also leads to meaningful dialogue about what good writing is. Answering the following questions can do a great deal to demystify writing prompts as well as show students how to use all the information available to them. One of the things we've noticed about students' approaches to writing on demand is that they frequently overlook critical statements and directions that could guide their work. Teaching them to answer these context analysis questions will make them alert to valuable cues.

ONLINE
6.1

Five Key Context Analysis Questions

1. What is my *time limit?*
2. What kinds of *writing aids* are available to me? Is there a rubric, a writing checklist, a list of dos and don'ts?
3. What are the targeted *skills?* What particular thinking or writing skills does this test require? What standards are being assessed?
4. What kind of *format* is expected? Will a five-paragraph essay work here, or is some other format, like a letter, required?

5. What *specialized expectations* are implicit in this particular writing task? For example, is length or audience specified?

Each of these questions will help students think more systematically about writing on demand (and will be addressed later in this chapter), but questions about time loom largest for both students and teachers. There are two different types of time constraints—externally imposed limits and internally imposed limits. Externally imposed limits, such as those set by test makers, hang over the entire experience of writing on demand because limited time is *the* factor that distinguishes writing on demand from all other types of writing. However, some tests have no externally imposed time limits, so students must set internal limits by estimating the proper length of time to write. Teachers tell us that in such situations, students often write too little.

Writing in the Context of Limited Time

It's true that deadlines exist for all writers. Sometimes the deadline is set by another person, and sometimes it is set by writers themselves. Teachers and editors frequently give writers a specific time by which they must complete an assignment. "The paper is due on Friday," or "We need this for our fall catalog," they might say. Writers also give themselves time limits. The three of us established deadlines for ourselves as we worked on this book. After looking at our calendars and considering other responsibilities, we agreed on a series of dates by which we would draft specific chapters.

It's useful to remember the deadlines all writers face when we think about the time constraints imposed by writing on demand. Donald Murray has this to say about deadlines: "Writers write and they get the writing done because they have deadlines. I am told that the term comes from an actual line drawn outside of a prison's walls. When prisoners crossed the deadline they were shot. Dead. And that's the way I feel about deadlines. They must be met or I will face professional death" (2000, 17). While not like death exactly, deadlines for writing on demand can feel pretty threatening, and many students do worry about how to meet them. We think it is valuable to give students explicit strategies to help them deal with the time dimension of writing on demand. Accordingly, the following section offers several ways to help students prepare for the time constraints of writing tests, and the remaining sections return to the other issues raised by the context analysis questions.

Developing Fluency

Watch students when they are writing in class. Some will gaze out the window, as if waiting for a muse to bring them inspiration. Some will scribble furiously, pause to scan quickly, and then go back and scratch out what they've just produced. Some will stare at their paper and, pressing down on their pens, carve words one by one, pausing to read and reread multiple times. Looking closely at students' behavior when they are doing an in-class assignment will reveal a lot about their habits of writing.

Knowing about students' composing habits is an important part of helping them become more effective in timed writing situations. Research on writing processes shows that there is no single way for all writers to proceed. Some revise extensively while others do more planning in their heads and revise less. Some have rituals for writing, like sharpening pencils or straightening their desks. Some focus on the lead or first paragraph, working to get it just right before they proceed. Regardless of the way they work, all writers go through some version of the writing process described in Chapter 2. They plan, they write drafts, they revise, and they polish their work.

The effectiveness of students' writing processes often depends on their fluency. In its simplest terms, *fluency* means the number of words a writer produces in a given amount of time. Of course, merely writing fast or having a high words-per-minute (WPM) rate doesn't mean you're producing high-quality writing, but research shows that students who can produce more words per minute actually write better than those who operate at a lower WPM rate (Kasper-Ferguson and Moxley 2002).

One of the first things a teacher can do to help students prepare for timed writing, while also enabling them to become better writers, is to encourage them to increase their WPM rate. Frequent or daily freewriting in class is a very good way to increase students' WPM rate, and keeping a record of their growth across several months or even throughout an entire year can motivate them to continue increasing their fluency. Here's how Kathleen, a ninth-grade teacher, does it:

> I designate ten minutes at the beginning of class on Mondays, Wednesdays, and Fridays for freewriting. I set a timer and tell students to start writing. Early in the year I give students topics to write about, and later in the year I let each student choose a topic for the whole class. This helps them get to know one another better and adds to their motivation.
>
> Each time we do this exercise I tell my students to keep writing continuously, even if they can't think of what to say next. [I say,] "Just write, 'I don't know what to say,' over and over until you think of something." I tell them it's important to keep the pen moving and trust that their minds will keep up with their hands.

> When they have finished writing, I tell them to count the number of words they have written and record it. At the end of each week they add their WPM for each day to a line graph. We keep a class chart on the bulletin board so we can see how everyone's WPM changes as the months go by. Students continue to write more and more throughout the year. There doesn't seem to be an upper limit.

Many teachers we know follow similar procedures to help students become more fluent writers by increasing their WPM rates. When students increase the number of words they can write in a given amount of time, they do more than simply push the pen faster. They learn to avoid getting tangled in complicated syntax and begin to see themselves as writers who do not need to stop and pause over each sentence. The fluency students develop from writing exercises like these carries over to other writing, enabling them to produce more words in various contexts, including writing on demand. Fluency is a confidence builder, and confidence breeds success.

Complicating Fluency

Fluency can mean more than producing a certain number of words per minute. It also refers to the capacity to generate and develop ideas in writing. In other words, fluency can be about the form and content of writing as much as the number of words produced. Accordingly, we recommend ways to enhance this dimension of fluency also. The writing produced in ten-minute writing exercises like the one described earlier can be used as the basis for developing a more complicated form of fluency. Students can use exercises from the following list, trying a different selection of writing with each exercise.

Things to Do with Ten-Minute Drafts

1. Reread your ten-minute draft and underline the phrases or sentences that seem most promising to you. Write for another ten minutes, using these phrases or sentences in the first line of the new selection.

2. Make a list of the points you made in a ten-minute writing. Then try to rearrange the points in a coherent order. Add any new ideas that occur to you.

3. Reread your ten-minute draft and try to compose one sentence that describes your main point.

4. Choose a ten-minute draft that you are comfortable sharing with others and read it to a classmate. Ask that classmate to tell you what she or he thinks are the main ideas in your draft.

5. What are the key terms in your ten-minute draft? Put each of these into a cluster diagram and try to add additional terms to each.

6. Reread your ten-minute draft, paying particular attention to sentence structure. How many different sentence types (simple, compound, complex, compound-complex) do you find? (See Chapter 7 for a discussion of sentence types.) Revise your draft to include more variety in sentence structure.

7. Underline the verbs in your ten-minute draft. How many are verbs of *being (am, are, is, was, were, be, being)*? (See Chapter 7 for a discussion of *being* verbs.) Try substituting more descriptive verbs for these.

8. Examine word choice in your draft. Underline words that you find especially well chosen.

9. Do you see any words repeated over and over in your draft? If you do, find alternatives for them.

10. Look at the verb tenses you have used on your draft. If they are mostly past tense, try shifting them into present or future tense and consider how the effect of the piece changes.

Doing exercises like these ten can help students look more analytically at their own writing and, at the same time, develop syntactic and conceptual fluency so that they are able to use a variety of sentence structures and generate more ideas about a given topic.

Writer's Notebook

Think about the exercises you have done with your ten-minute drafts and focus on the one(s) you found most helpful. Then write about the exercise(s) that helped you generate the most ideas and explain why they did.

Planning Writing

As the discussion of writing processes in Chapter 2 shows, planning is an essential part of writing. Writers think about what they will write, sketch ideas out using various methods, and begin an ongoing process of shaping those ideas into a coherent whole. Many students assume that there is no time for planning within the constraints of writing on demand. They seize their test booklets, scan the instructions, and begin scribbling furiously. Such students are usually disappointed with the results of their efforts, and a lack of planning or prewriting is part of the problem. While it is true that timed tests require first-draft writing and do not allow time for revision, the draft can be carefully planned. Students who do best on writing tests are the ones who allocate a significant portion of the available time to planning.

They seize their test booklets, scan the instructions, and begin scribbling furiously... [and] are usually disappointed with the results.

First, of course, students need to read the prompt and directions very carefully as they begin planning. Asking the context analysis questions will help them determine how to proceed, and in later sections we will talk about ways to answer these questions. Here, however, we will focus only on the question about time. The following sequence can help students understand how to proceed once they know how much time they have.

Planning to Use Time in a Writing Test

ONLINE 6.2

1. Note how long you have to complete the writing selection.
2. Look at the clock and write the following on a piece of paper:
   - time writing test begins
   - time that marks one quarter of the available minutes
   - five minutes before test must be completed
3. Use the first quarter of available time to plan your writing. This includes reading the prompt and instructions, answering the context analysis questions, prewriting, and developing a thesis or main point.
4. When the clock indicates that a quarter of the time has elapsed, consider where you are in the planning process. If necessary, you can take a few more minutes to finalize your thoughts.
5. Start writing your response after no more than one-half of the available time has elapsed.
6. As you write, glance at the clock occasionally and keep looking at your thesis and prewriting to keep them in the forefront of your mind.
7. Five minutes before the end of the test, draw your writing to a close.
8. In the last few minutes, reread and proofread your writing, making corrections, inserting missing words, or deleting unnecessary ones. Changes that are inserted or deleted neatly are acceptable—in most cases you will not have a lot of extra time, so do not try to recopy the entire selection.

Students who follow a protocol like this one report that they feel much less stressed about writing on demand. We think this is because they are taking control of the time available rather than letting time constraints control them. It's also important, of course, to be sure that students have strategies they can employ to make the best use of the time they allot to planning. As is true of most strategies for test taking, planning time for writing on all occasions improves the experience for both students and teachers.

Invention

It may seem counterintuitive to talk about invention or prewriting in the context of writing on demand, but prewriting is even more essential when time is limited because students don't have time to head in a wrong direction and then start over. They need to plan their writing carefully, and strategies of prewriting can help them do that. Some test booklets actually have a page designated as the prewriting page while others do not. Either way, students will feel a stronger connection between their other writing and a writing test if they learn to prewrite for writing on demand.

As Chapter 2 explains, prewriting takes many forms. Writers need to learn which forms work best for them, and one of the things teachers can do for their students is help them make choices about which form of prewriting to use. Here, for example, is a prompt students can consider in terms of how they might begin to generate ideas for writing.

> Many professional athletes and celebrities, e.g., movie stars and musical recording artists, receive multimillion-dollar salaries. Many people believe these salaries are excessive; others believe they are justifiable.
>
> Write an editorial for your local newspaper in which you defend or oppose the salaries of athletes and/or celebrities. (Delaware State Department of Education 2000, Grade 10 Writing Prompt)

This prompt comes with the following questions, designed to help students focus and plan their writing.

- What athletes and/or celebrities do you know who earn multimillion-dollar salaries?

- What reasons can you develop to support multimillion-dollar salaries?

- What reasons can you develop to oppose multimillion-dollar salaries?

- Which of your reasons are supported by facts?

- Which of your reasons are emotional?

- Do you want your editorial to support or oppose the salaries of athletes and/or celebrities?

Many prompts do not include questions like these to help with planning writing, so one prewriting strategy teachers can propose is for students to work with the prompt alone to generate a list of questions writers might ask themselves as they begin planning their writing. In addition, students writing in response to the prompt about multimillion-dollar salaries could choose from among several other prewriting strategies. They could cluster ideas around advantages of multimillion-dollar salaries and disadvantages of multimillion-dollar salaries, allowing the specific reasons and details to emerge in the circles that build out from these two categories. They could do quick freewrites on these two issues and then underline the ideas that emerge. They could create a list of ideas or reasons under each topic. Here's an example:

Advantages of Multimillion-Dollar Salaries	*Disadvantages of Multimillion-Dollar Salaries*
• Motivate youth to aspire to careers in sports, music, and drama • Give artists and athletes freedom to pursue creative approaches to their work • Generate public interest in sports and the arts • Enable athletes and artists to become philanthropists	• Create unrealistic expectations among youth • Make ticket prices much higher and often unaffordable for average people • Make sports and arts inaccessible for many people • Too many athletes and artists don't know how to use their money effectively for others

If students have used prewriting or invention throughout the year, they will know which strategy works best for them, and they will be able to implement it quickly.

➥ Writer's Notebook

Think about your various approaches to prewriting and identify the one that works best for you. Now explain, using a piece of writing you have done recently, how this strategy helped you. Be specific.

Asking a few students to share how different strategies work for them may help the non-prewriters see the advantages of various prewriting techniques.

Thesis Development

The directions for the prompt about professional athletes specify that students develop a thesis along with an introduction, transitions, and a conclusion. The process of prewriting often helps students develop a thesis statement or main point, and once they have decided on a thesis, they may want to do more prewriting or alternate between prewriting and thesis development as they plan.

One way or another, however, students do need to develop a thesis or central point in response to most of the prompts used in writing tests. Frequently, prompts require students to take a position when there could be good arguments made on either side, as the list of advantages and disadvantages in the previous section shows. With this prompt on athletes' salaries, one possible thesis would be "Although there are many advantages for athletes' high salaries, the disadvantages outweigh them." Another thesis could be the reverse, where the student argues for the advantages of high salaries, privileging them over the disadvantages. Still another possibility would be a thesis like this: "Because there are a number of advantages and disadvantages to high salaries for athletes, there is no one best response. The decision should depend upon the individual athlete and how he or she used the money."

Once students have identified a thesis and done some prewriting, they can proceed with writing the actual response. Continually referring back to their prewriting and thesis statement will help them stay focused and deal with the stress of having to write under time pressures. Students who have developed strategies like these for dealing with limited time in writing tests report that the pressure of time constraints is much reduced. Limited time is, of course, only one feature of the context that surrounds prompts on writing tests. We will now turn to another.

Considering Writing Aids

The second item in the context analysis questions deals with the writing aids that often accompany prompts in writing tests. Writing aids provide valuable information that can guide students toward greater success in writing on demand. Let's consider the environment of a prompt:

Write an essay explaining why experience is the best teacher.

By itself, this prompt doesn't provide a great deal of guidance to writers, but if a checklist like the following is added, there is a much richer context from which students can draw.

Checklist for Writers

- Does writing focus on the assigned topic?

- Is writing thoughtful and interesting?

- Does each sentence contribute to your composition as a whole?

- Are your ideas clear and easy for the reader to follow?

- Are ideas developed so that the reader is able to gain a good understanding of what you are saying?

- Did you proofread your writing to correct errors in spelling, capitalization, punctuation, grammar, and sentence structure?

Students often look at these aids as suggestions, but our analysis of scoring rubrics in Chapter 8 reveals that they should be looked at more as mandates. For example, students may feel that the question Does each sentence contribute to your composition as a whole? means that they should write sentences on the topic, but, as we show in Chapter 8, the rubric requirements for sentences are much higher. Not only do the sentences have to be on the topic, but there needs to be explicit connections between evidence and the thesis, transition sentences between major ideas, and all of this has to be expressed in sentences that are varied and clear. What students may find confusing about such a list, though, is deciding *when* they should remember each suggestion. Conscientious students might spend at least as much time analyzing the checklist as they spend with the actual prompt. For most, the biggest hurdle is, of course, transference. Even if capable of doing all of the tasks listed in the checklists, students may have trouble correlating the suggestions with work done in class. The following six-trait analytic rating guide—or some similar rubric—can help students connect the prompt's checklist with what they already know.

MINILESSON

Goal: To show students how to connect what they know with the features highlighted in the writing aids that accompany prompts for writing tests.

Talking Points:

- Read more than just the prompt in a writing test because writing aids and checklists contain valuable information.

- It's worth taking time to understand the information in checklists and other writing aids.

- The six-trait guide (or other classroom rubric) can help you understand checklists and writing aids.

Activity:

Use Online 6.3, available from the companion website. Copy onto an over-head transparency, and ask your students to match up the items in the writing prompt checklist with the analytic rating guide. Write their responses on the transparency. There will probably be some disagreement about where the items in the checklist should be placed, but it might end up something like this:

ONLINE 6.3

Six-Trait Analytic Guide for Evaluating Writing

Traits	*Checklist*
	Higher-Order Concerns
1. Ideas and content	• Write about the assigned topic.
	• Make your writing thoughtful and interesting.
	• Make sure that each sentence you write contributes to your composition as a whole.
	• Write about your ideas in depth so that the reader is able to develop a good understanding of what you are saying.
2. Organization	• Make sure that your ideas are clear and easy for the reader to follow.Make sure that each sentence you write contributes to your composition as a whole.
3. Voice	
	Lower-Order Concerns
4. Word choice	
5. Sentence structure	• Proofread your writing to correct errors in spelling capitalization, punctuation, grammar, and sentence structure.
6. Writing conventions	

Alternatively, students could complete this matching exercise in small groups, which would carry the added benefit of discussing or debating about the placement of suggestions. Either way, this kind of discussion connects best practices with test preparation.

Questions for discussion might include the following:

- Do any of the suggestions fit in more than one category? What are your reasons for placing the suggestion where you did?

- Are there any categories *not* addressed by this exam? Why do you think they were not included?

- What do the test makers seem to value least about the essays? What do they seem to value most?

- Do you think this test fails to measure any important writing skills? Why or why not?

- What kind of essay would meet these expectations?

- Do you feel you could write this kind of essay? Why or why not?

Assessment:
Ask students to write a brief paragraph about what they have learned regarding the way a piece of writing might be evaluated.

Going through this minilesson helps students see writing checklists as more than mere suggestions. Student begin to see that the prompt environment can be as important as the prompt itself to their understanding of what is expected of them. Instead of checklists, writing aids sometimes consist of rubrics that indicate how writing will be scored. Here, for example, is a sample scoring guide that might go with an expository writing prompt:
The student

- marshals evidence to support a central claim;

- conveys information and ideas from both primary and secondary sources;

- makes distinctions between the relative significance of specific facts and ideas;

- anticipates and addresses readers' possible misunderstandings and expectations, and

- uses language and terms accurately.

Students could match items on this scoring guide with a rubric they know well, just as was done in the previous minilesson. Translating terms that appear on test checklists into language from familiar rubrics will help students connect what they know with the requirements of a particular test.

Sometimes, of course, test makers do not provide any writing checklists or lists of requirements. Teachers can prepare students for such situations by reinforcing generic rubrics in regular class work so that students can internalize them. Teachers can summarize the features of writing that they value most and show how they are represented in the rubric. If the qualities of a good essay are discussed throughout the school year and used regularly with writing assignments, students will feel confident that they know these qualities. It will also help them understand that even though a prompt does not include a writing checklist, the test graders might have one, and the test probably has just as high expectations for the writing being evaluated as a test that does include a checklist.

If the qualities of a good essay are discussed throughout the school year and used regularly with writing assignments, students will feel confident that they know these qualities.

Considering Targeted Skills

The third question in context analysis may be the most difficult for students to answer. If asked, "What particular thinking or writing skills is this test targeting?" they may respond with blank looks, because answers to this question often draw on concepts and materials that students don't know about. Most secondary school students rarely think about the terms of their own learning; as mentioned in Chapters 3 and 4, they rarely think metacognitively. In part, this is because student learning goals and disciplinary standards remain outside their view.

We believe that students can become better learners—and better writers—if they can begin to think about their own learning, about the skills that they are in the process of acquiring. They can develop this capacity by writing about their own processes of writing. Here, for example, is a format for journal entries that will help students become more aware of their own learning.

> ### Writer's Notebook
>
> Create a two-column notebook in which you record two things: the processes or steps you go through as well as the skills you need to complete a piece of writing. Be specific.

**ONLINE
6.4**

Steps and Skills

Steps I Went Through in Writing My Essay	Skills I Needed to Complete These Steps
• Came up with a topic	• Listing, brainstorming
• Generated supporting details	• Mapping, cubing

Another way teachers can help students understand more about their own learning and the skills they need as writers is to share with them district goals or standards for student writing. Alternatively, teachers can share the National Council of Teachers of English standards with students, discussing the skills each of the standards requires.

Standards for the English Language Arts
Sponsored by NCTE and IRA

The vision guiding these standards is that all students must have the opportunities and resources to develop the language skills they need to pursue life's goals and to participate fully as informed productive members of society. These standards assume that literacy growth begins before children enter school as they experience and experiment with literacy activities—reading and writing, and associating spoken words with their graphic representations. Recognizing this fact, these standards encourage the development of curriculum and instruction that make productive use of the emerging literacy abilities that children bring to school. Furthermore, the standards provide ample room for the innovation and creativity essential to teaching and learning. They are not prescriptions for particular curriculum or instruction. Although we present these standards as a list, we want to emphasize that they are not distinct and separable; they are, in fact, interrelated and should be considered as a whole.

1. Students read a wide range of print and non-print texts to build an understanding of texts, of themselves, and of the cultures of the United States and the world; to acquire new information; to respond to the needs and demands of society and the workplace; and for personal fulfillment. Among these texts are fiction and nonfiction, classic and contemporary works.

2. Students read a wide range of literature from many periods in many genres to build an understanding of the many dimensions (e.g., philosophical, ethical, aesthetic) of human experience.

3. Students apply a wide range of strategies to comprehend, interpret, evaluate, and appreciate texts. They draw on their prior experience, their interactions with other readers and writers, their knowledge of word meaning and of other texts, their word identification strategies, and their understanding of textual features (e.g., sound-letter correspondence, sentence structure, context, graphics).

4. Students adjust their use of spoken, written, and visual language (e.g., conventions, style, vocabulary) to communicate effectively with a variety of audiences and for different purposes.

5. Students employ a wide range of strategies as they write and use different writing process elements appropriately to communicate with different audiences for a variety of purposes.

6. Students apply knowledge of language structure, language conventions (e.g., spelling and punctuation), media techniques, figurative language, and genre to create, critique, and discuss print and non-print texts.

7. Students conduct research on issues and interests by generating ideas and questions, and by posing problems. They gather, evaluate, and synthesize data from a variety of sources (e.g., print and non-print texts, artifacts, people) to communicate their discoveries in ways that suit their purpose and audience.

8. Students use a variety of technological and information resources (e.g., libraries, databases, computer networks, video) to gather and synthesize information and to create and communicate knowledge.

9. Students develop an understanding of and respect for diversity in language use, patterns, and dialects across cultures, ethnic groups, geographic regions, and social roles.

10. Students whose first language is not English make use of their first language to develop competency in the English language arts and to develop understanding of content across the curriculum.

11. Students participate as knowledgeable, reflective, creative, and critical members of a variety of literacy communities.

12. Students use spoken, written, and visual language to accomplish their own purposes (e.g., for learning, enjoyment, persuasion, and the exchange of information).

Several of the NCTE standards do not address writing directly, but together they show how skills of reading and writing connect. And, of course, a number of the standards speak about writing specifically. Focusing a discussion with students on one item, such as Standard 4, could enhance their understanding of the skills they need in order to communicate effectively with audiences such as peers, teachers, and community members. Here are some questions that might be used in such a discussion:

• How does your use of conventions like sentence structure, punctuation, and spelling change if you write about the same event to your peers and to your teachers? What do you need to know to be able to make these changes?

- How do you vary your word choice if you're writing a formal letter for a job application or writing a friend to describe your dream job? What skills help you write these two different letters?

- *Style* is difficult to define even though we recognize it when we see it. What are the features that contribute to your individual style as a writer? How did you learn these things?

Considering Format

The easiest answer to the question What kind of format is expected? is *the five-paragraph theme.* As George Hillocks Jr. reminds us, the five-paragraph format is often implied and often rewarded (2003, 68–69). The time constraints of writing on demand make this familiar, formulaic format particularly appealing for students because they don't have to think very much about how to use it. The pattern of introduction, three body paragraphs, and conclusion is one most students have used many times, and in a high-stakes test its familiarity is appealing. Furthermore, this form is appropriate in a number of situations. Prompts like the following can be addressed with a five-paragraph theme:

- Write an essay explaining to a corporation how a piece of equipment it produces would be useful to your school.

- Write an essay describing a person whom you find inspiring.

- Write an essay about a childhood experience that helped shape the person you are today.

Although the essay format is the most common one in writing tests, the five-paragraph version of the essay is not always the best choice. For one thing, a student's writing might not naturally fall into five paragraphs. The prewriting the student does in response to the prompt may suggest another structure or pattern. For example, on an AP exam, the reader may find the five-paragraph structure too formulaic, preferring a more organic and sophisticated construction. Nevertheless, students must understand that the reader will expect a clear sense of beginning, middle, and end when reading the essay. One way to equip students to develop an alternative structure is to read selections of nonfiction and talk about how they are put together. The language of some prompts dictates an alternative format. Here, for example, are verbs that are commonly used in prompts. Each suggests approaches to topics as well as variations in format:

Verbs	*Strategies for Responding*
compare	Show similarities as well as differences; use details and examples.
define	Give an explanation of the term and supply enough detail to demonstrate understanding.
discuss	Consider important characteristics and include examples.
evaluate	Assess strengths, weaknesses, advantages, and limitations.
explain	Use facts and details to make the topic clear and understandable.
justify	Give reasons and evidence to support an action, decision, or policy.
list	Use most-to-least or least-to-most organization.
summarize	Review all major points.

Considering Specialized Expectations

The line between format and specialized expectations about length, paragraphing, and other physical details of writing is not clear. For example, a directive to use a five-paragraph theme could appear in a list of specialized expectations even though we would ordinarily think of this as an issue of format.

Specialized expectations can be easy to overlook because they are not always presented explicitly. For example, a page after the prompt for one state test we looked at was completely blank except for directions in a small box at the top of the page and directions in a small box at the bottom of the page. The top box said, *"Use this prewriting page to plan your composition."* The bottom box said, *"Make sure that you write your composition on the two lined pages in the answer document."* Many students simply skipped this page and went on to write their essays. Some of them probably didn't use prewriting as a regular part of their composing. Others may have skipped it because they didn't think it counted on the test. Still others were probably nervous about having enough time to write the actual essay. Whatever the reasons, some of the students who flipped past the prewriting page missed the directions and the implied expectations about a two-page essay and wrote much shorter pieces.

Students can learn to recognize that directions do not always say one paragraph, or five paragraphs, or *one* lined page. In this case the directions tell students to write the composition on "two lined pages," and those directions, combined with the suggestion "Write about your ideas in depth so that the reader is able to develop a good understanding of what you are saying," should communicate that a well-developed essay—not a paragraph or two—is called for.

Another kind of specialized expectation emerges from the content of writing tests. Many state writing tests have prompts that reflect the literary influence in their curricula. Here, once again, is a prompt that calls upon students' knowledge of literature. We analyzed the prompt itself in Chapter 3; now we will analyze the context:

Writing Assignment

Often in works of literature there are characters—other than the main character—whose presence in the work is essential.

From a work of literature you have read in or out of school, select a character, other than the main character, who plays a key role. In a well-developed composition, identify the character and explain why this character is important.

This prompt clearly tests more than just writing ability—it tests students' understanding of literature. The test makers assume the student has read a work of literature (and probably more than one, since the student is to select one), can remember it, and knows enough about the characters to be able to write persuasively about a character that is not the main character. It also assumes the writer will agree that this secondary character is important.

In states that include literature-based prompts on exams, students must think about more than just preparing to write. Students must be cued to the fact they will be asked about something they have read, and they will not have access to that work of literature during the exam. Preparation might include working with teachers at other grade levels to make sure students know well in advance that they might be asked to write about the literature studied in previous grades. It would also be useful to know which works students have studied so they can do an exercise like the following one to review the works they have read in the past few years.

Grade	Work of Literature	Protagonist	Antagonist	Other Characters
9	To Kill a Mockingbird	Atticus Finch	racist Southern society, as exemplified by the Ewells	Jem, Scout, Boo Radley, Calpurnia
	The Odyssey	Odysseus	Poseidon	Penelope, Telemakhos, Athena
	The Education of Little Tree	Little Tree	prejudiced white men	Grandpa
	Romeo and Juliet	Romeo and Juliet	Tybalt, the feud	Mercutio
	I Heard the Owl Call My Name	Mark Brian	prejudiced whites	Marta, other members of Kwakiutl tribe
10	Antigone	Antigone	Creon	Ismene
	Macbeth	Macbeth	Macduff, Malcolm	Lady Macbeth, Duncan, Banquo
	Les Miserables	Jean Valjean	Inspector Javert	Fantine, Cosette, Thènardier
	Bless Me, Ultima	Antonio, Ultima	Tenorio, Trementina	Luna family, Antonio's school friends

Students could work in groups to recall the characters, and then they could work on a writing assignment that required them to write about characters intertextually, a great exercise even if they're not preparing for an exam. Alternatively, they might use old prompts or make up similar ones, such as the following:

Characters in literature often have a fatal flaw. Identify one character and his or her fatal flaw. Explain how the flaw influenced the outcome of the conflict.

Generating a list of flaws—pride, indecision, and impatience—will diversify this prompt and help students see they have an entire menu of choices. Using this prompt as part of a unit assessment not only is good practice in our usual course of studies but does double duty as exam preparation. Again, good teaching and test preparation are not contradictory but complementary.

Yet another set of specialized expectations appears in prompts that deal with reading. Let's take a look at a prompt that deals with a reading selection.

Directions: Read the following selection. The title is "The Ojibwa Corn Hero." Using specific information from the narrative, explain why Wunzh deserves to be considered a hero.

The Ojibwa Corn Hero

When the youth Wunzh reached the proper age, his father built him a lodge in a remote place where he could fast undisturbed and find his guardian in life. It was the spring of the year and, in the first days of his fast, Wunzh walked the woods each morning, musing on the first shoots of plants and flowers, coming alive in the warming earth.

He hoped this would store his mind with pleasant thoughts for his dreams each night. Often, on these strolls, he found himself wondering how these plants grew, some of them sweet like berries, others poisonous, yet others full of medicine. Perhaps, if he knew more about such things, he could help his people. Perhaps they might not have to rely on the luck of the hunt or the occasional fish caught from opaque waters.

As the days went by, Wunzh grew too weak for such wanderings and instead lay in his lodge, praying that he would dream of something that would help his people. In his increasing dizziness, he permitted himself the thought that while the Great Spirit had made all things, including the people, he could have made things a bit easier for them.

On the third day of his fast, as he lay in his lodge, he saw a figure descend from the sky—a figure richly dressed in yellow and green garments of many shades, with a great plume of golden feathers waving on its head. With dreamlike grace, it arrived in Wunzh's lodge.

"The Great Spirit sent me to you, my friend," said the figure. "He takes note that your prayers are unusual. You don't seem to want the glory of the warrior, but instead merely something for the good of your people." The visitor went on to explain that this was possible. The condition was that Wunzh wrestle with his visitor.

At first, Wunzh's heart sank. He was already weak from fasting. What hope did he have . . . ? But gathering his courage, he engaged the figure, and they wrestled until Wunzh felt utterly exhausted. Abruptly, the figure stopped, smiled and said, "That is enough for now. You did well, and I will come again to try you." He disappeared, ascending into the light of the sun.

The following day he came again and once again challenged Wunzh, who by now was even weaker. But it seemed that the weaker his body was, the greater his courage and determination. Again they wrestled, long and hard, and again the visitor broke it off, promising to come again for the final trial. Wunzh collapsed in exhaustion near death.

The next day, after the third and final trial had begun, the heavenly visitor stopped and declared himself beaten. He sat down next to the youth and told him the Great Spirit was pleased with his courage. Now he would receive the instructions he had prayed for.

"Tomorrow," the visitor said, "is your seventh day of fasting. Your father will come with some food for strength and I will come again and you will win. Afterward, you must strip my clothes from me, put me on the ground, and take away all the weeds. Then you must bury me there. Do not let weeds grow there, but come from time to time and see if I have returned. And then you will have your wish and be able to teach your people what you want them to know."

In the morning Wunzh's father came with food, and the youth said he would wait until sundown to eat it. And when the visitor came again, Wunzh seized him with strength that amazed the youth, threw him down on the ground, and stripped away his rich green and yellow clothes. Seeing that the figure was dead, he buried him as he had been told to, and returned to his father's lodge to eat.

In the days that followed, Wunzh would go off unannounced to the spot where he had buried his friend and keep the weeds away. Toward the end of the summer, he came to the spot and found that his old lodge had disappeared. In its stead was a tall, graceful plant, with clusters of yellow on its side, long green leaves, and a graceful plume of gold nodding from the top.

"It is my friend," Wunzh said to himself, and suddenly knew his friend's name: Mondawmin. He ran to fetch his father and told him that this was what he had dreamed for in his fast. If the people cared for his friend the way Wunzh instructed, they would no longer have to rely only on the hunt or the waters. With that, he showed his father how to tear off the yellow clusters, as he had torn off the garments before, and he showed how to hold the ears to the fire to turn them brown. The whole family then gathered for a feast upon this newly grown presence in their lives, and expressed their lasting thanks to the spirit, the beautiful visitor, who had given it to them.

And so corn came into this world.

The scoring guide for this prompt indicates that responses will be scored twice, once for reading comprehension and once for the quality of the writing. However, since reading comprehension is demonstrated through writing, it is difficult to untangle the two. Here is the scoring guide for the quality of writing:

The ten-point description is divided into two parts. Stylistic and rhetorical aspects of writing (topic, idea, and development) are scored on a six-point scale, and Standard English conventions are scored on a four-point scale.

The key terms *topic, idea,* and *development* can be compared to categories like *central claim* and *organization* that appear on rubrics we have examined elsewhere in this chapter, and teachers can help students see the similarities between this and other scoring guides.

The reading comprehension scoring guide focuses more directly on the Wunzh text:

Score	*Description*
4	Response provides an in-depth explanation of why Wunzh deserves to be considered a hero. Some knowledge of the characteristics or conditions of a hero is demonstrated (journey, struggle, etc.). The explanation includes specific, relevant information from the myth.
3	Response provides an explanation of why Wunzh deserves to be considered a hero. The explanation includes relevant information that lacks some specificity or development.
2	Response provides a partial explanation of why Wunzh deserves to be considered a hero, with limited, incomplete, or partially correct information from the myth included.
1	Response provides a minimal or vague statement about Wunzh or heroes.
0	Response is totally incorrect or irrelevant.

Although the topic of the reading passage is prominent in this guide, the language about its presentation uses terms like *specific, relevant,* and *development,* which can be found in many scoring guides for writing. Helping students see these similarities will provide them with strategies for success with reading and writing tests.

Key Points for Reflection

Although discussing context analysis questions helps students understand the requirements of the environment within which the prompt appears, we must not forget that preparation for on-demand writing begins long before such discussions. In the case of Lynn Amelio, one of the students quoted at the beginning of this chapter, the most useful preparation was the journal, a daily writing habit that began in sixth grade. Another student, Denali Seidel, who was younger than the other students in the class, spoke confidently after taking the exam: "I felt ready for the test because I've had a very writing-intensive year. I can't say I really 'studied' for the test. I just came to school alert and ready. Nothing surprised me—it was pretty much what I expected. I felt ready for it." We want our students to feel this confidence, a confidence that comes from writing instruction based on best practices, combined with an understanding of what to expect when approaching any timed writing situation.

Finally, teachers might consider talking with students about their experiences after having taken a timed writing exam. As the quotations at the beginning of this chapter show, such conversations are valuable for both students and teachers. Students get an opportunity to reflect on their experience, and teachers learn more about what gave their students confidence on the exam as well as where they struggled. In doing this, however, teachers need to be aware of the testing protocol, because some exams dictate that there be no discussion of the actual content of test questions for security reasons. Insights drawn from conversations about tests can help teachers plan instruction that will prepare students to read and respond to the various writing aids and targeted skills and use instructions about format and specialized expectations, all of which create the context of prompts in timed writing tests. Accordingly, we believe:

- All writers face deadlines, and the constraints of timed writing tests are different in degree but not in kind.

- Prompts in writing tests appear in a context, and students need to learn how to draw useful information from that context.

- Best practices emphasize that students need to be aware of their own processes of writing, and attending to context fosters that awareness.

- We can learn about writing tests from listening to students talk about their experiences with them.

WORKS CITED

Hillocks Jr., George. 2003. "Fighting Back: Assessing the Assessments." *English Journal* 92 (4): 63–70.

Kasper-Ferguson, Stephanie, and Roy A. Moxley. 2002. "Developing a Writing Package with Student Graphing of Fluency." *Education and Treatment of Children* 25 (2): 249–67.

Murray, Donald M. 2000. *Writing to Deadline: The Journalist at Work.* Portsmouth, NH: Heinemann.

Writing in Sentences

7

When it comes to language, nothing is more satisfying than to write a good sentence. It is not fun to write lumpishly, dully, in prose the reader must plod through like wet sand. But it is a pleasure to achieve, if one can, a clear running prose that is simple yet full of surprises. This does not just happen. It requires skill, hard work, a good ear, and continued practice, as much as it takes Heifetz to play the violin. The goals, as I have said, are clarity, interest, and aesthetic pleasure.

—BARBARA TUCHMAN

Sentences matter. Writers know this, and it is also true that rubrics and people who evaluate writing tests give high value to sentences. This high value is traditional and long-standing. In fact, the ancestor of today's rubrics for writing assessment was developed more than forty years ago by three researchers at the Educational Testing Service (ETS). In 1961 Paul Diederich, John French, and Sydell Carlton attempted to find points of agreement and disagreement about writing quality among fifty-three readers by analyzing their comments. These comments were organized into fifty-five categories, and the fifty-five categories were arranged under seven headings, one of which was sentence structure.

1. ideas
2. style
3. organization
4. paragraphing
5. sentence structure

6. mechanics

7. verbal facility (Diederich, French, and Carlton 1961)

Years later, a 2001 rubric used by the Northwest Regional Educational Lab echoed this list. Here is the Northwest Lab's rubric for Six Plus One Trait Writing, and again, sentences matter:

1. ideas

2. organization

3. voice

4. word choice

5. sentence fluency

6. conventions

7. presentation

Sentences were important to writing assessment in 1961, and they remain important today. Regardless of whether they are described in terms of *structure* or *fluency*, sentences matter. A sampling of rubrics for state assessments demonstrates the importance assigned to sentences in evaluating writing on demand.

Each of the following statements describes the sentence features necessary to receive the highest score on a piece of writing in that particular state.

• Variety in sentence structure and length enhances effect. (Kentucky Holistic Scoring Guide)

• Language use: the extent to which the response reveals an awareness of audience and purpose through effective use of words, sentence structure, and sentence variety. (New York Scoring Guide)

• Style: Precise, illustrative use of a variety of words and sentence structures to create consistent writer's voice and tone appropriate to audience. (Pennsylvania Writing Assessment Domain Scoring Guide)

• Sentence Fluency:
    Sentence construction makes meaning clear.
    Sentences are purposeful and build upon each other.

> The writing has cadence; the writer has thought about sound as
>   well as meaning.
> Sentences vary in length and structure.
> Fragments are used only for style or effect.
> Dialogue, if used, sounds natural. (Alaska Comprehensive System
>   of Student Assessment)

- Conventions: Papers receiving higher scores follow conventions of punctuation, capitalization and spelling, and use a variety of sentence structures to present ideas. (Scoring Rubric for Florida Comprehensive Assessment Test)

Most state scoring guides contain statements like these, and together they show the importance of sentences in the evaluation of writing on demand. Furthermore, research shows that people who evaluate writing on demand pay particular attention to the quality of sentences (Broad 2003). Of course, sentence structure and sentence mechanics by themselves don't impress evaluators or general readers, and one of the mistakes many writing teachers make is to focus on sentence-level concerns too early in the writing process. But the quality of sentences interacts with the overall organization of a piece of writing. If an essay is well organized it receives a superior score only when sentence structure is impressive (Kellogg 1994).

Examination of rubrics and of research on the scoring practices of evaluators reveals some common features that can help guide students toward becoming better writers *and* preparing them to do well on timed writing assessments. Although the specific details vary from one form of assessment to another, we can identify common features of the sentences in writing that receives high scores from evaluators. They are, of course, features that mark all good writing. They can be described most succinctly by the two terms—*structure* and *fluency*—that appear in the ETS and Northwest Lab rubrics. *Structure* refers to features like variety, effectiveness, and, of course, correctness. *Fluency* likewise connotes variety, but it also includes the connections among sentences. Fortunately, both structure and fluency can be taught through direct instruction.

Some people think that embracing a program of process writing means avoiding all direct instruction. We agree that enlightened writing instruction should not focus on decontextualized sentence drills and endless worksheets, but we do think that helping students understand how sentences work can make them better writers and, along the way, help them do well on timed writing assessments. Research shows that many sentence-based pedagogies lead to greater variety and coherence in student writing (Connors 2000). The strategies described here can help students develop variety and cohesion in their sentence making.

Making Choices in Sentences

Composing sentences, like much else in writing, is about making choices. An expanded repertoire of sentence-making strategies means that writers can make choices. They are not bound to use the same one or two sentence patterns throughout an entire essay. They can choose from among a variety of syntactic structures, selecting on the basis of the effects they want to have. *Rhetoric,* defined by Aristotle as finding all the available means of persuasion, suggests ways to help writers think about what they want to achieve with a given selection.

> *Composing sentences, like much else in writing, is about making choices.*

One set of choices centers on the audience. Rhetoric tells us that a good writer always considers the audience. Since most students write for teacher and/or evaluator audiences, it is reasonable to assume that the audience will be looking for qualities that are valued on commonly used rubrics. Of the six or seven features that appear on most rubrics—ideas, organization, style/voice, word choice, conventions/mechanics, fluency/structure, and verbal facility/presentation—all depend on choices made at the sentence level.

Word choice is probably the most obvious because we combine individual words to create sentences. The use of an apt word to express an idea will always be impressive to a reader, and strong verbs are particularly helpful. In fact, word choice contributes to qualities that readers associate with verbal facility and/or good presentation of ideas because appropriate language gives writing an authoritative quality. Readers tend to trust and respond positively to writers who use words well.

Attention to conventions and mechanics at the sentence level also contributes to the quality of verbal facility and presentation because smoothness in syntax and lack of obvious errors present well. On the other hand, simple correctness in sentence structure does not equate particularly well with high scores from readers. High scores result from an amalgam of word choice, syntax, and verbal facility. A string of perfectly correct sentences can be flat and tedious. This, in turn, leads to the issue of style or voice, which is the most difficult feature of writing to define. Style is what gives writing its individuality and makes it interesting and even fun. The quality of sentences shapes the effectiveness of style. Consider, for example, Tuchman's second sentence from the chapter opening: "It is not fun to write lumpishly, dully, in prose the reader must plod through like wet sand." This sentence is interesting to read. Organization extends beyond the sentence level, but it is made visible with the connectors that tie one sentence to another. Look, for instance, at how

Tuchman connects her second sentence with her third: "But it is a pleasure to achieve, if one can, a clear running prose that is simple yet full of surprises." In addition to setting up the contrast between writing bad sentences and writing good ones, the image of the clear running prose contrasts with that of the wet sand. Ideas extend across an entire piece of writing, but they find most explicit expression in individual sentences.

Each of these features, key in any evaluation of writing, is shaped by a writer's choices within individual sentences. Choosing the right words, constructing syntax to convey meaning effectively, demonstrating fluency, creating a style or voice that engages the reader, avoiding obvious errors of usage, cueing the reader about the connections between sentences, making ideas clear and convincing—each of these choices contributes to the effect a piece of writing has on its audience. This is especially true when that audience is an evaluator reading a writing test.

Another set of choices in writing centers on the purposes of the text. Sentence-based aspects of wording, syntax, fluency, style or voice, correctness, connections, and ideas all require consideration of *why* a given selection is being written. What does the writer want the language *to do?* In the case of writing tests, the answer appears easy: to get the highest possible score. While that may be true, a more comprehensive statement of purpose can be developed from careful examination of the writing prompt. As Chapter 3 shows, every prompt suggests something about purposes, as well as audience and subject, for writing, and sentence-level decisions should include consideration of these purposes.

One of the ways that writing prompts signal something about purpose is in their directives about genre. When a prompt says, "Write to convince your principal to accept your point of view on the effect watching TV has on grades," it's clear that writers are being asked to make an argument. On the other hand, when a prompt says, "Explain why you do your job or chore," writers know they need to write an expository essay, and explanation becomes part of the purpose. Choices about sentence features will differ for each type of writing.

We offer this discussion of choices at the sentence level because *correctness* is often the most prominent term in discussions of sentences. While we acknowledge that errors can be a problem, we affirm that sentences are more about good choices than about correctness. Accordingly, this chapter includes a number of strategies to help students learn to make choices as they are writing.

Word Choice

Here is an excerpt from a discussion among evaluators: "'Plethora?' Did you teach him that word? That's an awfully big word for this age" (Broad 2003,

57). The evaluator is clearly impressed by this "big word" and sees both the writing and the writer in positive terms because of it. This evaluator shows that it is a good thing for students to use vocabulary that stretches them because maturity in word choice will be judged favorably.

What can we conclude? Word choice is one of the sentence-level features that improves writing and can lead to a higher score on writing tests.

Word choice is one of the sentence-level features that improves writing and can lead to a higher score on writing tests.

Choosing the Right Word

Besides striving for effective words, writers must also select the correct words. The chart below lists some of the words that students typically confuse. Learning to use the correct word in each case can enhance word choice.

ONLINE 7.1

Commonly Confused Words

Words	Meaning	Example
accept	agree to or willingly receive	Frank accepted the award.
except	not including	All the painters except June were finished.
affect	to influence	The quiz grade affected Sam's GPA.
effect	the result of an action	The medicine had a great effect on my performance.
alot	not a word	*Never use.*
a lot	always two words	The fish ate a lot of food.
beside	at the side of	She sat beside me in class.
besides	in addition to	There are other card games besides poker.
borrow	receive on loan	May I borrow your pen?
lend	give out temporarily	I will lend you my badge.
bring	move toward or with	I'll bring your newspaper over.
take	move away from	Take your trash to the dump.
capital	wealth or resources	The interest on your capital will support you.
capitol	building where lawmakers meet	We met on the steps of the Capitol.

Words	Meaning	Example
disinterested	impartial	Members of the board should be disinterested when they make policy decisions.
uninterested	indifferent	Many people are uninterested in classical music.
elicit	to draw out	Torture usually elicits answers.
illicit	unlawful	The detective watched for illicit activity.
farther	more distant	The road went farther than I realized.
further	additional	The scientist needs to do further investigation.
former	first of two things mentioned previously	Alex and Chris are both good skiers; the former in downhill and the latter in slalom.
latter	second of two things mentioned previously	
imply	suggest without stating directly	Are you implying that John is lazy?
infer	draw a conclusion from evidence	When you gave away your ticket, I inferred that you didn't want to go to the concert.
it's	contraction for *it is*	It's a beautiful day.
its	possessive form of *it*	The team played its top rival.
lay	to place	Susan will lay your book on the table.
lie	rest in a flat position	The cat likes to lie in the sun.
loose	not securely attached	The loose door hinge squeaked.
lose	to misplace	Be careful not to lose your ring down the drain.
moral	lesson about standards or nature of life	Here's the moral of the story.
morale	attitude or mental condition	After winning the championship, the team's morale soared.
precede	come before	The king precedes his subjects.
proceed	go forward	Now we'll proceed into the dining room.

Words	Meaning	Example
principal	most important or head of an organization	The principal of the high school suspended everyone involved in the demonstration.
principle	basic standard	Coach Evans believes in the principle of fair play.
raise	to lift or make something go up	Raise your hand if you plan to attend.
rise	to go upward	My bread rises in three hours.
real	actual or true	Mary's real motive was envy.
really	in reality or in fact	Will the train really come?
set	to place	Set your suitcase over there.
sit	to occupy a seat or specific place	Let's sit together on the plane.
stationary	standing still	Stationary bicycles are good for exercise.
stationery	writing paper	There's stationery in my desk.
than	introduces second part of a comparison	June is older than Frank.
then	next in order	Eat your lunch and then we'll go to the movie.
their	possessive pronoun	They gave the guard their passes.
there	adverb of place	John is standing over there.
they're	contraction of *they are*	They're our new neighbors.

Choosing Effective Words

There are usually several "right" words for a given sentence, and writers can choose from among them, depending upon the effects they want to create. Usually, specific and concrete words are more effective than abstract and general ones. *Aspen* is better than *tree; heavy, wet snow* better than *weather; cracked* better than *damaged by.* In other words, a sentence that reads *The aspens cracked under the heavy, wet snow* is better than this: *The trees were damaged by the weather.* Students can learn to use more specific and concrete language if they aim for words that describe what they can see, hear, touch, smell, and taste.

> **➥ *Writer's Notebook***
> ➥
> ➥ Keep a list of sparkling words (words that are new and interesting to you) that
> ➥ you might be able to use in your writing. Watch for them when you are reading.
> ➥ Often they will be the words you have to look up in a dictionary.
> ➥

Strong verbs also play an important role in effective word choice. As a first step, encourage students to eliminate forms of the verb *to be*: *am, be, are, is, was,* and *were*. Another set to cut includes *has, have,* and *had*. One way to begin limiting the use of words like these is to ask students to mark each appearance in a piece of their own writing and then come up with more powerful alternatives. The following selection, written by a tenth-grade student, demonstrates how this might be accomplished:

> The most valuable course I have taken in my school career *is* Spanish. Many people choose to take foreign languages just to graduate with an advanced diploma, but I take the course because it *is* fun, and educational. The most upcoming foreign language *is* Spanish, and the Hispanic population *is* dominating. An advanced Spanish language study can possibly help me get along in the future.

Once students see how much they rely on the verb *to be,* they are more motivated to learn about alternatives. Consider the effect of substituting stronger verbs for the recurring *is:*

> Spanish stands out as the most valuable course in my school career. Many people choose to take foreign languages just to graduate with an advanced diploma, but I take the course for fun and education. Spanish dominates the foreign languages spoken in this country, and the Hispanic population continues to grow. An advanced Spanish language study can possibly help me get along in the future.

This selection could benefit from further editing, but the addition of strong verbs is a first step.

MINILESSON

Goal: To show students how to revise sentences to use more strong verbs.

Talking Points:

• The quality of sentences matters a lot in the way readers evaluate writing.

- Strong verbs add significantly to the quality of sentences.

- Verbs of being (*am, be, are, is, was,* and *were*) along with *had* and *has* should be eliminated where possible.

ONLINE
7.2

Using Strong Verbs

For each sentence, replace the weak verb with a strong one that creates a vivid image. Keep the same information, but rearrange or add to it if you wish. See the example in *a*.

a. She has hair that is long and stringy.
   Her hair hangs below her waist in threadlike tendrils.
b. My brother is kind to me.
c. The teacher is totally boring.
d. The party was fun.
e. The gym was crowded with athletes.
f. She was happy with her report card.
g. When her best friend moved away, Jane was sad.
h. My high school has a great band.
i. We were the best in the dance competition.
j. Toni Morrison is a good writer.

Activity:

Hand out copies of the worksheet (available on the companion website) and have students complete them individually. Then have students meet in small groups to compare their revisions of sentences *b–j* and write on the board the best for each from their group. The whole class can compare and discuss the several "best" versions.

Assessment:

After students have completed this exercise, you can ask them to revise some of their own sentences. One way to facilitate this process is to put together a collection of sentences that have weak verbs drawn from student papers and ask students to revise them; students nearly always recognize their own sentences in lists like these. Then they can swap drafts and underline weak sentences for one another to revise. Finally, they can identify and revise weak sentences in their own drafts.

Another area where students can improve verb usage is in selections where they include quotations from literature or other sources. The continual repetition of *says* does not enhance the quality of sentences. The following list provides alternatives students can use with quotes:

- suggest

- state

- contend

- note

- exclaim

- assert

- elaborate

- shout

- detail

- explain

Avoiding Repeated Words

It's easy to lapse into using the same word more than once in a sentence. Occasionally repetition can be effective, as in a sentence like this: *Stress rules my life: tension with my parents, tension with my teachers, tension with my friends.* Generally, however, repeating the same word makes sentences clumsy and ineffective, as the following examples, drawn from student writing, show:

- This story is told using careful word usage.

- This section of the essay concludes with the conclusion of the episode.

- It centers itself around a central story in a very intriguing way.

Variety in Sentences

One of the characteristics of good writing that gets high marks from evaluators of writing tests is variety in sentence structure. Of course, syntactic variety is partly shaped by word choice. Using strong verbs often leads writers to move away from repeating the following pattern:

One of the characteristics of good writing that gets high marks from evaluators of writing tests is variety in sentence structure.

NOUN [SUBJECT]   VERB   ADJECTIVE [COMPLEMENT]

The large building   was   red and brown.

At the same time, however, making good syntactic choices requires thinking about the audience. Writers need to consider where they want to direct the audience's attention and then create the syntax to accomplish their goals. Consider, for example, the following sentences:

Lacrosse is my sister's sport. It is strenuous and challenging.

This linear form, putting one subject-verb-complement sentence after another, is typical for many inexperienced writers, and this form makes it difficult for the writer to direct the audience's attention to the connection between the features of lacrosse and the game itself. Here is an alternative:

Lacrosse, strenuous and challenging, is my sister's sport.

Putting the adjectives *strenuous* and *challenging* in the same sentence instead of adding that information in a separate sentence focuses the reader's attention on the nature of lacrosse and makes it easier to move on to another sentence like this:

It attracts some of the strongest athletes in our school.

These two sentences direct the audience to qualities of the sport. If the writer wants to focus the audience in a slightly different way, an alternative like this can be used:

Attracting some of the strongest athletes in our school, lacrosse is my sister's strenuous and challenging sport.

Here the audience is directed to think more about the implications of lacrosse for a school's athletic program. In other words, syntactic choices are linked to quality in writing because they play such a key role in demonstrating the writer's purposes and directing the audience's attention. Students who write well and receive high scores on writing tests know how to use a variety of syntactic forms. One of the ways students can learn to use more variation in sentence structure is to analyze their own writing to see what sentence types they use most commonly. The following chart gives students a lens for looking at their own writing.

Identifying Sentence Types

ONLINE
7.3

Sentence Type	Features	Example	Symbol
Simple	One independent clause (can have compound subject and/or compound predicate)	Traders and buyers hurry to the center of town and usually arrive at the same time.	S
Compound	Two or more independent clauses but no dependent clause. Independent clauses may be joined by a comma and a coordinating conjunction or by a semicolon with or without a conjunctive adverb	The guide dog stopped suddenly, so he did not fall into the hole. Rain poured for ten days; therefore, the festival had to be cancelled.	CD
Complex	One independent clause and one or more dependent clauses	She read the newspaper because she wanted to learn more about the candidates for mayor.	CX
Compound-complex	Two or more coordinated independent clauses and at least one dependent clause	He majored in biology, but he became so fascinated by language that he changed to English.	CD-CX

Here is how a student used the chart in Online 7.3 to examine the sentence patterns in his own writing. This was an essay Joe had revised several times before he did the analysis of sentence variety, and here is what he found:

Sentense Combining Essay

ONLINE
7.4

Adversity

Adversity has played a major role in my life.[S] I was born with collapsed lungs, chronic asthma, jaundice, and amniotic band syndrome which claimed four of the digits on my left hand.[CX] My mother realized that many obstacles had to be overcome before I, her new baby, could thrive.[S] I persevered through two weeks of surgery but was finally allowed to go home.[CX]

Overcoming adversity has become an inspiration in my life.[S] I have discovered that the missing digits on my left hand are not a limitation but a motivation.[S] I have played both baseball and soccer at the high school level, have reached a typing speed of eighty words per minute, and have strung my guitar backwards so that I can play music.[S] In spite of these triumphs the greatest adversity was yet to come.[S]

The morning of December 12, 2000 brought an immeasurable amount of pain and suffering into my life.[S] My mother served as my hope and my inspiration; she was a tutor, a mentor, a role model, and a friend.[CD] Our bond was torn apart, however, when a house fire claimed her life and broke my heart.[CX]

Using sentence-type analysis, this student realized that even though the length of his sentences varied, he relied heavily on one type—the simple sentence. The implication is clear for this writer: although there are a number of good qualities in this piece, the writer can improve it tremendously by using a greater variety of sentence types.

Writer's Notebook

Find and record one interesting sentence each day. Copy the sentence in your writer's notebook, then analyze it and explain how it achieves its effect.

The fact is that most writers prefer one sentence type—even unconsciously—and simply becoming aware of that preference can help them introduce more variety into their writing. In addition, many writers favor particular forms of a given type of sentence. For example, one person may like to begin many complex sentences with the dependent clause *(Although it was a cold day, the children went swimming.)* rather than putting it at the end of the sentence. Another person may love the coordinating conjunction *and,* using it continually to connect two independent clauses in a compound sentence. Once students have identified the types of sentences they most commonly use, the next step is to look for recurring patterns within those types.

When Joe looked carefully at the simple sentences in his essay he saw how most of them began with the same noun-verb pattern *(Adversity has played; My mother realized; I was born; I persevered).* He could see that he used the same pattern again and again within his sentences. When he read his essay aloud, he heard how the noun-verb pattern at the beginning of each sentence began to sound repetitive. He realized that he needed to use additional sentence types and patterns in his writing.

Of course, simple sentences can be very effective. Consider, for example, the sentence "This does not just happen" in the opening selection by Barbara Tuchman. Positioned after three relatively long complex sentences, this short simple sentence encourages the reader to pause before turning to the two final sentences. Students will use sentence variety effectively when they consider the outcomes they want to achieve. The following steps, then, can lead to successful use of sentence variety:

1. Learn to identify the four major sentence types—simple, compound, complex, and compound-complex.

2. Consider how the syntax of these types will direct the reader's attention.

3. Identify sentence types in one's own writing.

4. Analyze the patterns of sentence types in one's own writing.

5. Consider what arrangement of sentence types will achieve the desired effect.

Sentence Combining

Many students routinely employ the simple sentence and the compound sentence, using *and* as a coordinating conjunction. To introduce a greater variety of sentence structures into their writing, students need to learn new patterns, and sentence combining can help. Research (Connors 2000; Hunt 1965; Mellon 1969; O'Hare 1973) shows that sentence combining is a very effective way of helping students learn to write more complex sentences, and with the ability to write more complex sentences comes the capacity to introduce greater sentence variety in any piece of writing, including writing on demand.

Sentence-combining exercises can help students broaden their sentence sense.

Cued Sentence Combining

Sentence-combining exercises can help students broaden their sentence sense. The first type, shown below, cues students by indicating the word they should use in combining the two sentences.

Cued Sentence Combining

ONLINE 7.5

Combine each pair of sentences into one sentence, using the word in parentheses, as shown in the example below:

1. Willa Cather wrote about life in the American West. She was raised in Nebraska. (use *who*)
   Willa Cather, who was raised in Nebraska, wrote about life in the American West.

2. My family moved to California. My father became a disk jockey. (use *when*)

3. All the sophomore girls traveled to Detroit. In Detroit they had a concert. (use *where*)

4. The burglar opened the closet door carefully. He was looking for a locked box. (use *and*)

5. Bald eagles are a protected species. The population of bald eagles is growing annually. (use *but*)

6. Soccer is often played in the spring. It is also played in the fall. (use *or*)

7. The price of the new CD has been increased. It is possible to purchase it with a money-saving coupon. (use *but*)

8. The boy carried water bottles for the football team. He was called Water Boy. (use *who*)

9. Oklahoma was the destination of the Cherokee people who were forced to move out of the Southeast in the early nineteenth century. It was called Indian Territory before it became a state. (use *which*)

10. Commercial airplanes consume a lot of fuel. Some newer planes have been made more fuel efficient. (use *although*)

Open Sentence Combining

A less structured form of sentence combining gives students a series of short sentences and asks them to combine them however they like. Usually students come up with several variations of combinations, and they can learn more about sentence variety by looking at one another's combinations in pairs or in small groups. They come to understand that there is no single right way to put sentences together and that different writers want to achieve different effects. The following exercise helps them see alternatives to their own combinations.

**ONLINE
7.6**

Open Sentence Combining

Combine the following sets of sentences into one. Compare your sentence with those written by other students in your group.

Set One

1. There was a car accident.
2. More than twenty cars were involved.
3. There was fog on the highway.
4. The cars ran into one another.
5. The cars couldn't move.
6. Rescue vehicles had a hard time getting there.

7. Sirens blared and lights flashed.
8. The accident injured a dozen people.

Set Two

1. The wedding was over.
2. The guests were tired.
3. The guests were happy.
4. The bride and groom were ready to leave.
5. The guests got into their cars.
6. Their cars filled the parking lot.
7. They laughed and talked.
8. Suddenly the parking lot was empty.

Set Three

1. My desk is cluttered.
2. It is covered with papers.
3. It is covered with books.
4. My assignment is somewhere on the desk.
5. I can't find my assignment.
6. My teacher will be angry if I turn my assignment in late.
7. My teacher will lower my grade on the assignment.
8. I wish I could find my assignment.

Exercises like these can help students learn how to put sentences together differently and broaden their repertoires for writing. By focusing on individual sentences that have already been identified as needing elaboration, they can develop various strategies for composing syntactically interesting and diverse sentences.

The next step is for students to learn to recognize the need for sentence combining in longer selections of writing. Initially, it usually works best for students to work with a selection written by another student because they will be more able to see the places that need development. The essay on pages 173 and 174 (Online 7.4 on the companion website) is a good selection for students to start with because it contains so many sentences that would benefit from the expansion of sentence combining. From there students can move on to consider paragraphs or essays written by classmates and, eventually, selections of their own writing. With a background in sentence combining, students can begin to identify their own particular patterns of sentence structure and work on increasing the variety of their sentences. The importance of doing this cannot be overemphasized because sentence variety is one of the top features that rubrics identify and test evaluators look for.

Cumulative Sentences

Sentence combining offers one way to help students develop the ability to vary their syntactic patterns, but other strategies are also available. One of these is to teach students the cumulative sentence. This pattern begins with an independent clause that is amplified by a series of free modifiers. Here are some examples:

The flame edged up the match.
to
The flame edged up the match, driving a film of moisture and a thin strip of darker grey before it.

The skaters are filling the rink.
to
The skaters are filling the rink, the girls gliding and spinning, the boys swooping and daring, their arms flapping like wings.

The baby cried.
to
Lusty-voiced, red-faced, with flailing legs and arms, the baby cried, wild as a hornet, tiny as a cat.

The NASCAR phenomenon has swept the country.
to
The NASCAR phenomenon has swept the country, involving great numbers of car enthusiasts, drawing ever larger audiences, attracting big money from advertisers, enveloping even Barbie in its uniform.

The modifiers that follow the main clause add considerable detail, and they ask the writer to observe closely and choose words carefully. As Francis Christensen, an early proponent of the cumulative sentence, put it, writing cumulative sentences requires "verbal virtuosity and syntactical ingenuity" (1963, 160). Exercises like the following can help students develop cumulative sentences.

ONLINE
7.7

Cumulative Sentence Exercise

Add at least three free modifiers to these main clauses, varying the position of the modifiers. Try to include as much sensory detail as possible.

1. Four women in red walked to the podium
2. Then I heard the siren blare

3. She raised her hand
4. The feather bed beckoned me
5. Five sparrows huddled near the bird bath
6. The speaker paused
7. Joan could play the piano for hours
8. The old man's eye remained fixed on me
9. Ocean swells moved rhythmically toward us
10. The little girl stood at the top of the stairs

Compare your cumulative sentences with someone else's, considering the kinds of details each of you added to the main clause.

Returning to the "Adversity" piece, we can see how the introduction of a few cumulative sentences can add to its syntactic variety. Take, for example, the final sentence of the first paragraph: *I persevered through two weeks of surgery but was finally allowed to go home.* This sentence could be revised to *I persevered through two weeks of surgery, pricked senseless by long needles, caught in a tangle of tubes, blinded by the light that shone night and day over my incubator, before I was finally allowed to go home.*

Another sentence that could be revised into cumulative form is the first one in Paragraph 3: *The morning of December 12, 2000 brought an immeasurable amount of pain and suffering into my life.* Here is one possible revision: *Freakish and stealthy, with exquisite precision, the morning of December 12, 2000, brought an immeasurable amount of pain and suffering into my life, upending my days, haunting my nights.* Once students are comfortable with exercises like the one above, they can turn to their own writing for independent clauses that can be revised into cumulative sentences.

Imitation

Imitation offers still another way to give students the ability to make choices about sentences. As we use it here, imitation does not mean simply copying the work of others; it means using models to generate creative ideas about syntax (see Chapter 5 for a related discussion about reading closely). One of the most common maxims is that good writers read widely. While it's true that extensive reading contributes to the quality of writing, the connection between the two can be strengthened if students are encouraged to see the texts they read as treasure troves to be mined for examples of effective, even arresting, sentences.

Recognition

The first step in a pedagogy of imitation is *recognition*, seeing sentence patterns. Teachers can always give students models for imitation exercises, but it is much more effective if students become collectors of sentences themselves.

One way to help them get started with the process of recognition is to suggest patterns they might seek out. For example, students could begin with a list like the one in Online 7.8. While the technical terms may be unfamiliar—even off-putting—to students, the content is important. In the case of AP students, they are accountable for being able to identify these terms in the multiple-choice section of the exam and to apply them in the essay portion. The following rhetorical labels and definitions can help students see that there are recognizable patterns with a long history of use and, further, that they can learn those patterns for writing effective sentences.

ONLINE 7.8

Sentence Patterns

Type	*Features*	*Example*
Multiple repetitions (anaphora)	Repetition of the same word(s) at the beginning of successive clauses	Our class has worked on school spirit for four years—four years of pep rallies and bonfires, four years of cookie sales and tag days, four years of cheering ourselves hoarse.
Phrase reversal (chiasmus)	The second half of a sentence reverses the order of the first	When the going gets tough, the tough get going.
Interrupted repetition (diacope)	Repetition of a word or phrase with one or more words in between	Give me bread, oh my jailer, give me bread.
End repetition (epiphora)	Repetition of a word or phrase at the end of several clauses	When I was a child, I spoke as a child, I understood as a child, I thought as a child.
Apparent omission (occupatio)	Emphasizing a point by seeming to pass over it	I will not mention her extravagance, her luxurious wardrobe, her credit card debts, her loyalty to fashion designers—austerity is her new mode.
Part-whole substitution (synecdoche)	Substitution of part for the whole	All hands on deck.
Triple parallels (tricolon)	Pattern of three parallel phrases	I came, I saw, I conquered.
Verb repetition (zeugma)	One verb governs several objects, each in a different way	Here thou great Anna, whom three realms obey, dost sometimes counsel take—and sometimes tea.

Writer's Notebook

Try to find sentences in your reading that follow some of the classical patterns described in the Sentence Patterns chart. Record them and share them with your classmates.

Copying

Once students become adept at recognizing sentences worth imitating, they can move to the next step in the imitation process: *copying*. This means actually transcribing the sentence word for word with all its punctuation. Some teachers find it useful to have students keep journals or commonplace books into which they copy sentences that impress them. The location doesn't matter, but the process of copying does. Research shows that the connections among the hand, the eyes, and the brain, which are all engaged in copying, foster learning, and students can actually begin to learn new sentence patterns through the act of copying (Emig 1977).

Understanding

Understanding is the next step in the process of imitation. Once students have found (or been given) and copied effective sentences, they can analyze the sentences to figure out how they are constructed. The following chart provides a model they can use to analyze their sentences. By giving each sentence a name, describing its features, and including the sentence itself as an example, students develop a broader understanding of how sentences can be constructed.

Sentence Patterns

ONLINE
7.9

Type	Features	Example
Reversal	State idea negatively and then positively	The trouble is not with the facts; the trouble is that clear inferences have not been drawn from the facts.
Command	Use imperative voice at the beginning of a sentence to attract attention	Never mind that the teacher gave him a pass; he was still suspended for skipping class.
Repeating	Repeat words for emphasis	I scream for ice cream, you scream for ice cream, we all scream for ice cream.

Creative Imitation

Creative imitation is the final step in the process. At this point students are ready to generate sentences of their own, using the sentences of others as models. Like the experience of copying, this part of the process helps them develop new sentence sense because they are physically, visually, and mentally involved in creating new syntax. Here are some examples of creative imitations of sentences from Mark Twain's *Huckleberry Finn:*

> *Original sentence:* It was a mighty nice family and a mighty nice house too.
> *Imitation:* It was a mighty nice burger and a mighty nice rest'raunt too.
>
> *Original sentence:* It was beautiful to hear that clock tick and sometimes when one of these peddlers had been along and scoured her up and got her in good shape, she would start in and strike a hundred and fifty before she got tuckered out.
> *Imitation:* It was grand to see that clown smile, and sometimes when one of these girls had been waiting on a young'un standing in front of that counter, she would hand him a placemat with the clown grinning from one side to the other.

Imitation's progression from recognition of sentence patterns, to copying various patterns, to understanding patterns by analyzing them, to creatively imitating them helps students learn to produce as well as appreciate new sentence types.

Cohesion

Knowing how to make choices about the syntax of individual sentences gives student writing authority and fluency that convinces readers and impresses evaluators. But individual sentences cannot stand alone. Connections between them also deserve attention. Research shows that cohesion is another feature of sentences that matters to evaluators. Essays that use the greatest number of cohesive ties—words and phrases that create transitions between sentences—typically receive higher scores than those that use only a few (Faigley and Witte 1981).

Essays that use the greatest number of cohesive ties . . . typically receive higher scores.

Many of the strategies students can learn through imitation will also help them develop stronger cohesion in their writing. Here are some examples:

Strategy	*Example*
repeat key words	The band director emphasized precision. When he introduced a new formation, he gave section leaders precise directions about location.
repeat sentence patterns	Because my brother was good at science, everyone in my family expected me to be at home in the lab. Because my sister was a great musician, they thought I should join the band.
use synonyms	In the Internet world some people take on alternate identities. These disguises can help them cheat others.

There are, of course, a number of words that signal relationships between sentences, and helping students become familiar with them is another way to develop cohesion in their writing. One approach to transitional words and phrases is to consider the circumstances when they are most likely to be useful. The following chart shows some of these.

Occasions for Using Transitional Words

ONLINE
7.10

Occasions for Creating Cohesion	**Transitional Words and Phrases**		
Narrations or descriptions or processes that include time	after again always before	during every time finally meanwhile	next the next day then while
Descriptions that convey relationships among things or people	around behind below	here in front of in the center	on the side of on top of over
Explanations of the relative importance of things or ideas	first more important	less important mainly	second
Comparing and contrasting	also as either . . . or in the same way yet	on the contrary unlike than likewise neither . . . nor	similarly also however instead but

Occasions for Creating Cohesion	Transitional Words and Phrases		
Describing cause-and-effect relationships	although because consequently	as a result if, then for this reason	since so that therefore
Introducing examples	as for example	namely like	such as to illustrate
Signaling emphasis	indeed in fact	in other words	
Offering more information	in addition moreover	similarly besides	also furthermore

Key Points for Reflection

This chapter has suggested several ways of teaching students how to write more effective sentences. Each of these strategies offers writers choices, and together they create a repertoire that expands the number of options available for each writing task. They give students access to what Barbara Tuchman describes as the satisfaction of writing "a good sentence." Whether at the level of words, syntax, or intersentence connections, the choices students make will shape meaning as well as style and tone. These choices, in turn, will influence how student writing is judged by teachers, the general public, and those who evaluate writing on demand. We believe:

- Sentence-level instruction improves the writing of all students.

- Learning to produce good sentences helps students demystify writing.

- Variety in sentence structure is an attribute of good writing that is recognized by test evaluators and teachers alike.

- Cohesive ties strengthen writing.

WORKS CITED

Broad, Bob. 2003. *What We Really Value: Beyond Rubrics in Teaching and Assessing Writing*. Logan: Utah State University Press.

Christensen, Francis. 1963. "A Generative Rhetoric of the Sentence." *College Composition and Communication* 14 (3): 155–61.

Connors, Robert J. 2000. "The Erasure of the Sentence." *College Composition and Communication* 52 (1): 96–128.

Diederich, Paul B., John W. French, and Sydell T. Carlton. 1961. "Factors in Judgments of Writing Ability." *ETS Research Bulletin (61–15)*. Princeton: Educational Testing Service.

Emig, Janet. 1977. "Writing as a Mode of Learning." *College Composition and Communication* 28 (2): 122–28.

Faigley, Lester, and Stephen Witte. 1981. "Analyzing Revision." *College Composition and Communication* 32 (4): 400–414.

Hunt, Kellogg W. 1965. *Grammatical Structures Written at Three Grade Levels*. Urbana, IL: NCTE.

Kellogg, Ronald T. 1994. *The Psychology of Writing*. New York: Oxford University Press.

Mellon, John. 1969. *Transformational Sentence-Combining: A Method for Enhancing the Development of Syntactic Fluency in English Composition*. Urbana, IL: NCTE.

O'Hare, Frank. 1973. *Sentence Combining: Improving Student Writing Without Formal Grammar Instruction*. Urbana, IL: NCTE.

8 Scoring Writing

For excellence, the presence of others is always required.

—HANNAH ARENDT

Much has been written about the process of writing—prewriting, drafting, peer feedback, revising, and publishing—but what about postprocess? At some point, most writing receives a grade or a score—what then? Often, teachers don't talk about scoring with students. Even though teachers regularly share writing process terminology with students and create ways for student writers to publish their work, they rarely involve students in scoring systems. The thinking that guides marginal comments and end notes, the rationales for the grades assigned, the scoring guides or rubrics that lead to the scores—all of these remain largely outside student awareness. Teacher talk does, of course, include discussion of grading. We have heard grousing (and participated in it ourselves): "I spent all weekend grading their papers, and they didn't even look at them!" or "It's like they didn't even read my comments from the last essays—I saw all the same mistakes again!" Comments like these convince us that students need to understand and participate in grading or scoring writing so they can benefit more fully from teacher grades and prepare themselves for the scoring of writing on demand.

Throughout this book, and particularly in Chapter 4, we have emphasized the importance of making assessment a visible part of writing instruction. If students have learned some of the terminology of assessment, participated in peer response writing groups, and considered various rubrics and other scoring systems, they will be ready to take part in some scoring of writing themselves. We believe that involving students in actual grading and/or scoring will help them understand more fully the criteria for good writing. In our own experiences as teachers, the most powerful moments of learning about assessing writing have come in scoring sessions when we have debated about what number or letter to give a specific paper. In these sessions the truth of Hannah Arendt's point about excellence has seemed most compelling. Pushed to explain to our peers why a paper deserves a B or a 4, we have come to understand scoring systems much more fully. We believe students deserve the same opportunity.

Student understanding of scoring seems especially important in the current context of multiple high-stakes writing tests. We have often heard students say some version of, "I know just what I need to write to get an A from Ms. Smith." Other students murmur, "I don't have a clue why Ms. Smith gave me a C." Subjectivity and personal relationships do insinuate themselves into our grading of students we've come to know in our classes, and we assume this is true for other teachers too. For us, the creation, the discussion, and the use of rubrics and other scoring systems offer a counterbalance to these forces, helping us to be more fair in our grading. For our students, scoring writing offers a way to become better readers of teachers' grades and comments as well as to prepare for writing pieces that will be scored by someone they have never met.

> *Students need to understand and participate in grading or scoring writing so they can benefit more fully from teacher grades and prepare themselves for the scoring of writing on demand.*

Beginning to Use Rubrics in the Classroom

Teachers who have started to use rubrics in the classroom are pleasantly surprised to find an increase in precise vocabulary among students in peer and teacher conferences, decreased student complaints about grades, and better accountability when discussing grading with colleagues, administrators, and parents. Creating a rubric for an assignment seems like just more work for teachers' already busy lives, but time spent drafting a rubric can easily be saved in the actual grading of essays. Also, one can create a rubric in the amount of time it takes to have just one conference with a student confused about a grade.

Teachers who have never developed a rubric should remember that creating the first one can take time, but with experience the process gets faster. It's also useful to remember that teachers don't need to "rubricize" everything. One can start with an essay exam or a research paper and go from there. Better yet, once a class has begun to use rubrics, students can help develop them, thereby increasing their understanding—and acceptance—of the grades they receive.

Often, teachers have some kind of scoring guide or check sheet already in place to help grade assignments. We call these proto-rubrics. Here is an example:

Example 1: Compare-Contrast Essay Check Sheet

Introduction   _____
Body   _____
Comparison   _____
Conclusion   _____
Usage   _____

This check sheet is useful because students are reminded to be organized in their essays and to attend to writing conventions. Students might use this check sheet as a reminder of what they need to do, and teachers might use it as a way of determining whether students have indeed completed the requirements. Obviously, this is a fairly simple check sheet. One for, say, a research paper, can be much longer as well as more detailed and specific.

A check sheet like Example 1 does not tell students how much of their grade has to do with each of the requirements. In the next example, the teacher has designated weighting for each of the items on the check sheet.

Example 2: Compare-Contrast Essay Scoring Guide

Introduction   _____(10%)
Body   _____(20%)
Comparison   _____(30%)
Conclusion   _____(10%)
Usage   _____(30%)

This proto-rubric can now be called a *scoring guide* instead of a check sheet because the percentage of the grade is designated for each requirement. Some teachers create scoring guides that use points instead of percentages, breaking the categories down into more requirements, as in this example:

Example 3: Compare-Contrast Essay Scoring Guide

I. Introduction (10 points)

    Hook   _____/5
    Clarity of topic   _____/5

II. Body (50 points)

    Paragraph 1
      Three similarities   _____/15
    Paragraph 2
      Three differences   _____/15
    Sentences regarding topic   _____/10
    Transitions   _____/10

III. *Conclusion (10 points)*

    Summary of points   ____/5
    Clincher sentence   ____/5

IV. *Usage (30 points)*

    Spelling   ____/5
    Usage   ____/5
    Sentence structure   ____/10
    Punctuation   ____/10

    TOTAL POINTS: ____/100

In Example 3 the teacher has broken down the percentage for each category into points for doing specific tasks, like making the topic clear. Such a score sheet can be an improvement over a letter grade for demystifying the grading process for students. For example, if a student got very few points for punctuation under the *Usage* heading, he or she would have a clearer idea of what contributed to lowering his or her grade.

Refining the Rubric

One of the difficulties that can emerge in developing rubrics is the temptation to continue to expand the categories to deal with unanticipated inadequacies in student papers. For example, what if a student has three examples, but one is not as strong as the others? Or what if the statements about the topic don't correlate with what is discussed in the body of the paper? These and similar issues are not directly addressed by the scoring guide in Example 3. Teachers often respond by trying to expand their guides to anticipate every possible problem.

We have seen teachers add more and more descriptors to a scoring guide like the one in Example 3 (which is already nearly a page long). While we understand and sympathize with the problem, we don't think efficiency should be compromised. A too-long list of features on a scoring guide makes grading more difficult, not easier. Another difficulty one can run into is having a student challenge the scoring guide by saying, "Look, I have a sentence about my topic right here. Why did I get only three points for it?" As teachers, we can imagine that the sentence about the topic might be deficient in any number of ways, but in the student's eyes, this scoring guide indicates only whether a statement about the topic is included, not how good it is. For this reason, we define a true rubric as a scoring guide that includes references to the *quality* of the writing. Here is a simple example that is fundamentally different from the scoring guide in Example 3:

Example 4: Essay Rubric

	4	3	2	1
Introduction	excellent	good	fair	poor
Body	detailed	developed	minimal	poor
Conclusion	strong	good	adequate	unacceptable
Usage	adheres to most conventions	deviates from conventions 3–4 times	deviates from conventions 5–7 times	deviates from conventions 8 or more times

With this kind of simple rubric, students get some idea of the required features of the essay as well as of the required quality of each feature. For example, the body should be not just developed but also detailed to receive a top score. A new problem arises, however: how to convert the score to a grade. Some teachers simply add up the number of top scores for the total (in this case, four scores of four equals sixteen) and divide the student total into that total. For example, 14/16 equals 87.5 percent, a letter grade of B. By showing how the relative values of these categories can be converted into a number, teachers can demonstrate that grades are not simply pulled out of the sky. With this or any scoring system, it is entirely possible for two students to get exactly the same grade for vastly different reasons. Teachers who grade papers with diverse strengths know that not all writing graded a B is a B for the same reason.

Furthermore, the issue of usage or adherence to conventions of Standard Written English is problematic. While it is useful to quantify deviations from conventions because it helps distinguish levels of student ability, it is important to consider what is being counted. That is, eight instances of the same problem—such as misspelling the same word multiple times or consistently failing to capitalize a proper noun or continually missing subject-verb agreement—is not the same as eight *different* problems in usage. One of the issues teachers need to negotiate, then, is how to count deviations from conventions in a way that recognizes this difference. One alternative we have used is to consider six instances of the same error as three errors on the rubric. At any rate, the point remains that students who receive the same score can do so for very different reasons, and a detailed rubric will make those reasons visible, as the examples of Student 1 and Student 2 show.

Example 5: Two Scored Essay Rubrics

Student 1	4	3	2	1
Introduction	excellent	**good**	fair	poor
Body	**detailed**	developed	minimal	poor
Conclusion	strong	**good**	adequate	unacceptable
Usage	adheres to most conventions	deviates from conventions 3–4 times	**deviates from conventions 5–7 times**	deviates from conventions 8 or more times

Total score for Student 1: 12/16 = 75% (Add bold scores)

Student 2	4	3	2	1
Introduction	excellent	**good**	fair	poor
Body	detailed	**developed**	minimal	poor
Conclusion	strong	good	**adequate**	unacceptable
Usage	**adheres to most conventions**	deviates from conventions 3–4 times	deviates from conventions 5–7 times	deviates from conventions 8 or more times

Total score for Student 2: 12/16 = 75% (Add bold scores)

This rubric is helpful to a student like Student 2 above, who might think a C is a C is a C and yet wonder why another student with lots of grammar mistakes can get the same grade. Sometimes teachers want to use a rubric like the previous one, but weight it according to their own priorities with each particular assignment. In such a case, points can be added to categories, as in Example 6:

Example 6: Essay Rubric

Introduction (10 points)	excellent (9–10 points)	good (8 points)	fair (6–7 points)	poor (5 and below)
Body (50 points)	detailed (45–50 points)	developed (40–44 points)	minimal (35–39 points)	poor (34 and below)
Conclusion (10 points)	strong (9–10 points)	good (8 points)	adequate (6–7 points)	unacceptable (5 and below)
Usage (30 points)	adheres to most conventions (27–30 points)	deviates from conventions 3–4 times (25–26 points)	deviates from conventions 5–7 times (22–24 points)	deviates from conventions 8 or more times (21 or less)

Rigid use of rubrics can send the message that writing is a process of accumulating points rather than creating a work in which many elements combine seamlessly together for a certain effect.

Adding up the points on a rubric like this gives students a number of points out of one hundred, but tracking points at this level of precision is difficult and can lead to arithmetic errors. Some papers inevitably challenge the rubric by creating a situation where the points don't add up to a grade that corresponds to the teacher's holistic sense of what the grade should be. We have found that it is usually possible to adjust for this within the rubric itself, usually by relying on categories like *Body* or topic-specific categories. We think it's worth pausing over this point because rigid use of rubrics can send the message that writing is a process of accumulating points rather than creating a work in which many elements combine seamlessly together for a certain effect.

Using Rubrics with Students

Because we think of a good piece of writing as ultimately greater than the sum of points assigned by individual categories, we prefer to move from simpler rubrics like the one in Example 4 to a more complex one like that in Online 8.1. The descriptors for each quality of writing invite more holistic thinking about writing, even though they do assign points for each category. The difficulty with a rubric like the one below is that it takes a while to learn. We have found that students can become adept at using it, however, if they spend enough time with it. And we believe it is worth the time because students who have internalized a detailed rubric like this one will have an enhanced understanding of the complexities of writing.

ONLINE 8.1

Rubric

	5 (highest)	4	3	2	1 (lowest)
Ideas/ Content	Clear, focused, and interesting. Holds the reader's attention. Relevant detail enriches the central idea.	Clear and focused, but not as interesting as a top-scoring paper. Support could be stronger.	Clear and focused, though may not be captivating. Support is attempted but may be limited or out of balance with main ideas.	May have a focus but lacks clarity or changes midpaper. Details may not directly support the main ideas.	The paper lacks a central idea or purpose or forces the reader to make inferences based on very sketchy details.

	5 (highest)	4	3	2	1 (lowest)
Organization	Organization enhances the central idea or theme. The structure is compelling, moving the reader through the text.	The organization is clear but perhaps formulaic.	The reader can readily follow what's being said, but the overall organization may sometimes be ineffective or too obvious.	At times, the reader has difficulty following the ideas because of lapses in organization.	Organization is haphazard and disjointed. The writing lacks direction, with ideas, details, or events strung together helter-skelter.
Voice	The writer speaks directly to the reader in a way that is individualistic and engaged. Clearly the writer is involved and is writing to be read.	The reader senses the person behind the words. It is engaging but not as expressive as a top-scoring essay.	The writer seems sincere but not fully involved in the topic. The result is pleasant, acceptable, sometimes even personable, but not compelling.	Voice is inconsistent. At times the writer seems engaged in the topic, and at other times, not.	The writer seems indifferent, uninvolved, or dispassionate. The writing is flat, lifeless, stiff, or mechanical. It may be overly technical or jargonistic.
Word Choice	Words convey the intended message in an interesting, precise, and natural way. The writing is full and rich, yet concise.	Writer shows a competent command of diction. Words are sometimes carefully chosen.	The language is quite ordinary, but it does convey the message. Often the writer settles for what's easy, producing a "generic" paper.	For the most part, word choice is sufficient to convey the message, but at times choices are incorrect.	Vocabulary is limited and so vague that only a general message comes through. Writer gropes for words to convey meaning.
Sentence Structure	Writing has an easy flow and rhythm. Sentences are well built, with strong, varied structure that makes for expressive oral reading.	Sentences are correct and varied but not carefully constructed to showcase the meaning.	Sentences are mechanical rather than fluid, lacking rhythm or grace. Some awkward constructions force the reader to slow down or reread.	Lapses in correct sentence structure are beginning to impede the reader's understanding of the text.	The paper is difficult to follow or read aloud. Sentences tend to be choppy, incomplete, rambling, irregular, or just very awkward.

	5 (highest)	4	3	2	1 (lowest)
Writing Conventions	Conventions are used effectively to enhance meaning. Errors are so minor that the reader can easily skim over them.	Competent command of language, but some errors keep this essay from being a top-scoring essay.	Writing convention errors begin to impair readability. Errors do not block meaning but tend to be distracting.	Errors in writing convention begin to impede meaning.	Numerous errors in conventions repeatedly distract the reader and make the text difficult to read.

The best way to understand a rubric is to use it, and we have found two complementary ways that students can comfortably increase their understanding of the whole rubric: in whole-class holistic scoring sessions and in small-group analytic trait scoring sessions. In the minilessons that follow, we show how this can be accomplished.

MINILESSON

Goal: To help students develop a holistic understanding of the rubric in Online 8.1 through a whole-class scoring session.

Talking Points:

- We understand rubrics when we use them to score actual writing.

- It is possible to see the connection between rubrics and the way a piece of writing combines elements of good writing when essays are scored holistically in a whole-group setting that allows for discussion of and reflection on scoring.

- Scoring writing is done best with others.

Activities:

1. Make an overhead transparency of the rubric in Online 8.1 (see companion website) and show it to the class, highlighting the six main categories.

2. Hand out a sample essay for students to read and score. While it would be best to use a sample that addresses a prompt you have

given, perhaps from a different year or a different section of the course, you could use the following prompt and student sample.

ONLINE 8.2

Sample Student Essay

Prompt: Do you agree or disagree with the new state law requiring the pledge of allegiance to be recited in school each day?

Saying the Pledge: Is it Legally Right?

I disagree with the bill requiring the public schools of Alaska to recite the Pledge of Allegiance daily in the classroom. My major opposition to this bill is the law of separation of church and state, and how this disobeys the law immensely. Also it depletes classroom time further, and some statements do not register in all areas to all people of the United States.

In the pledge of Allegiance it says "in one nation under god", many people in many different religions do not acknowledge "God" as their supreme ruler and do not pray to him, but another higher being. Also if one religion is represented by saying god, all other religions are supposed , under law, to be represented.

Another major reason I oppose the reciting of the Pledge of Allegiance daily in the public classroom is that it further depletes the teaching and learning time given to teachers and students. As teachers already complain that they do not have sufficient time to complete their assigned curriculum and then with the Pledge of Allegiance it further lessens the teaching time available to work on projects, class work, or lecturing.

To me the entire Pledge of Allegiance is not even correct. As it states "With liberty and justice for all", which in America is the way life is supposed to be, but in actuality doesn't happen. Children in inner-city schools, immigrants, and homeless people do not receive the same rights and justice that those of us who live in middle class America enjoy. In my opinion a student feels he or she need to recite the pledge of Allegiance daily to fulfill their duty as American citizens, then I feel they should either make time at home, or before class starts in the morning. As it should be a personal choice if one feels they need to renew their patriotism daily or if we know it enough from when we recited it daily in second grade.

These are just some of the reasons I feel that the Pledge of Allegiance should not be recited by requirement in classrooms in the high school level daily as Bill: CSHB 192 states it should.

3. Have students score the sample paper using the rubric in Figure 8.1, encouraging them to write a well-reasoned justification for their

score using the language of the rubric. Here is a sample score sheet to go over with them. Online 8.3 on the companion website has room for them to practice justifying scores.

**ONLINE
8.3**

Essay Score Sheet

Category	Score	Justification
Example: Ideas/content	2	The essay has a promising idea, but it doesn't really appear until the conclusion. Because there is no clear focus stated in the introduction, it is difficult to evaluate the effectiveness of the support. The essay is not particularly long, either; ideas need more development.
Ideas/content		
Organization		
Voice		
Word choice		
Sentence structure		
Writing conventions		

4. After students have read the sample and scored it according to the rubric, collect or call for the scores and write the range on the board or on an overhead transparency.

5. Begin the process of norming, or finding the score that can be supported by everyone, including you. For example, suppose for *Ideas and content,* you have the following scores written:

Score	5	4	3	2	1
Ideas and Content	||	|||||	||||||||	|||		

It will be interesting for students to see the range of scores represented visually, especially to see what score was given by the majority. Call on students who gave each score to justify their choice. Next, ask the students who gave it a five if they are willing to lower their score based on what they have heard. Then ask the students who gave it a one if they could raise their scores. If students are not willing to change right away, ask students who chose the other scores to try to convince them. Also, give the students a chance to justify their scores, if they wish to. Through debates it may be possible to narrow the range and arrive at a score through consensus. In the process, students will come to a better understanding of the rubric and see the connection between the language of the rubric and the score given.

Assessment:

To assess how the whole-class holistic scoring session went, ask students to turn over their score sheets and respond to the following writer's notebook prompt. This will give them a chance to reflect on the norming process they just went through and give you a chance to assess how much they have learned about scoring writing.

Writer's Notebook

What did you learn from participating in this rubric activity? What was most confusing or difficult about it? If you changed your score, what made you do so?

While the whole-class holistic scoring session is summative in nature, students can also work with rubrics to give formative feedback to each other, which can then be used for revision. We describe how this can work in the minilesson that follows.

MINILESSON

Goal: To help students develop an analytic understanding of the rubric in Online 8.5 by focusing on just one category in the rubric and use this understanding to give peer feedback.

Talking Points:

- Today you will use your rubric and your group members to score anonymous student papers.

- You and your group will be responsible for one category—like voice or usage—on the rubric.

- It is important that you give each paper your best attention, stay focused on your trait, write a clear and detailed justification for your score, and sign your name at the bottom of your score. If you are unsure of how to evaluate the paper, ask another group member to read and evaluate it too.

- When you are finished scoring the paper, pass it on to the next group immediately. We need to avoid creating a bottleneck of papers, so keep them moving!

Activities:

1. Show students the overhead transparency of the rubric in Online 8.1 again, and tell them that this time they will specialize in one of the six categories of writing.

2. Explain that they are going to deepen their understanding of this rubric by working with one category of a more detailed version of the rubric (see Analytic Trait Rubric) and taking a position at one of the stations on a sign-up sheet like the one that follows. Emphasize that students at each station will be viewed as experts, so it will be important for them to sign up for a category for which they feel well prepared. You may want to help direct students in this sign-up process, since you already know their strengths and weaknesses. Make a form like this, with just enough sign-up spots to distribute students equally among stations:

ONLINE 8.4

Sign-up Sheet for Peer Feedback Stations

Station 1: Ideas and content	Station 2: Organization	Station 3: Voice	Station 4: Word choice	Station 5: Sentence structure	Station 6: Writing conventions
1.	1.	1.	1.	1.	1.
2.	2.	2.	2.	2.	2.
3.	3.	3.	3.	3.	3.

3. Ideally, you will be able to arrange tables or group desks like Figure 8.1 on page 199.

   At each table, each student should have a copy of the overall rubric available for reference (Online 8.1). In addition, students should have the section for that trait that they will be scoring from the Analytic Trait Rubric (Online 8.5). At Station 6 (writing conventions), make grammar handbooks available for reference.

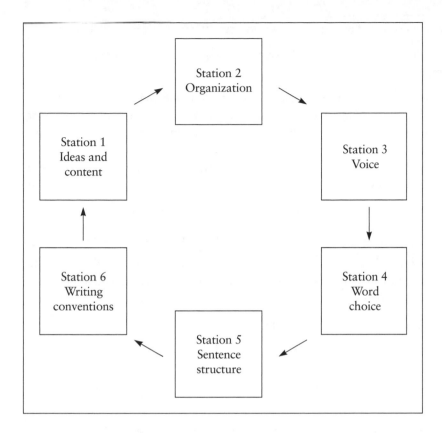

FIGURE 8.1

4. Tell students to read over the page of the rubric that covers the trait they will be evaluating and talk with their group members about what each descriptor means. (You should probably circulate from group to group during this process to field their questions.)

Analytic Trait Rubric

ONLINE 8.5

Ideas and Content

5   The paper is clear, focused, and interesting. It holds the reader's attention. Relevant anecdotes and details enrich the central theme or story line.

* The writer seems to be writing from experience and shows insight and a good sense of how events unfold and of how people respond to life and to each other.

* Supporting, relevant details give the reader important information that he or she would not personally bring to the text.

- The writing has balance; main ideas stand out.

- The writer seems in control and envelops the topic in an enlightening, entertaining way.

- The writer works with and shapes ideas, making connections and sharing insights.

3   The paper is clear and focused, even though the overall result may not be captivating. Support is attempted, but it may be limited, insubstantial, too general, or out of balance with main ideas.

- The writer may or may not be writing from experience, but either way, he or she has difficulty going from general observations to specifics.

- The reader can often second-guess the plot or main points of the text.

- Ideas, though reasonably clear, often tend toward the mundane; the reader is not sorry to see the paper end.

- Conclusions or main points seem to echo observations heard elsewhere; only on occasion do they seem to be the writer's own thinking.

- Supporting details tend to be skimpy, general, or predictable.

- The writer is beginning to define the topic but isn't there yet.

1   The paper lacks a central idea or purpose or forces the reader to make inferences based on very sketchy details.

- Information is very limited or simply unclear.

- Details do not ring true; they evolve from clichés, platitudes, or stereotypes.

- Attempts at development may be minimal or clutter up the text with random thoughts from which no central theme emerges.

- The writer has not begun to define the topic in any meaningful or personal way.

Organization

5   The organization enhances and showcases the central idea or theme. The order, structure, or presentation is compelling and moves the reader through the text.

- Details seem to fit where they are placed; sequencing is logical and effective.

- An inviting introduction draws the reader in and a satisfying conclusion leaves the reader with a sense of resolution.

- Organization flows so smoothly that the reader hardly thinks about it.

3   The reader can readily follow what's being said, but the overall organization may sometimes be ineffective or too obvious.

- The introduction and conclusion are recognizable, though not so well crafted as the reader might wish.

- Placement or relevance of some details leaves the reader occasionally confused.

- The paper sometimes moves along at a good pace, but at other times it bogs down in trivia or glosses over important ideas.

- Transitions sometimes work well; at other times, connections between ideas seem unclear.

- Despite problems, the organization does not seriously get in the way of the main point or story line.

1   Organization is haphazard and disjointed. The writing lacks direction, with ideas, details, or events strung together helter-skelter.

- There is no clearly identifiable introduction or conclusion.

- Transitions are very weak, leaving connections between ideas fuzzy, incomplete, or bewildering.

- Noticeable gaps in information confuse and confound the reader.

- Pacing is consistently awkward, so that the reader feels either mired down in trivia or rushed along at a breathless pace.

- Lack of organization ultimately obscures or distorts the main point.

Voice

5   The writer speaks directly to the reader in a way that is individualistic, expressive, and engaging. Clearly the writer is involved in the text and is writing to be read.

- The paper is honest and written from the heart. It has the ring of conviction.

- The language is natural yet provocative; it brings the topic to life.

- The reader feels a strong sense of interaction with the writer and senses the person behind the words.

- The projected tone and voice clarify and give flavor to the writer's message.

3   The writer seems sincere but not fully involved in the topic. The result is pleasant, acceptable, sometimes even personable, but not compelling.

- The writer seems to weigh words carefully, to keep a safe distance between writer and reader to avoid risk, and to write what he or she thinks the reader wants.

- The writing tends to hide rather than reveal the writer.

- The writing communicates in an earnest but fairly routine manner and only occasionally amuses, surprises, delights, or moves the reader.

- Voice may emerge strongly on one occasion, only to shift or disappear a line or two later behind a facade of general, vague, or abstract language.

1   The writer seems wholly indifferent, uninvolved, or dispassionate. As a result, the writing is flat, lifeless, stiff, or mechanical. It may be (depending on the topic) overly technical or jargonistic.

- The reader has no sense of the writer behind the words and no sense of a real desire on the part of the writer to communicate.

- The writer seems to speak in a kind of monotone that flattens all potential highs or lows of the message.

- The writing communicates on a functional level at best, without moving or involving the reader at all.

- Delivery is so consistently flat that the reader may find it hard to focus on the message even when the wording seems reasonably clear and correct.

Word Choice

5   Words convey the intended message in an interesting, precise, and natural way. The writing is full and rich, yet concise.

- Words are specific and accurate; they seem just right.

- Imagery is strong.

- Powerful verbs give the writing energy.

- Vocabulary may be striking, but it's natural and never overdone.

- Expression is fresh and appealing; slang is used sparingly.

3   The language is quite ordinary, but it does convey the message. It's functional even if it lacks punch. Often the writer settles for what's easy or handy, producing a sort of "generic" paper stuffed with familiar words and phrases.

- The language communicates but rarely captures the reader's imagination.

- The writer rarely experiments with language; however, the paper may have some fine moments.

- Attempts at colorful language often seem overdone, calculated to impress.

- Images lack detail and precision.

- Clichés, redundancies, and hackneyed phrases are common.

- A few key verbs may liven things up, but equally often verbs are general or predictable.

1   The writer struggles with a limited vocabulary, groping for words to convey meaning. Often the language is so vague and abstract or so redundant and devoid of detail that only the broadest, most general sort of message comes through.

- Words are consistently dull, colorless, or abstract.

- Monotonous repetition or overwhelming reliance or worn, threadbare expressions repeatedly cloud or smother the language.

- Often words simply do not fit the text. They seem imprecise, inadequate, or just plain wrong.

- Imagery is very fuzzy or absent altogether; the text is "peopled" only with generalities.

- Verbs are weak and few in number. Forms of *to be* and *to have* predominate.

Sentence Structure

5   The writing has an easy flow and rhythm when read aloud. Sentences are well built, with consistently strong and varied structure that makes expressive oral reading easy and enjoyable.

- Sentence structure reflects logic and sense, helping to show how ideas relate.

- The writing sounds natural and fluent; it glides along with one sentence flowing effortlessly into the next.

- Sentences display an effective combination of power and grace.

- Variation in sentence structure and length adds interest to the text.

- Fragments, if used at all, work well.

- Dialogue, if used, sounds natural.

3   Sentences tend to be mechanical rather than fluid. The text hums along efficiently for the most part, though it may lack a certain rhythm or grace, tending to be more pleasant than musical. Occasional awkward constructions force the reader to slow down or reread.

- Connections between phrases or sentences may be less fluid than desired.

- The writer shows good control over simple sentence structure but variable control over more complex structures.

- Sentences sometimes vary in length or structure, but for the most part, the writer falls into a pattern and sticks with it.

- Fragments, if used, sometimes seem the result of oversight.

- Dialogue, if used, sometimes rings true, but sometimes sounds forced or contrived.

- Sentences, though functional, often lack energy.

- Some parts of the text invite expressive oral reading; others may be a bit stiff.

1   The paper is difficult to follow or read aloud. Sentences tend to be choppy, incomplete, rambling, irregular, or just very awkward.

- Nonstandard English syntax is common. Word patterns are often jarring and irregular and far removed from the way people usually write or speak.

- Sentence structure does not generally enhance meaning; in fact, it may obscure meaning.

- Many sentences seem disjointed, awkward, confused, or nonsensical.

- Word patterns may be monotonous, as in repetitive subject-verb or subject-verb-object patterns.

- The text does not invite and may not even permit expressive oral reading.

Writing Conventions

5   The writer demonstrates a good grasp of standard writing conventions (grammar, capitalization, punctuation, usage, spelling) and uses them effectively to enhance meaning. Errors tend to be so few and so minor that the reader can easily skim right over them unless specifically searching for them.

- Paragraphing tends to be sound and to reinforce the organizational structure.

- Grammar and usage are correct and contribute to clarity and style.

- Punctuation is smooth and guides the reader through the text.

- Spelling is generally correct, even on more difficult words.

- The writer may manipulate conventions—particularly grammar—for stylistic effect.

- The writing is sufficiently long and complex to allow the writer to show skill in using a wide range of conventions.

- Only light editing would be required to polish the text.

3   Errors in writing conventions, while not overwhelming, begin to impair readability. While errors do not block meaning, they tend to be distracting.

- Punctuation may be incorrect or missing altogether.

- Spelling is usually correct or reasonably phonetic on common words.

- Problems with usage are not severe enough to distort meaning, but usage does not offer as much precision in meaning as it could.

- The writer may show reasonable control over a very limited range of conventions, but the text may be too simple or too short to reflect real mastery of conventions.

1   Numerous errors in usage, sentence structure, spelling, or punctuation repeatedly distract the reader and make the text difficult to read. In fact, the severity and the frequency of errors tend to be so overwhelming that the reader finds it very difficult to focus on the message and must reread for meaning.

- The writer shows very limited skill in using conventions.

- Basic punctuation (including terminal punctuation) tends to be omitted, haphazard, or incorrect.

- Spelling errors are frequent, even on common words.

- Extensive editing would be required to polish the text.

5. Student groups will then evaluate one trait in the papers written by their peers. To prepare for this, remove names from the essays, assign an identifying number to each essay, and attach a score sheet like the one below (Online 8.6). Remaining with their groups, students each read several essays, conferring with group members if they are uncertain about the score and handing a scored paper to the next group before starting to score another.

Peer Feedback Sheet

ONLINE 8.6

ESSAY #_____
GROUP 1: IDEAS AND CONTENT   5   4   3   2   1

_____
_____
_____
_____

Reader:_____

GROUP 2: ORGANIZATION   5   4   3   2   1

_____
_____
_____
_____

Reader:_____
GROUP 3: VOICE   5   4   3   2   1

_____
_____
_____
_____

Reader:_____

GROUP 4: WORD CHOICE   5   4   3   2   1

_____
_____
_____
_____

Reader:_____

GROUP 5: SENTENCE STRUCTURE   5   4   3   2   1

_____

_____

_____

_____

Reader:_____

GROUP 6: WRITING CONVENTIONS   5   4   3   2   1

_____

_____

_____

_____

Reader:_____

Assessment:

You can collect the peer responses first and read them over to assess students' facility in using a rubric to give feedback on papers. Alternatively, you could give the essays and feedback sheets back to the writers and ask them to revise their essays. If doing the latter, consider having the students complete the following writer's notebook prompt to help them reflect on their writing process and to help you evaluate the utility of the peer feedback session.

Writer's Notebook

What kinds of changes did you make to your essay after seeing the peer feedback sheet? What did you find most useful about your peers' comments? What did you find least useful? Are there any scores you strongly disagreed with? If so, why? What did you learn about rubrics and writing processes from engaging in this peer feedback session?

We like to share a synthesis of student responses as a whole class to reinforce what students' peers are finding useful about their comments and what they are finding lacking.

The value of this lesson is that it reinforces learning about the rubric at the same time that it provides students with detailed comments on their writing. Each student has his or her paper read six times and receives detailed feedback in each category. This should give students plenty to work on for their next revision.

Once students have become comfortable scoring essays on one trait or category of the rubric, they can move to another, and eventually, they can work as individual evaluators, reading a paper and deciding on scores for all six categories. Moving toward this expanded scoring strengthens their understanding of the many factors that writing comprises, and it also gives them insight into the ways evaluators of *their* writing tests might proceed.

As a closing note, we have allowed students to revise based on peer feedback from this minilesson, but the process can also be adapted to having students take multiple practice timed-writing tests with no revision, as in the Advanced Placement model that follows (see page 211).

State Writing Tests

Students benefit from learning about scoring systems when their own writing will be subjected to this kind of evaluation. Having students study rubrics like those in Online 8.1 and Online 8.5 and asking students to use them to evaluate pieces of writing helps them understand how scoring works at the same time that it gives them new ways to think more generally about the quality of writing. One form of writing on demand faced by many students is a state-mandated writing test. Teachers can usually obtain detailed information—including sample questions, rubrics, and examples of student responses—from their state department of education. Typically the state writing test is linked to standards and benchmarks for English language arts, so it is a good idea to begin by sharing the state standards with students. Here, for example, are Florida's *Sunshine State Standards for Writing:*

Typically the state writing test is linked to standards and benchmarks for English language arts, so it is a good idea to begin by sharing the standards with students.

Standard l: The student uses writing processes effectively.

1. Selects and uses appropriate prewriting strategies, such as brainstorming, graphic organizers, and outlines.

2. Drafts and revises writing that is focused, purposeful, and reflects insight into the writing situation; has an organizational pattern that provides for a logical progression of ideas; has effective use of transitional devices that contribute to a sense of completeness; has support that is substantial, specific, relevant, and concrete; demonstrates a commitment to and involvement with the subject; uses creative writing strategies as appropriate to the purposes of the paper; demonstrates a mature command

of language with freshness of expression; has varied sentence structure; has few, if any, convention errors in mechanics, usage, punctuation, and spelling.

3. Produces final documents that have been edited for correct spelling; correct punctuation, including commas, colons, and common use of semicolons; correct capitalization; correct sentence formation; correct instances of possessives, subject-verb agreement, instances of noun-pronoun agreement, and the intentional use of fragments for effect; and correct formatting that appeals to readers, including appropriate use of a variety of graphics, tables, charts, and illustrations in both standard and innovative forms.

Standard 2: The student writes to communicate ideas and information effectively.

1. Writes text, notes, outlines comments, and observations that demonstrate comprehension and synthesis of content, processes, and experiences from a variety of media.

2. Organizes information using appropriate systems.

3. Writes fluently for a variety of occasions, audiences, and purposes, making appropriate choices regarding style, tone, level of detail, and organization.

A class could look at standards from its own state (they can usually be obtained from the state department of education's website) and discuss the qualities of writing that are given preeminence. Florida's standards, for example, give clear emphasis to processes of writing and to rhetorical and formal features of writing. Starting with state standards, one can then turn to the rubric used in state writing tests. In the case of the Florida standards, for instance, putting them next to the rubric used to evaluate the writing portion of the Florida Comprehensive Assessment Test shows how these standards are translated into criteria for assessing writing. Here is the rubric:

Six points. The writing is focused and purposeful, and it reflects insight into the writing situation. The organizational pattern provides for a logical progression of ideas. Effective use of transitional devices contributes to a sense of completeness. The development of the support is substantial, specific, relevant, and concrete. The writer shows commitment to and involvement with the subject and may use creative writing strategies. The writing demonstrates a mature command of language with freshness of expression. Sentence structure is varied, and few, if any, convention errors occur in mechanics, usage, punctuation, and spelling.

Five points. The writing is focused on the topic, and its organizational pattern provides for a logical progression of ideas. Effective use of transitional devices contributes to a sense of completeness. The support is developed through ample use of specific details and examples. The writing demonstrates a mature command of language, and there is variation in sentence structure. The response generally follows the conventions of mechanics, usage, punctuation, and spelling.

Four points. The writing is focused on the topic and includes few, if any, loosely related ideas. An organizational pattern is apparent, and it is strengthened by the use of transitional devices. The support is consistently developed, but it may lack specificity. Word choice is adequate, and variation in sentence structure is demonstrated. The response generally follows the conventions of mechanics, usage, punctuation, and spelling.

Three points. The writing is focused but may contain ideas that are loosely connected to the topic. An organizational pattern is demonstrated, but the response may lack a logical progression of ideas. Development of support is uneven. Word choice is adequate, and some variation in sentence structure is demonstrated. The response generally follows the conventions of mechanics, usage, punctuation, and spelling.

Two points. The writing addresses the topic but may lose focus by including extraneous or loosely related ideas. The organizational pattern usually includes a beginning, middle, and ending, but these elements may be brief. The development of the support may be erratic and nonspecific, and ideas may be repeated. Word choice may be limited, predictable, or vague. Errors may occur in the basic conventions of sentence structure, mechanics, usage, and punctuation, but commonly used words are usually spelled correctly.

One point. The writing addresses the topic but may lose focus by including extraneous or loosely related ideas. The response may have an organizational pattern, but it may lack a sense of completeness or closure. There is little if any development of the support ideas, and the support may consist of generalizations or fragmentary lists. Limited or inappropriate word choice may obscure meaning. Frequent and blatant errors may occur in the basic conventions of sentence structure, mechanics, usage, and punctuation, and commonly used words may be misspelled.

Unscorable. The paper is unscorable because

- the response is not related to what the prompt requested the student to do,

- the response is simply a rewording of the prompt,

- the response is a copy of a published work,

- the student refused to write,

- the response is illegible,

- the response is written in a foreign language,

- the response is incomprehensible (words are arranged in such a way that no meaning is conveyed),

- the response contains an insufficient amount of writing to determine if the student was attempting to address the prompt, or

- the writing folder is blank.

A close reading of this rubric reveals how many features of writing named in the *Sunshine State Standards* are included in the rubric. Notice, for example, how the category *focus* is described in each of the six score points. It is possible to trace a direct line between many of the terms in the standards and the criteria included in the rubric. A similar pattern of connection is evident between the standards and rubrics used by many states, and students can benefit from seeing how the rubric for their state writing test evolved from the standards.

Once students have compared state standards with the rubric used to evaluate the state writing test, they can use the state rubric to evaluate their peers' writing as they did using the rubric in Online 8.1. States typically release prompts used in prior years, and students can write in response to one of these, perhaps even in a timed-writing context, and then score one another's essays using the state rubric.

Many teachers do not, of course, teach AP courses, but the prompts and scoring system merit the attention of anyone who is interested in connecting best practices with strategies for success on writing tests.

The Advanced Placement Exams

The Advanced Placement (AP) tests of the College Board include two that focus on English: the English Language and Composition exam and the English Literature and Composition exam. As the titles suggest, both exams require writing, but since the English Language and Composition exam is the one typically used to exempt students from the first-year writing course at college, we will focus on it.

Many teachers do not, of course, teach AP courses, but the prompts and scoring system merit the attention of anyone who is interested in connecting best practices with strategies for success on writing tests. The AP requires students to write forty-minute essays, and rubrics are designed for specific prompts. Students can benefit from working with the level of complexity offered by AP prompts, and it is also valuable for them to see how rubrics can address specifics of a given prompt. Here, for example, is an AP prompt:

An AP Prompt

ONLINE
8.7

In his 1998 book *Life in the Movies: How Entertainment Conquered Reality,* Neal Gabler wrote the following:

> One does not necessarily have to cluck in disapproval to admit that entertainment is all the things its detractors say it is: fun, effortless, sensational, mindless, formulaic, predictable, and subversive. In fact, one might argue that those are the very reasons so many people love it. At the same time, it is not hard to see why cultural aristocrats in the nineteenth century and intellectuals in the twentieth hated entertainment and why they predicted, as one typical nineteenth century critic railed, that its eventual effect would be "to overturn all morality, to poison the springs of domestic happiness, to dissolve the ties of our social order, and to involve our country in ruin."

Write a thoughtful and carefully constructed essay in which you use specific evidence to defend, challenge, or qualify the assertion that entertainment has the capacity to "ruin" society.

Students, whether or not they are in AP classes, can benefit from analyzing a prompt like this rhetorically, using the strategies discussed in Chapter 3. They would also benefit from writing a response to it, and they could then score one another's essays using the AP guide. The scoring guide for this question follows. It is general enough to be used with a variety of essays, but the references to "ruin society" demonstrate that it was designed for the entertainment prompt.

Scoring Guide

9 Essays earning a score of 9 meet the criteria for 8 papers and, in addition, are especially sophisticated in their argument or demonstrate particularly impressive control of language.

8 Essays earning a score of 8 recognize the complexity of the claim that entertainment has the capacity to "ruin" society and successfully establish and support their own position by using appropriate evidence to develop their argument. Their prose demonstrates an

ability to control a wide range of the elements of effective writing but is not flawless.

7 Essays earning a score of 7 fit the description of 6 essays but are distinguished by more complete or more cogent argumentation or a more mature prose style.

6 Essays earning a score of 6 demonstrate an adequate understanding of the claim and adequately establish and support their own position about entertainment's ability to "ruin" society. Their arguments are generally sound and provide sufficient evidence, but they are less developed or less cogent than essays earning higher scores. The writing may contain lapses in diction or syntax, but generally the prose is clear.

5 Essays earning a score of 5 may have a less adequate understanding of the claim and/or may offer limited, inconsistent, or unevenly developed positions of their own. The writing may contain lapses in diction or syntax, but it usually conveys the writer's ideas adequately.

4 Essays earning a score of 4 respond to the prompt inadequately. They may have difficulty understanding the claim or establishing their own position and/or may use evidence that is inappropriate or insufficient to develop their own position. The prose generally conveys the writer's ideas but may suggest immature control of writing.

3 Essays earning a score of 3 meet the criteria for the score of 4 but demonstrate less success in developing their own position or less control of writing.

2 Essays earning a score of 2 demonstrate little success in understanding the claim and/or in developing their own position. These essays may misunderstand the prompt, fail to present an argument, or substitute a simpler task by merely responding to the question tangentially with unrelated or inappropriate evidence. The prose often demonstrates consistent weaknesses in writing, such as a lack of development or organization, grammatical problems, or a lack of control.

1 Essays earning a score of 1 meet the criteria for the score of 2 but are especially simplistic in their argument or are weak in their control of writing.

0 Indicates an on-topic response that receives no credit, such as one that merely repeats the prompt.

— Indicates a blank response or one that is completely off topic.

One of the benefits of working with AP prompts and rubrics is that their relative complexity offers another way to help students develop a meta-cognitive understanding of their own writing processes. Here is how one teacher set up a reflective and self-regulating system of peer holistic scoring for the practice timed essays the students wrote in class:

1. Students wrote a practice forty-minute essay in response to the AP entertainment prompt.

2. The teacher collected the essays, removed the names, and photocopied them. (To remove the possibility of handwriting identification, one can used typed papers, but it is more authentic to use handwritten ones since the test, as of this writing, is administered without the use of computers.)

3. The teacher helped students learn to use the rubric by

   • discussing the language of the rubric, focusing on terms like *cogent argument* and *lapses in diction* that may have been unfamiliar to students

   • considering the similarities between the rubric and the prompt, paying particular attention to the complexity of the claim about entertainment ruining society

4. The teacher had the whole class use the rubric to score one paper and compare scores by using the following method:

   • writing all the scores on the board

   • considering the range of scores represented

   • asking students to explain the scores they gave

   • inviting students at extreme ends of the range of scores to consider changing their scores

   • explaining this process of coming to agreement on scores as *norming,* a process that evaluators undergo each time they score writing tests.

After students have participated in an initial norming session, similar to the one described in the first minilesson in this chapter, they can benefit from further experience with norming, and they can work with more of the papers written by the class in response to the entertainment prompt. They could, for

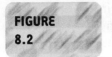

FIGURE
8.2

Range Finding

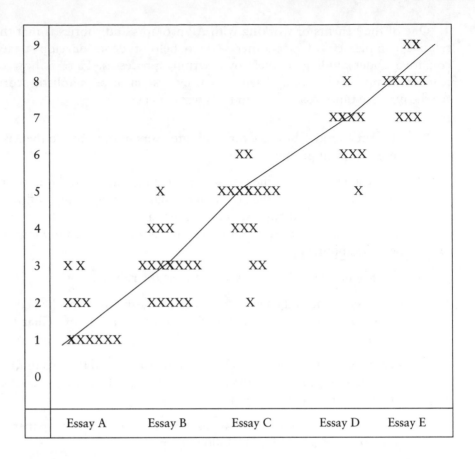

example, read and score two or three more essays as homework and then participate in another round of norming in class the next day. Alternatively, they could try norming within small groups, coming to consensus on the score for each essay.

Range Finding

If student responses to the prompt by Gabler appear to cover a broad range of scores, students can also participate in range finding. By showing how students' scores for several papers cluster, range finding helps students (like adult evaluators) see the development of agreement among evaluators. Teachers can select five essays that cover all or most of the range of scores from 1 through 9 and ask students to read and score them. Alternatively, the teacher can select sample essays from another source.

When students report their scores, the teacher can ask for all the scores for each essay in turn and put each score on a chart like the one in Figure 8.2 rather than using the numerical scores.

If the norming has been successful, a pattern like the one in Figure 8.2 will emerge, and students will have visual evidence that they have learned to rank papers within a range with some degree of accuracy. If students receive grades correlated with scores (A = 1, B = 3, C = 5, D = 7, E = 9) it will boost their confidence immensely, and they will begin to see that grading essays is not merely subjective. They will also begin to understand a complex rubric from the inside, which will make them better evaluators of their own writing. Perhaps most important, they will also begin to trust their peers to give a fair score, which is invaluable for teachers who want to make scoring a regular part of class work. A writing assignment like the following writer's notebook will provide useful information about student confidence and impressions.

Writer's Notebook

What is the most important thing you have learned about scoring writing from your experiences with the AP prompt and rubric? Describe your level of confidence in the scores produced by your peers and explain how you came to feel this way.

Scoring Regularly

Teachers who want to make scoring a regular part of writing instruction can introduce a variety of rubrics, have students help develop assignment-specific ones, or use a familiar one consistently. Regardless of the way the rubric is selected or developed, students can learn a good deal about writing by continually participating in scoring sessions. The following strategies can make the scoring process go smoothly:

1. Assign each student a number and record the name and number for each essay on a chart like the following one.

2. Give students their numbers and ask them to use the number instead of a name on papers that will be scored.

3. Ask students to submit two copies of each essay that will be scored.

4. Give the copies of each student essay to two graders (each student will have two essays to score).

5. Tell graders to score the essays and write a justification for the score, tying their justification to the language of the rubric they are using.

6. Collect the scores and enter them on the chart.

Student Name	Number on Essay	Grader 1's Name and Score	Grader 2's Name and Score

If the two graders' scores are the same or vary by only one point on a 1–9 scale, the score can be entered on the chart and perhaps even translated into a grade, thus reducing the teacher's paper load. If the scores vary by more than one point, the teacher can meet briefly with the two graders to discuss their differences and help the graders agree upon a score.

Evaluators who score papers for any writing test need to participate in continual renorming. Our experience as evaluators for writing tests is that renorming occurs almost daily, and students likewise need regular opportunities to renorm their scoring. Teachers can do this by having the entire class score one paper or by having students work in small groups in which they are required to come to consensus on a given essay.

The benefits of continued scoring throughout the year are several.

The benefits of continued scoring throughout the year are several. Students gain an insider perspective on how graders score papers in writing tests. They become more adept at evaluating writing and gain confidence that they and their peers can make good judgments about the quality of writing. They learn to use more precise language to describe features of writing, and all of these abilities carry over to other contexts, including writing on demand.

The best evidence for our claims comes in the form of testimony offered by students themselves. Here, for example, is a reflection written by a student who participated in a scoring session with his classmates. Demetrius, the student, was asked to write about whether he felt the score assigned by his peers was fair, and he wrote the following response:

> I believe my score was almost fair. I received an 8, but I think I should have gotten a 7 because I didn't particularly like my word choice and my hold of language. I figure that I could have used either better figurative language or shown greater control of the essay. I look at it now and it seems rather bland, but of course I'm not cutting myself any slack because of the 40-minute handicap. Anyway, I was satisfied with my work though.

Demetrius' written reflection showed that he had internalized some concepts from the rubric, such as *word choice*, *figurative language,* and *control of language*. It also showed that Demetrius had a great degree of ownership of his writing. Since no points were given for what was said on the reflection, we can safely say that Demetrius' engagement in this reflection was not grade motivated. By being able to step back and critique his own work, he acquired an important skill for his future writing—that of taking critique from others and also being a good self-critic.

Another student, Arianna, showed similar engagement in her written reflection:

> Yes, I think my essay deserved the 5 that it received. My diction and syntax could definitely use some improvement, considering that some phrases and sentences were hard to read. I also agree that I lack in discussion of my thesis. My essay doesn't discuss ironic uses or attitude. I believe I had a good thesis, which allows me to receive that score of 5. I feel I had an adequate understanding of Sontag's attitude toward and use of metaphor. I also agree that I didn't clearly demonstrate the relationship between details of the passage and the attitudes and use. I feel I could discuss more effectively Sontag's use of metaphor. I could also work on my organization and develop my thesis more clearly. I would also write in a more sophisticated tone.

Arianna was a student for whom the frequent scoring sessions and reflective writings were especially useful. At the beginning of the year, she did not have a clear understanding of what essay prompts were calling for, and in this mid-year reflection, one can see that she had developed a good grasp of what the prompt demanded along with a pretty accurate assessment of her ability to meet those demands. She continued to work on bringing her writing into line with expectations, and frequent opportunities to evaluate writing and reflect on that evaluation were particularly useful for her. Students like Arianna and Demetrius not only learn more about writing through scoring but also become much less dependent on their teachers and begin to trust their own ability to evaluate writing.

Key Points for Reflection

Although peer response writing groups are common in writing classes, few teachers engage students in actually scoring the writing of their peers. Yet learning about rubrics and using them to score one another's writing can help students become better writers as well as enhance their ability to evaluate their own work and that of their peers. In the process, students can begin to see the connections between standards and the scoring guides used by evaluators; they can learn to use more precise language to describe any piece of writing; and they can develop confidence in their ability to describe the quality of writing. Accordingly, we believe:

- Rubrics provide useful information about what is valued in writing.

- Students can learn about rubrics in order to both respond to peer writing and reflect on their own writing.

- Students can be trained, as adult evaluators are, to score each other's writing reliably.

- Students' development as writers can be enhanced by scoring writing.

Success with Writing on ACT, SAT, AP, and Essay Exams

Nothing goes by luck in composition. It allows of no tricks. The best you can write will be the best you are.

—HENRY DAVID THOREAU

Experience has shown me that there are no miracles in writing. The only thing that produces good writing is hard work.

—ISAAC BASHEVIS SINGER

Success comes to a writer, as a rule, so gradually that it is always something of a shock to him to look back and realize the heights to which he has climbed.

—P. G. WODEHOUSE

We wish we could say that we had the perfect trick or that we could show teachers how to enact a miracle in students' writing, but Thoreau and Singer have it right—hard work is essential in writing, hard work for both teachers and students. Nevertheless, success is possible. The principles we have outlined in this book will help students perform well on writing tests at the same time that they become good writers, especially if these principles are infused into an already sound writing program that students have engaged in for several years. Our aim has been to highlight those features of best practice that are most applicable to writing on demand. To summarize, the main principles of writing on demand are the following:

[Our] principles . . . will help students perform well on writing tests . . . especially if these principles are infused into an already sound writing program.

- thinking backward

- engaging the processes of writing

- analyzing the rhetorical features of prompts

- understanding forms of assessment

- reading closely

- analyzing the prompt environment

- working at the sentence level

- involving students in scoring writing

Most of this book has suggested ways of applying these principles to writing instruction in general. In this final chapter we address ways of employing these principles for specific forms of writing on demand—the ACT, the SAT, AP Literature and Composition exams, and essay exams.

ACT Writing Test

The ACT Writing Test expects students to demonstrate the skills important for the college courses they will soon take, skills such as forming an opinion, supporting it with appropriate evidence for the audience, organizing and making connections between ideas, and expressing themselves in clear, effective language. It asks students to demonstrate their accomplishment as writers, not their aptitude for writing. Accordingly, everything teachers do to prepare student writers matters. As a first step, a class might look at a successful student response to an ACT test question and think backward about possible prompts and writer strategies that might have led to the writing of this response. Here is one sample essay; others can be found on the ACT website at *www.act.org*.

ONLINE
9.1

Sample Essay from ACT Website

Many high schools have adopted dress codes that set guidelines for what students can wear in the school building. Many people disagree with these policies. Though arguments can be made for either side, my opinion is that a dress code can have a very positive outcome for several reasons.

First of all, a dress code promotes student equality and acceptance. High school students are at a vulnerable age when they want to be accepted. If a teenager feels as though they don't belong, it can lead to serious emotional problems. Some students get so upset that they withdraw from family, their grades fail, and they may become hostile. The shootings at Columbine High School were the response of two boys who felt unaccepted. Students following a dress code would look more alike. This helps all students feel like part of a group as well as eliminates problems of not wearing the "right" clothes for students affected by poverty who can't afford to.

Second, a dress code eliminates distractions in the classroom. Students who wear tight clothing could be uncomfortable and not able to concentrate. Some students may feel peer pressure to wear revealing clothes they believe are immodest just because it's in style. This would make them uncomfortable in a different way but also keep them from concentrating. Tight and revealing clothes can also affect the rest of the students especially the opposite sex, by catching the eye and causing people to think about things other than what they should be learning.

Lastly, a dress code can contribute to students' education by teaching students how to dress for the working world. Since most students will have to work sometime after they graduate, it's important that they know what to wear for a job. A dress code can teach students to distinguish between what is appropriate to wear and what is not.

While many people are afraid dress codes restrict personal freedom it is important to remember that a dress code is only for school and that students can express their individual style on their own time. Since a dress code in school can make students feel more accepted, decrease distractions in the classroom and help students prepare themselves for a job; it's not surprising that many schools have adopted dress codes.

In discussing a sample essay, teachers can refer to "thinking backward," the concept introduced in Chapter 1. Questions to be discussed could include the overall impression created by the essay, its most effective features, and the ways it can be compared with other pieces of writing. Then teachers might invite student writers to work with a sample prompt.

MINILESSON

Goal: To help students familiarize themselves with the requirements of the ACT Writing Test using on-demand writing principles.

Talking Points:

- The prediction and reflection you'll do in your writer's notebooks will help you prepare for and process your learning in this lesson.

- We'll use the prompt analysis questions (see Chapter 3 for a detailed discussion) to think about possible prompts and rubrics for the essay we'll be reading.

• We'll use the context analysis questions (see Chapter 6 for a detailed discussion) to discover the context of the prompt, which will bring out hidden or implicit requirements of the essay exam.

Activities:

Writer's Notebook

Write in response to the following questions:

• What do you think you will be asked to do on the ACT Writing Test?

• What skills do you think will be tested?

• How do you feel about writing an essay under timed conditions?

To reinforce the value of this writing, teachers can give students a chance to share their responses in pairs, in small groups, or with the whole class. Teachers could list skills on the board for later discussion.

Once students have had an opportunity to write about their expectations of the ACT, they can test them with sample writing prompts like this one:

> Your college administration is considering whether or not there should be a physical education requirement for undergraduates. The administration has asked students for their views on the issue and has announced that its final decision will be based on how such a requirement would affect the overall educational mission of the college. Write a letter to the administration arguing whether or not there should be a physical education requirement for undergraduates at your college.
>
> In your essay, take a position on this question. You may write about either one of the two points of view given, or you may present a different point of view on this question. Use specific reasons and examples to support your position. (Do not concern yourself with letter formatting; simply begin your letter, "Dear Administration.")
>
> In an actual testing situation, your response will be evaluated by how well you formulate an assertion and support it with a coherent and logical argument.

As a first step, students can use the prompt analysis questions to understand the text of the prompt more fully. As always, we include typical student responses to the question.

1. What *mode* of writing is this prompt calling for, and how do we know?

   The prompt asks students "to write a letter to the administration arguing whether or not there should be a physical education requirement for undergraduates at your college." The word *arguing* points to the rhetorical mode of argumentation.

2. What is the *topic*?

   The student's assertion about whether or not there should be a physical education requirement for undergraduates.

3. Is there an intended *audience* for the writing task?

   Yes, students are asked to address their arguments to a hypothetical administrator at their hypothetical college. Students should think about what this imagined individual's stake might be in both sides of the argument. How are college administrators different from high school administrators? Would a college administrator be interested in requiring a physical education course? Why or why not? What is the best tone to take to convince this audience?

4. What is the *purpose* of writing about this issue?

   To persuade the administrator over to the student's position about the physical education requirement.

5. What is my *role* as a writer in achieving the purpose?

   To use the best reasons and examples possible to persuade the student's audience.

After students have analyzed the sample ACT prompt, the class can turn to context analysis with the same prompt:

1. What is my *time* limit?

   Thirty minutes.

2. What kinds of *writing aids* are available? Is there a rubric, a writing checklist, a list of dos and don'ts?

   Every ACT prompt is accompanied by the paragraph that begins "In your essay take a position on this question." Clearly the test emphasizes students' ability to select a viewpoint and offer arguments that support it.

   This would be a good time to examine the scoring guide for the ACT Writing Test to develop a further understanding of what evaluators will be considering as they read student essays.

Scoring Guide from ACT Website

Score = 6

Essays within this score range demonstrate effective skill in responding to the task.
The essay shows a clear understanding of the task. The essay takes a position on the issue and may offer a critical context for discussion. The essay addresses complexity by examining different perspectives on the issue, or by evaluating the implications and/or complications of the issue, or by fully responding to counter-arguments to the writer's position. Development of ideas is ample, specific, and logical. Most ideas are fully elaborated. A clear focus on the specific issue in the prompt is maintained. The organization of the essay is clear: the organization may be somewhat predictable or it may grow from the writer's purpose. Ideas are logically sequenced. Most transitions reflect the writer's logic and are usually integrated into the essay. The introduction and conclusion are effective, clear, and well developed. The essay shows a good command of language. Sentences are varied and word choice is varied and precise. There are few, if any, errors to distract the reader.

Score = 5

Essays within this score range demonstrate competent skill in responding to the task.
The essay shows a clear understanding of the task. The essay takes a position on the issue and may offer a broad context of discussion. The essay shows recognition of complexity by partially evaluating the implications and/or complications of the issue, or by responding to counter-arguments to the writer's position. Development of ideas is specific and logical. Most ideas are elaborated, with clear movement between specific statements and specific reasons, examples, and details. Focus on the specific issue in the prompt is maintained. The organization of the essay is clear, although it may be predictable. Ideas are logically sequenced, although simple and obvious transitions may be used. The introduction and conclusion are clear and generally well developed. Language is competent. Sentences are somewhat varied and word choice is sometimes varied and precise. There may be a few errors, but they are rarely distracting.

Score = 4

Essays within this score range demonstrate adequate skill in responding to the task.
The essay shows an understanding of the task. The essay takes a position on the issue and may offer some context for discussion. The essay may show some recognition of complexity by providing some response to counter-arguments to the writer's position. Development of ideas is adequate, with some movement between general statements and specific reasons, examples, and details. Focus on the specific issue in the prompt is maintained throughout most of the essay. The organization of the essay is apparent but predictable. Some evidence of logical sequencing of ideas is apparent, although most transitions are simple and obvious. The introduction and conclusion are clear and somewhat developed. Language is adequate, with some sentence variety and appropriate word choice. There may be some distracting errors, but they don't impede understanding.

Score = 3

Essays within this score demonstrate some developing skill in responding to the task.

The essay shows some understanding of the task. The essay takes a position on the issue but does not offer a context for discussion. The essay may acknowledge a counter-argument to the writer's position, but its development is brief or unclear. Development of ideas is limited and may be repetitious, with little, if any, movement between general statements and specific reasons, examples, and details. Focus on the general topic is maintained, but focus on the specific issue in the prompt may not be maintained. The organization of the essay is simple. Ideas are logically grouped within parts of the essay, but there is little or no evidence of logical sequencing of ideas. Transitions, if used, are simple and obvious. An introduction and conclusion are clearly discernible but underdeveloped. Language shows a basic control. Sentences show little variety and word choice is appropriate. Errors may be distracting and may occasionally impede understanding.

Score = 2

Essays within this score range demonstrate inconsistent or weak skill in responding to the task.

The essay shows a weak understanding of the task. The essay may not take a position on the issue, or the essay may take a position but fail to convey reasons to support that position, or the essay make take a position but fail to maintain a stance. There is little or no recognition of a counter-argument to the writer's position. The essay is thinly developed. If examples are given, they are general and may not be clearly relevant. The essay may include extensive repetition of the writer's ideas or of ideas in the prompt. Focus on the general topic is maintained, but focus on the specific issue in the prompt may not be maintained. There is some indication of an organizational structure, and some logical grouping of ideas within parts of the essay is apparent. Transitions if used are simple and obvious, and they may be inappropriate or misleading. An introduction and conclusion are discernible but minimal. Sentence structure and word choice are usually simple. Errors may be frequently distracting and may sometimes impede understanding.

Score = 1

Essays within this score range show little or no skill in responding to the task.

The essay shows little or no understanding of the task. If the essay takes a position it fails to convey reasons to support that position. The essay is minimally developed. The essay may include excessive repetition of the writer's ideas or of ideas in the prompt. Focus on the general topic is usually maintained, but focus on the specific issue in the prompt may or not be maintained. There is little or no evidence of an organizational structure or of the logical grouping of ideas. Transitions are rarely used. If present, an introduction and conclusion are minimal. Sentence structure and word choice are simple. Errors may be frequently distracting and may significantly impede understanding.

No Score

Blank, off-topic, or illegible

3. What are the *targeted skills*? What particular thinking or writing skills does this test require? What standards are being assessed?

   Students must be able to think critically, take a position, and support this position persuasively while keeping in mind a hypothetical audience.

4. What kind of *format* is expected? Will a five-paragraph essay work here, or is some other format, like a letter, required?

   Students are asked to use the format of a letter, starting with the salutation "Dear Administrator." The ACT is not a minimum-proficiency exam, and college-bound students will be taking it in competition with each other for college admission. Therefore, it is likely students will have to write an essay that is more sophisticated in structure than the five-paragraph essay in order to compete for a top score. In using the letter format—salutation, body, closing—students should keep in mind that this is not a personal letter, and therefore, they should avoid writing too informally.

5. What *specialized expectations* are implicit in this particular writing task? For example, is length or audience specified?

   There is an implicit expectation that students will address the following line from the prompt: "The administration has asked students for their views on the issue and has announced that its final decision will be based on how such a requirement would affect the overall educational mission of the college." The close reader will logically want to address the connection between the overall requirement and the mission of the college, since that connection is what the administration's decision will be based on and students are tasked with persuading the administration. The test evaluators are probably expecting strong reasons and examples, as well as fluent writing.

After discussing context analysis with students, teachers might ask the class, "Where do we go from here? Now that we have analyzed the prompt and the context, what is our next step in preparing to write the essay?" Students will probably reply that they need to select a position to take. As a class, they could brainstorm possible positions to take, possibly listing them on the board. Then teachers could ask students to choose one position and ask questions to generate material:

• What are the reasons I can use to support my position?

• What examples and support can I use to back up my position?

A visual organizer like the following might be useful to students:

Argument Essay Template

ONLINE
9.3

My position on the topic: I oppose the PE requirement

Reasons My Position Is Valid	*Examples to Back Up My Reasons*
1. College requirements should focus on academics	1. High tuition makes each credit expensive
	2. Students can participate in athletics or join a gym
2.	1. 2.
3.	1. 2.

Students will, no doubt, generate varying numbers of reasons and supports for the position they might take. Once everyone has brainstormed enough material to be able to write the essay, you might walk them through the rest of the process of completing it, beginning by discussing the circumstances in which evaluators will be working. Given the sheer volume of essays, readers will have to work quickly, and students should think about how they can make their work clear and easy for the readers. In particular, they might review the importance of varying sentence structures and using transitional words effectively (see Chapter 7).

After students have completed their essays, preferably using the thirty-minute time limit so they can get a feel for how much they can accomplish within that amount of time, they can use the ACT scoring guide (see Online 9.2) to rate one another's essays. The process of using the scoring guide will give them further insight into how evaluators will look at their writing.

As a final step, students can return to their writer's notebooks and consider what they thought at the beginning of this exploration of the ACT writing test.

Writer's Notebook

Read over your first writer's notebook entry.

- How right were you in your predictions about what you will be asked to do on the ACT essay exam and what skills will be tested? What did you learn from our analysis of the prompt and the scoring guide?

- How have your feelings about writing an essay under timed conditions changed? What is your plan for writing on demand? Do you still have unanswered questions?

Assessment:

Reading the students' writer's notebook entries will allow you to assess student understanding of this lesson.

SAT Writing Exam

Before looking at the SAT writing exam, it is worth noting that the name of the SAT has changed in recent years. It was originally called the Scholastic Aptitude Test, implying that it measured students' capacity or ability to learn, their *aptitude,* rather than what they had already learned. Later the SAT was called the Scholastic *Assessment* Test, and now SAT does not stand for anything. Like the ACT Writing Test, the writing test in the SAT does not measure students' aptitude for writing; it measures what they can already do, what they have already achieved as writers. Students who have learned the principles of writing on demand within the context of writing instruction based on best practices will be well prepared to demonstrate what they have achieved as writers.

The SAT writing test is similar to the ACT in many ways, but it is slightly shorter. Students have twenty-five, rather than thirty, minutes to complete the essay. Teachers can find sample essays and prompts along with the scoring guide on the SAT website, *www.sat.com,* and students can benefit from thinking backward about essays, applying prompt analysis and context analysis to prompts, and using the scoring guide to assess one another's writing. Completing these steps, along with reinforcing the guiding principles of this book, will help students become more knowledgeable about the SAT writing exam and build their confidence as writers who can meet the challenge of demonstrating their proficiency in writing on demand.

Obviously, students will be under tremendous pressure to do well on the ACT and/or the SAT because it affects their entrance into college. Checking the ACT and SAT websites frequently for new information about prompts and scoring guides is important for giving students practice using prompt analysis and context analysis so they will understand what is required of them.

AP Exams

Even teachers who are not teaching an Advanced Placement course can find it useful to have students analyze prompts from the AP test. These prompts, typically more involved than those on other writing tests, can help students develop the ability to read and respond to a wide variety of writing tests. AP exams—Literature and Composition and Language and Composition—are designed to be ranked (1–9), so a holistic scoring guide is used, rather than an analytic rating guide. This test is not geared to state standards, but to the College Board's curriculum for the AP courses, a curriculum that aims to be similar to first-year college writing courses. Therefore, it is helpful to look at the description for each AP course.

Compared with other writing tests, prompts for the AP essays are very complex, so a significant amount of time and effort should be spent in having students analyze the prompts. Ideally, this analysis will be introduced early in the AP course so that students become familiar with the prompts' shape and complexity. There are other factors to note: in the Advanced Placement exams, students are asked to write three essays in 120 minutes, or 40 minutes per essay. The essay portion counts for 55 percent of the total score. The multiple-choice reading section counts for 45 percent. Partly because they have more time and partly because of the college-level demands, the expectations for students who write AP exams are higher.

It is immensely helpful to students if they have an awareness of what types of essays they can expect to write, even if they cannot know the exact topic. As with any timed writing task, anticipating the structure of the prompt saves precious time that can then be spent in the actual planning and writing of the essay. Those who score AP exams regularly indicate that students should be careful not to quote extensively from the passages. Summary does not have a place in these essays; rather, analysis is essential. In addition, readers of the AP exam often express a wish that students had taken more time and/or care in planning their essays. While readers understand that some students write their way into a higher score, the general consensus is that more effort needs to be put into prewriting. Scorers appreciate those students who are close readers—it is an essential skill for both types of AP exams.

Readers of the AP exam often express a wish that students had taken more time and/or care in planning their essays.

Students often wonder whether AP readers are expecting a five-paragraph theme. They are not. In our experiences as and discussions with exam readers, we found that evaluators respond most favorably to essays that are not formulaic and often make positive comments about essays that avoid the five-paragraph format, introducing more variety into the structure. Readers score several hundred essays on the same topic, so they appreciate variety in structure, especially structure that serves the student's individual ideas while still fulfilling the reader's desire for a clear beginning, middle, and end.

Perceptive analysis, persuasion, and support are other important features of top-scoring AP exams.

Students who have command of language, defined as minimal problems with usage, strength and variety in sentence structure, and a sophisticated vocabulary typically score well on AP exams. When readers see less use of the formulaic five-paragraph essay in the exams they read, they usually see that as a positive. Perceptive analysis, persuasion, and support are other important features of top-scoring AP exams. Students who read closely, think deeply, and write analytically are usually successful.

AP Language and Composition Exam

The AP Language and Composition exam focuses more on writing than on literature, and it tends to draw more from strong nonfiction writers in various disciplines for its prompts. AP Language and Composition students should be developing sophisticated reading strategies to complement their writing. Here are the common types of prompts on the AP language exam:

- *Analysis of a reading passage:* In this prompt, students are asked to identify a central focus or the attitude of the writer toward his or her subject and the particular rhetorical devices the author uses to convey that attitude. Sometimes the attitude is defined for the students, and sometimes they are asked to identify it for themselves. Sometimes the writing techniques—such as figurative language, narrative structure, tone, and diction—are defined for the student, and sometimes the student gets to choose which rhetorical devices to analyze.

- *Persuasive essay:* This prompt asks the student to defend, challenge, or qualify a particular assertion. Students are encouraged to use evidence from their reading, observation, or experience to support their assertions.

- *Comparison-contrast essay:* Students are given two short reading passages by different authors and asked to compare and contrast the two essays. The essays may be two different interpretations of the same topic, in which case students may be asked to compare tone, diction, structure, manipulation of language, metaphor, or any other rhetorical device.

As can happen with any of these exams, changes are continually being made to the length and format of the AP Language and Composition exam. For example, as of this writing, AP teachers were expecting the style analysis essay question to be replaced with a miniature document-based essay. In a document-based essay, students have several documents (short paragraphs, cartoons, posters, etc.) on a controversial topic and are asked to take a stand and use at least three of the documents to support their position in the essay. The open-ended essay asks students to defend, challenge, or qualify a controversial statement. Chapter 8 includes more discussion about the prompts used in the Language and Composition exam.

AP Literature and Composition Exam

There are three kinds of questions on the AP Literature and Composition exam:

- *Poetry question:* Students are given a poem to read and asked to write an essay dealing with some aspect of the poem, such as organization, use of imagery, or the significance of the title. If there are any difficult words in the poem or obscure allusions, these are usually glossed, but no other writing aids are given.

- *Prose question:* Students are given a prose passage to read and told to write an essay about some aspect of the passage, such as the attitude of the narrator toward a character, the development of a theme or concept within the passage, or the use of literary devices. Directions usually include admonitions about making specific references to the text, attending to diction, and including plenty of detail.

- *Open question:* This prompt poses a question, makes an assertion, or provides a short quotation. Students are then asked to address the prompt, using one of the literary works listed or a comparable work of their own choice.

Here is a prompt typical of the prose ones in the AP Literature and Composition test. The questions of prompt analysis and context analysis can help students understand it more fully.

Prompt Typical of AP Literature and Composition Test

The naturalist and explorer John Muir has left us a journal of his life and thoughts that is brimming with insight and brilliance. Analyze the following passage for its diction, tone and syntax. Explain how these elements are well suited to the theme of this passage.

> There is love of wild nature in everybody, an ancient mother-love ever showing itself whether recognized or not, and however covered by cares and duties.
>
> In God's wildness lies the hope of the world—the great fresh unblighted, unredeemed wilderness. The galling harness of civilization drops off, and the wounds heal ere we are aware.
>
> I am often asked if I am not lonesome on my solitary excursions. It seems so self-evident that one cannot be lonesome where everything is wild and beautiful and busy and steeped with God that the question is hard to answer—seems silly.
>
> In the mountains, free, unimpeded, the imagination feeds on objects immense and eternal.
>
> To the Indian mind all nature was instinct with deity. A spirit was embodied in every mountain, stream, and waterfall.

Prompt Analysis

1. What *mode* of writing is this prompt calling for, and how do we know?

    The mode is analysis/persuasion. This is indicated with the verb *analyze* in the prompt. Implicit in the directions is a call to persuade readers that one's description of Muir's point of view is a reasonable one, given the passage.

2. What is the *topic*?

    The topic is two pronged: first, students have to discuss Muir's use of diction, tone, and syntax, and then they need to explain how these are effective for the message he is conveying.

3. Is there an intended *audience* for the writing task?

    There is no explicit audience, but students should assume their essay will be read by college and high school teachers who are very familiar with the passage. Because thousands of other students are writing on this topic, students need to distinguish themselves by the perceptiveness of their analyses, the forcefulness of their arguments, and the maturity of their control of language. A formal tone is expected.

4. What is the *purpose* of this piece of writing?

    To demonstrate the student's ability to read the passage closely and discern Muir's point of view and to convince the reader that the student understands the way Muir uses language and rhetorical features to convey this point of view.

5. What is my *role* as a writer in achieving the purpose?

    The writer's role is to speak authoritatively about his or her understanding of the passage. The writer should be persuasive and organized in creating an essay that fulfills this purpose. It is important that each assertion about language and rhetorical devices is supported and that devices are not merely identified, but also shown to be connected to the overall effect of the piece.

After students have analyzed the sample AP prompt, teachers can ask them to use context analysis questions:

1. What is my *time* limit?

    Writers have forty minutes per essay.

2. What kinds of *writing aids* are available? Is there a rubric, a writing checklist, a list of dos and don'ts?

    Very little besides the prompt is given to students at the time of the exam, so it is important for them to have some experience beforehand working with an AP scoring guide so they will get an idea of what qualities of their writing are valued. Here is a generic AP rubric that can help students understand the expectations of AP readers.

Holistic Rubric

ONLINE
9.5

8–9 Superior papers are specific in their references, cogent in their definitions, and consider a multiplicity of views. These essays need not be without flaws, but they demonstrate the writer's ability to analyze with insight and understanding and to control a wide range of the elements of effective composition. At all times, they stay focused and demonstrate an awareness of audience. The writer provides specific support—mostly through direct quotations—and connects the specifics to an overall meaning.

6–7 These papers are less thorough, less perceptive, or less specific than 8–9 papers. The specifics are still connected to an overall meaning, but they are less developed. They are well written, but with less maturity and control. While they demonstrate the writer's ability to analyze, they reveal a more limited understanding and less control of academic discourse than do the papers in the 8–9 range.

5 The writer doesn't contribute to a new understanding of the topic for the reader; superficiality characterizes these essays. Discussion of meaning may be formulaic, mechanical, or inadequately related to the chosen details. Typically, these essays reveal simplistic thinking and/or immature writing. They usually demonstrate inconsistent control over the elements of composition and are not as well conceived, organized, or developed as the upper-half papers. However, the writing is sufficient to convey the writer's ideas, stays mostly focused on the prompt, and contains at least some effort to produce analysis, direct or indirect.

3–4 Discussion is likely to be unpersuasive, perfunctory, underdeveloped, or misguided. The meaning they deduce may be inaccurate or insubstantial and not clearly related to the question. Part of the question may be omitted altogether. The writing may convey the writer's ideas, but it reveals weak control over such elements as diction, organization, syntax, or grammar. Typically these essays contain significant misinterpretation of the question or the work they discuss; they may also contain little, if any supporting evidence, and practice paraphrase and plot summary at the expense of analysis.

1–2 These essays compound the weakness of the essays in the 3–4 range and are frequently unacceptably brief. They are poorly written on several counts, including many distracting errors in grammar and mechanics. Although the writer may have made some effort to answer the question, the views presented have little clarity or coherence.

    While there are many AP holistic rubrics readily available online or in test-prep books, a list of dos and don'ts is not as easy to find. Here are some suggestions we have gleaned from AP teachers and readers:

- A title is not needed. Maybe 5 percent of students include them, so students should feel free to do so if they wish, but it neither adds nor detracts from the score, so certainly not much time (if any) should be spent working on a title.

- Clear handwriting is appreciated, but students should not make the mistake of taking the time to recopy their essays in their best handwriting. It just needs to be legible. If it is not legible, then the ideas cannot be scored.

- Revision is acceptable. Students can just draw a line through material they want the reader to disregard and insert new material where appropriate.

3. What are the *targeted skills*? What particular thinking or writing skills does this test require?

    Analysis is probably the most important thinking skill for this prompt. Being able to write persuasively, with a good control of language, is also targeted.

4. What kind of *format* is expected? Will a five-paragraph essay work here, or is some other format, like a letter, required?

    No particular format is required on AP essay exams; rather, students are assessed on their ability to create an organizational structure that makes sense considering the complex demands of the prompt. While some students find a five-paragraph essay fits their purposes, sometimes those essays can sound too formulaic. Students should concentrate on making sure their essay is focused and has a clear beginning, middle, and end. They should use transitions and let the structure of the essay echo the weighting of their ideas. Readers understand that these are first-draft productions, and they are often admonished to reward the writer for what he or she does well. That means that students who start out weak can still end up with a score in the upper half if they write their way into good insights. Students would do well to leave a few minutes at the end to read over their essays and correct any glaring errors or repetitious word choice. Sometimes the focus can also be clarified at the beginning of the essay.

5. What *specialized expectations* are implicit in this particular writing task? For example, is length or audience specified?

    No particular length or audience is specified. Students would do well not to overly criticize or praise the writer whose work they are analyzing. Often, comments such as "The writer was unclear in showing his point of view" reflect more the reader's weakness than the writer's. Plot summary is frowned upon, as the AP readers have the passage right in front of them and have read it dozens of times. Students must deal with *all* parts of the prompt in their essays. Creativity is good, but creativity alone will not ensure a high score.

Because AP prompts are so complex, we recommend spending a good deal of time in class analyzing them with students. Beyond the consideration of the previous questions, it may be helpful to have students create visual representations of what they are being asked to do.

AP Prompt Analysis

Prompt:
The naturalist and explorer John Muir has left us a journal of his life and thoughts that is brimming with insight and brilliance. Analyze the following passage for its diction, tone and syntax. Explain how these elements are well suited to the theme of this passage.

superficial topic	Muir's ideas	(Use the space below to *identify* theme, language, and devices.)
global focus	theme of passage	*The hope of the world lies in wild nature*
secondary foci	analyze diction, tone, and syntax	*descriptive, metaphorical, complex*

Student's controlling idea:
Through his use of descriptive language, metaphors, and complex syntax, Muir conveys the idea that the hope of the world lies in wild nature.

By analyzing the prompt in this way, students can develop a working thesis for drafting their essays.

Another approach to helping students become not just familiar with prompts, but comfortable with them is to have them write their own AP-style prompts for reading passages. In our experience, this writing provides a useful assessment of students' understanding of AP prompts, and of prompts in general. Here are some examples of prompts that students developed for Orwell's essay "Why I Write":

> Write an essay analyzing how Orwell conveys what he feels is the greatest motivation for writers. Take into consideration his different style of organization, his word choice, and the choice of details in connection with his ideas about the reasons for which writers write.

> Write an essay in which you analyze the first two paragraphs of George Orwell's "Why I Write." Analyze Orwell's tone and overall attitude toward his experience writing as a child. Consider his diction, use of allusion, and ambiguity.

These students clearly understood the two-pronged approach in AP prompts because they were able to imitate that feature of the prompts. They also understood that one prong is global and the other has to do with language and structure. In the first student prompt, the global (or principal) focus is identifying what Orwell believes is the "greatest motivation for writers," and the secondary focus is considering organization, word choice, and details. In the second student prompt, identifying "Orwell's tone and overall attitude toward his experience writing as a child" is the global idea. The secondary idea is to "consider his diction, use of allusion, and ambiguity." The students who created the first prompt also had a sense that there is a connection between the global and secondary issues. They asked the writer to analyze the secondary idea "in connection with his ideas about the reasons for which writers write," in other words, in connection with their global idea. Although this student-generated prompt lacks the stylistic sophistication of AP prompts, the students showed that they understood the basics of what an AP prompt is supposed to do. The second prompt contains the two levels but does not show the connection between them. This lack of connection opens the door for further instruction because it suggests that students might not make connections between the two levels when producing essays for the writing test.

Open Questions

In addition to prompts about selections of prose and poetry, the AP Literature and Composition Exam includes what is called an open question, meaning that students can write about a literary work of their choice. Some students have the impression that a personal response is called for in the open question, but our discussions with AP readers indicate that that is not a good choice. The issue of literary merit often generates considerable conversation—and dispute—among readers. If students do not want to write on the works listed with the question (usually about thirty or so), they can choose a novel or play of "comparable literary merit." Students choose many works off the list; several readers counted more than two hundred different literary works chosen by students. Some choices, like *Cat in the Hat,* are clearly unacceptable because they are neither novels nor are they comparable to a work like *Hamlet.* Sometimes readers don't agree on which works make good choices for writing the open question essay. For example, one reader appreciated essays written on Zora Neale Hurston's *Their Eyes Were Watching God,* while another reader felt the work was not "rich" enough to yield a top-scoring essay. Usually a suitable choice is one that has distinctive voice and style, has social concerns, deals with basic truths, deals with ambiguity, and has layers of meaning. So, for the AP Literature and Composition exam, students not only have to be able to write well but also have to have the ability to select texts that meet these criteria. Students can choose a work that is not widely known, but they must be aware of their audience and argue their case that the work has literary merit because a given reader may not be familiar with the work they have chosen.

Here is a prompt typical of those used in the open question:

> When we get to the end of a novel or play, our reading should have created a consistent tone, and we should be mindful of how some aspects of life have been intensified or even changed.
>
> Choose a play or novel that sustains a consistent tone. In a well-written essay, identify the aspects of life that are intensified or changed by the ending and explain its significance to the work as a whole. You may select a work from the list below or another novel or play of literary merit.
> *Bless Me, Ultima; Candide; Ceremony; The Color Purple; Crime and Punishment; Cry, the Beloved Country; Emma; Great Expectations; The Great Gatsby; Heart of Darkness; Invisible Man; Jane Eyre; King Lear; Moby-Dick; The Piano Lesson; The Portrait of a Lady; Praisesong for the Widow; A Raisin in the Sun; Song of Solomon; The Stone Angel; The Tempest; Their Eyes Were Watching God; Twelfth Night; Wuthering Heights*

Like many of the open question prompts, students must learn to distinguish between background information and the actual directions for writing the essay. In this case, the penultimate line of the prompt, *In a well-written essay, identify the aspects of life that are intensified or changed by the ending and explain its significance to the work as a whole,* tells students what to write. Just as students are asked to make a connection between the global prong and secondary prongs in the AP language prompts, in the open question of the AP literature exam, students are asked to make a connection between the particular quality of the work and the work as a whole. Again, prompt analysis offers a good way to examine the prompt, and teachers might use these questions to structure a discussion with students:

1. What *mode* of writing is this prompt calling for, and how do we know?

    The verb *explain* in the directions suggests the expository mode, but experience reading these exams and talking with other readers tells us that students are also expected to be persuasive in their essays.

2. What is the *topic*?

    Students are to identify the aspects of life that are intensified or changed by the ending and explain its significance to the work as a whole. Because this is the open question, students can choose which text they will use in addressing this topic.

3. Is there an intended *audience* for the writing task?

    As with the AP language exam, there is no explicit audience, but students should assume their essay will be read by college and high school teachers who are very familiar with the passage. Because thousands of other students are writing on this topic, students should strive to distinguish themselves by the perceptiveness of their analyses, the forcefulness of their arguments, and the maturity of their control of language. A formal tone is expected.

4. What is the *purpose* of this essay?

    To show strong reading and literary criticism skills when choosing a work that contains the kind of ending described in the prompt and then to write persuasively in showing a connection between that ending and the larger meaning of the work.

5. What is my *role* as a writer in achieving the purpose?

    The writer's role is to be insightful and persuasive when discussing and developing the topic.

After students have analyzed the sample AP prompt, you could ask them to consider the questions of context analysis.

1. What is my *time* limit?

    Students have forty minutes to write the essay. Keep in mind that students write three forty-minute essays during the AP exam, as well as spend fifty-five minutes reading passages and answering questions about them on the multiple-choice portion of the exam.

2. What kinds of *writing aids* are available? Is there a rubric, a writing checklist, a list of dos and don'ts?

    As with the AP language exam, very little besides the prompt is given to the students at the time of the exam, so it is important for them to have some experience beforehand working with an AP scoring guide so they will get an idea of what qualities of their writing are valued. AP workshops are useful for getting the materials one needs to help students work with sample prompts and rubrics.

3. What are the *targeted skills*? What particular thinking or writing skills does this test require?

    Literary analysis is probably the most important thinking skill for this prompt. Good judgment in texts and interpretation of the ending of a work is also important. As with all AP prompts, being able to write persuasively, with a good control of language, is also targeted.

4. What kind of *format* is expected? Will a five-paragraph essay work here, or is some other format, like a letter, required?

No particular format is required on AP essay exams; rather, students are assessed on their ability to create an organizational structure that makes sense considering the complex demands of the prompt. While some students find a five-paragraph essay fits their purposes, sometimes those essays can sound too formulaic. Students should concentrate on making sure their essay is focused and has a clear beginning, middle, and end. They should use transitions and let the structure of the essay echo the weighting of their ideas. Readers understand that these are first-draft productions, and they are often admonished to reward the writer for what he or she does well. That means that students whose essays start out weak can still end up with a score in the upper half if they write their way into good insights. Students would do well to leave a few minutes at the end to read over their essays and correct any glaring errors or repetitious word choice. Sometimes the focus can also be clarified at the beginning of the essay.

5. What *specialized expectations* are implicit in this particular writing task? For example, is length or audience specified?

No particular length or audience is specified. Students would do well not to overly criticize or praise the writer whose work they are analyzing. Often, comments such as "The writer was unclear in showing his point of view" reflect more the reader's weakness than the writer's. Students must deal with *all* parts of the prompt in their essays. Creativity is good, but creativity alone will not ensure a high score.

Essay Exams

The writing tests we have described thus far are administered in secondary schools, and several mark the passage between high school and college. Essay exams are a genre of writing test that many students experience in high school and nearly all students encounter in higher education. We believe that students need preparation for this type of writing on demand also, especially since they will encounter essay exams in many different courses.

Essay Exams in High School

Essay exams or essay questions in high school vary quite a bit. In general, high school essay exams ask for more detailed and lengthier explanations than short-answer questions. Some prompts can be as complex as an AP essay exam prompt, requiring students to demonstrate content knowledge about literature read, an ability to think analytically, and command of language, as the following prompt demonstrates:

> Many of the novels we read this term deal with the conflict between moral versus civil law. Choose two novels and analyze the author's treatment of this idea. How does the author's use of tone, diction, plot, and/or characterization convey his or her ideas?

Students encounter essay exams in many of their classes, in addition to English, and teachers can help them understand how to demonstrate content knowledge as well as basic thinking skills. For example:

> We have studied several diseases this term. Choose two and compare and contrast them in terms of infection, progression, and treatment.

Some essay exam prompts are mainly focused on getting students to demonstrate content knowledge, as in this essay question typical of those often used in social studies classes:

> Describe three of the earliest river-valley civilizations.

As you can see, there is little here to guide the writer. Faced with an essay question like this, students will need to rely upon strategies of their own, and the questions of prompt analysis offer a useful way to begin. You might begin a discussion of this prompt by using these questions:

1. What *mode* of writing is this prompt calling for and how do we know?
   The directive to "describe" indicates that students are expected to include considerable detail and write in the genre typically called *description*, a subcategory of the mode of exposition.

2. What is the *topic*?
   Students can choose from among the various early civilizations studied, but the category of early river-valley civilizations will shape their choice of topic.

3. Is there an intended *audience* for the writing task?
   The teacher is the implied audience and here the teacher takes on the role of examiner, one who will be reading to determine if the student demonstrates mastery of the required information.

4. What is the *purpose* of writing about this experience?

   This essay question is designed to determine whether students have learned the material covered in class. Accordingly, the purpose for writing is to demonstrate learning of the specified material.

5. What is my *role* as a writer in achieving the purpose?

   Students writing in response to this prompt take on the task of re-assuring or convincing the teacher that they have learned about ancient civilizations.

After students have discussed the prompt itself, you could ask them to consider it in light of context analysis.

1. What is my *time* limit?

   Like most essay exams, this one does not specify a time limit, but managing time is key to success on a test like this. Strategies include scanning the entire test to see if point values have been assigned to various sections; determining the number of parts or questions on the entire test; and looking for cues in headings or titles in the test. Whatever the approach, students need to determine quickly how much time they can afford to spend on a question like this. Other factors in determining how much time to spend on this question are the following: whether this is the only essay question or one of many; whether there is an objective test section along with the essay section; and how much the teacher has weighted each section. For example, if the class period is sixty minutes, and the teacher has assigned 20 percent to the essay section and 80 percent to the objective section, the student should limit himself or herself to fifteen minutes or so to write the essay.

2. What are the *targeted skills*? What particular thinking or writing skills does this test require? What standards are being assessed?

   Memory and selection are the dominant thinking skills being assessed here. In order to answer the question, students need to recall characteristics of several ancient civilizations, choose three, and identify details about each. Writing skills include the ability to organize and present information quickly and clearly.

3. What kinds of *writing aids* are available? Is there a rubric, a writing checklist, a list of dos and don'ts?

   Since no writing aids are included with this question, students will need to rely upon their experience with other types of prompts to determine what criteria might be used to evaluate this prompt. If the school or district uses a common rubric, then this one could be used. Here is a sample generic rubric for an essay exam.

Generic Rubric

ONLINE 9.7

	4	**3**	**2**	**1**
Ideas/ content	Essay has a clear focus, ideas are compelling, there is good development and strong support	Focus is apparent, some development takes place and ideas offer support, though it may it not be consistent	Focus is not clear, ideas need development, and/ or more support is needed for ideas	No focus, lack of development and/or support, may be unacceptably brief
Organization	Introduction includes a strong thesis; clear topic sentences; smooth transitions between ideas; and strong closure	Clear introduction, body, and conclusion, although transitions could be smoother	Lapses in organization begin to detract from the meaning of the essay	Organization is unclear, or essay consists of one long paragraph with no sorting and grouping of ideas
Voice/word choice	Voice sounds like an individual, with consistency throughout the piece. Word choice is precise and sophisticated	Voice is good, though not superlative. Words are correct and are sufficient to convey meaning	Voice is inconsistent; word choice is not always correct	Voice may be inappropriate; words are carelessly chosen or just plain wrong
Sentence structure/ writing conventions	Sentence structure is correct and varied; few, if any, grammar errors	Sentence structure is generally correct, though not as varied as it could be; some grammar errors	Sentence structure errors require frequent rereading; grammar errors begin to impede meaning	Poor sentence structure; many grammar errors

4. What kind of *format* is expected? Will a five-paragraph essay work here, or is some other format, like a letter, required?

The requirement to write about three civilizations suggests at least three body paragraphs, and with an introduction and conclusion, a five-paragraph essay would serve well. To some extent the length of this essay will depend upon the time allotted to it within the whole test.

5. What *specialized expectations* are implicit in this particular writing task? For example, is length or audience specified?

While no expectations are explicitly mentioned, the form and context of this question suggest that originality will matter less than organization, creativity less than accuracy.

After students have analyzed the prompt in this way, you might ask them to bring to class examples of essay questions they have faced recently and do a similar analysis in small groups. In addition, you might ask a colleague who teaches a non-English class that regularly requires essay tests to visit your class and answer questions about the best way to respond to essay exams.

Essay Exams in College

Not all students will go immediately to college, but for those who do, the writing they do in high school lays the foundation for the writing they will do as they continue their education. This is particularly true of essay exams, since nearly every college student will be required to face at least a few tests that include essay exams. Some may have to produce dozens of them. The questions on college tests are similar to those on high school tests, but they tend to be a bit longer and more complex. For example, here is a prompt from a college English class:

> In our course on applied linguistics, which concept we studied will be of greatest use to you in your future studies and why?

Like many college essay exams, this question is deceptively simple. Students may think they are being invited to give a loosely structured personal response, but more likely, the professor is expecting a highly reasoned evaluation that demonstrates a solid learning of course theories, as well as an ability to apply that knowledge.

Here is another sample:

> Choose any two passages from the following texts by Theodore Dreiser, F. Scott Fitzgerald, John Steinbeck, and Sinclair Lewis. Compare and contrast the authors' articulation of and attitude toward the American Dream.

Like some high school prompts, the main thinking called for is analysis, but in this case, the number of texts under consideration is larger and more complex, and the student has to work on the additional level of a concept or theory that was widely discussed in class.

Let's apply our principles of writing on demand to this question from a political science course:

> What is the French concept of citizenship, and how does this concept apply to people born in France who are not of French ethnicity?

To give students an idea of how this question differs from the type they may have encountered in high school, teachers could use prompt analysis questions to examine it.

1. What *mode* of writing is this prompt calling for, and how do we know?

    Both parts of this question are looking for explanation (of French citizenship in general and French citizenship for special populations), so it would be reasonable to assume that exposition is the appropriate mode.

2. What is the *topic*?

    In the simplest terms, the topic is citizenship, in its various forms. At another level, because this is a class in political science, it is a question about nationhood, government, and the rights of various populations. These issues remain in the background but would shape a successful response.

3. Is there an intended *audience* for the writing task?

    While no audience is specified, the political science instructor is the implied audience, and this suggests the need to keep in mind issues that are especially important to those within the field. A political scientist would not, for example, be as interested in questions about social class (of various types of citizens) as would a sociologist.

4. What is the *purpose* of writing about this?

    This essay requires students to demonstrate their recall of information about French citizenship, and it also asks them to apply their knowledge to make distinctions.

5. What is my *role* as a writer in achieving the purpose?

    Student writers need to demonstrate their comprehension of the material and ability to apply what they know.

After students have analyzed the prompt, teachers could have them turn to context analysis questions to learn more about how to approach such a question.

1. What is my *time* limit?

   The amount of time available for this question will depend entirely upon the context in which it appears, whether it is the only question or one of several in a test. As is true for the high school test, it is key to begin by figuring out how much time can be allocated to this prompt.

2. What kinds of *writing aids* are available? Is there a rubric, a writing checklist, a list of dos and don'ts?

   As is characteristic of nearly all essay exams, no writing aids are provided, which means that students need to draw on their experience with writing aids from prompts that resemble this one.

3. What are the *targeted skills*? What particular thinking or writing skills does this test require? What standards are being assessed?

   This question asks students to demonstrate knowledge of citizenship and use that knowledge to analyze the status of a particular group. The writing skills required include the ability to explain clearly, synthesize ideas, and draw conclusions.

4. What kind of *format* is expected? Will a five-paragraph essay work here, or is some other format, like a letter, required?

   Given the complexity of the question, a five-paragraph essay would probably not be sufficient. Students would need to include a number of explanatory paragraphs in addition to an introduction that frames the issue of citizenship and a conclusion that comments on the status of those who are not ethnically French.

5. What *specialized expectations* are implicit in this particular writing task? For example, is length or audience specified?

   Length is specified only in the way that time is, by considering the context in which the question appears and determining how much space can be allocated to it. The audience, as has already been noted, will be reading from the perspective of a political scientist.

By expanding the application of our questions to college essay exams, we hope to have shown the utility of our approach as well as the importance of teaching not just for the test, but beyond the test.

Key Points for Reflection

This chapter has shown how any timed writing prompt can be approached using our principles for writing on demand. Our approach seeks to meaningfully connect testing imperatives with what we know to be best practice in our field. We have demonstrated how students can be guided to think backward from finished writing to consider rhetorical mode, topic, audience, purpose, role, writing aids, targeted skills, format, and implicit specialized expectations. Analyzing prompts with students teaches them the critical-thinking skills teachers always hope to impart, and in exploring each of the questions, students learn to think reflectively about their own writing practices.

Our goal has been to not only help students survive the test-intensive atmosphere in which they are being educated today but help them think deeply about the larger picture of their individual development as writers. We hope our student writers are like those that Wodehouse describes in the quotation at the beginning of this chapter: writers to whom success has come so gradually that they are shocked when they look back and realize the heights to which they have climbed. Self-reflection on their development is crucial for students to come to this realization. The frequent writer's notebook entries sprinkled throughout this book are one way we give students opportunities to pause and look back at how far they have come.

In making time to give students these opportunities, we help ourselves, as professionals, survive the testing mania as well. Looking critically at writing prompts and looking creatively at ways to help students address those prompts can help deepen the practice of teaching.

Looking critically at writing prompts and looking creatively at ways to help students address those prompts can help deepen the practice of teaching.

Lately, the demands on professional life can often seem to come from a "do more, have less" philosophy. There are more standards to meet, more legislation to learn about, more students in classes, more responsibilities for mentoring new professionals. All the while, there is less money as budgets are being cut across the country. The teachers we know often wonder how they can possibly do any more. The alternative we offer is not to do more but to do differently. We have tried to identify the areas in which English/language arts teachers already excel—teaching writing process, close reading, peer feedback, and so on—and highlight those that can best serve the requirements of writing on demand. Managing the workload wisely not only preserves health and sanity but also contributes to student success. When students are successful, neither they nor their teachers feel demeaned—they have met the demands. We believe:

- Analyzing the prompts and contexts of the SAT, ACT, AP, and essay exams helps teachers and students recognize and learn to respond to the particular demands of those exams.

- Writing-on-demand principles can be used to address prompts of many different grade levels, from secondary school to college, and at many levels of complexity within each grade as well.

- Preparing students to succeed on writing tests is not an additional time requirement, but something that can be accomplished through the best practice work that writing teachers already do.

Index